T0299499

JUST ONE PAN

Also by Jane Lovett:

The Get-Ahead Cook

Make it Easy

Jane Lovett

JUST ONE PAN

Over 100 easy and creative recipes for home cooking

Photography by Tony Briscoe

For darling Luce,

Thank you. x

OPINEL
INOX
OPINEL
SAVOIE FRANCE

Contents

Introduction

I have greatly enjoyed writing, developing and testing recipes for this book for many reasons. Not least because at the end of a busy day, when cooking supper isn't always an appealing thought, there is a joy in adding ingredients to one pan and letting it do all the work.

Having amassed an armoury of one-pan recipes, which I love cooking as much as we enjoy eating them (and to which I'm adding all the time), this way of cooking has become the new norm for me and the very reason I wanted to share them in this book. Not only does one-pan cooking allow for a bit of downtime as it cooks away on the stove or in the oven, perhaps with a glass in hand between work and supper, it also saves time on washing-up and affords more time to relax with family or entertain guests.

In fact, one pan becomes a bit addictive and I can't stop myself lobbing all sorts of combinations into pans and tins. Once you've caught the bug, I hope, like me, you might find yourself thinking of different themes and adding relevant ingredients. For example, a one-pan dish based on Spanish ingredients, such as smoked paprika, chorizo, black olives, a pouch of Spanish flavoured grains, almonds, garlic, sherry vinegar and so on, or perhaps a dish for Bonfire Night where you can create something tasty out of sausages, butternut squash and apples. You'll soon get the hang of it!

Ranging from the traditional full-English breakfast or fish and chips to a Sunday roast, there are numerous dishes that can be cooked in one pan. There is something for everyone in this collection of delicious recipes, from meat and fish dishes to meat-free, plant-based and vegetarian options. A few can be adapted to be made vegan, too. The recipes cover all occasions from quick, mid-week meals or suppers to family feasts, as well as snacks, salads and platters, and it goes without saying that one-pan cooking is a gift for entertaining.

Being a home cook, I have written this book very much for fellow home cooks. The recipes are straightforward, easy and achievable and require no specific cooking skills.

I hope many of the recipes will become weekly staples that you know you can rely on, enjoy and will love cooking as much as I have enjoyed developing, cooking and eating them with my family and friends. Furthermore, I hope you will have or gain the confidence to adapt and put your own stamp on these recipes as well as creating your own versions.

The Pros of One-pan Cooking

There are many pros to one-pan cooking which (incidentally) is much more versatile than it might sound and is so much more than the hackneyed idea of soups, tray bakes or casseroles. There are a wide variety of pots, pans and tins to choose from that most kitchens will have as a matter of course, and which offer different takes on one-pan cooking – many of which are used in these recipes and details of which I will delve into later.

One-pan cooking is time-saving, so cooks can enjoy a relaxed time before eating, it cuts down on washing-up (a major joy!), plus on the cooking side, the flavours gently meld together, creating a kind of magic that you don't always get using a mass of individual pots and pans.

The recipes in this book are all cooked in one pan, tin or dish. I have stuck to the 'rules' and essence of one-pan cooking; however, in the spirit of my desire to bring you an elevated, more interesting take on one-pan cooking, please do allow leeway for other utensils and kitchen equipment to be used where necessary. You may well choose to use more than one pan/tin/dish to suit your own purposes, too. For example, you may wish to brown nuts or seeds in a separate pan, while the main event is cooking in the oven. On this note, I have also offered ideas for salads, sauces, dressings or fresh bread for mopping. These are by no means necessary, just more options to complement the recipes. The broader theme remains though, to bring you the very best one-pan recipes, to make life simpler, minimise clutter and lighten the washing-up load.

Cook's Notes

- All eggs used in the recipes are large and free-range.
- All butter used in the recipes is lightly salted.
- Full-fat ingredients are used throughout the book, but you can substitute depending on personal preference.
- Herbs are all fresh unless stated as dried. Fresh or dried bay leaves can be used in relevant recipes.
- If you are vegetarian, please ensure that the cheese you use is suitable for vegetarians. Vegetarian options for alternative cheeses are mentioned in some recipes, but always check the packaging to be certain that the cheese is suitable.
- All recipes assume that raw ingredients are at room temperature before going into the oven.
- Ovens should be preheated to the specified temperatures. I used a non-fan (conventional) electric oven for all the recipes. Fan (and gas) oven temperatures are also given, but do consult your oven manual if using a fan oven (though generally the temperature is 20°C lower than the conventional one given, as shown in the recipes).
- Spoon measures are level unless stated otherwise. Use a set of measuring spoons for accurate measuring. A teaspoon is 5ml, a tablespoon is 15ml.

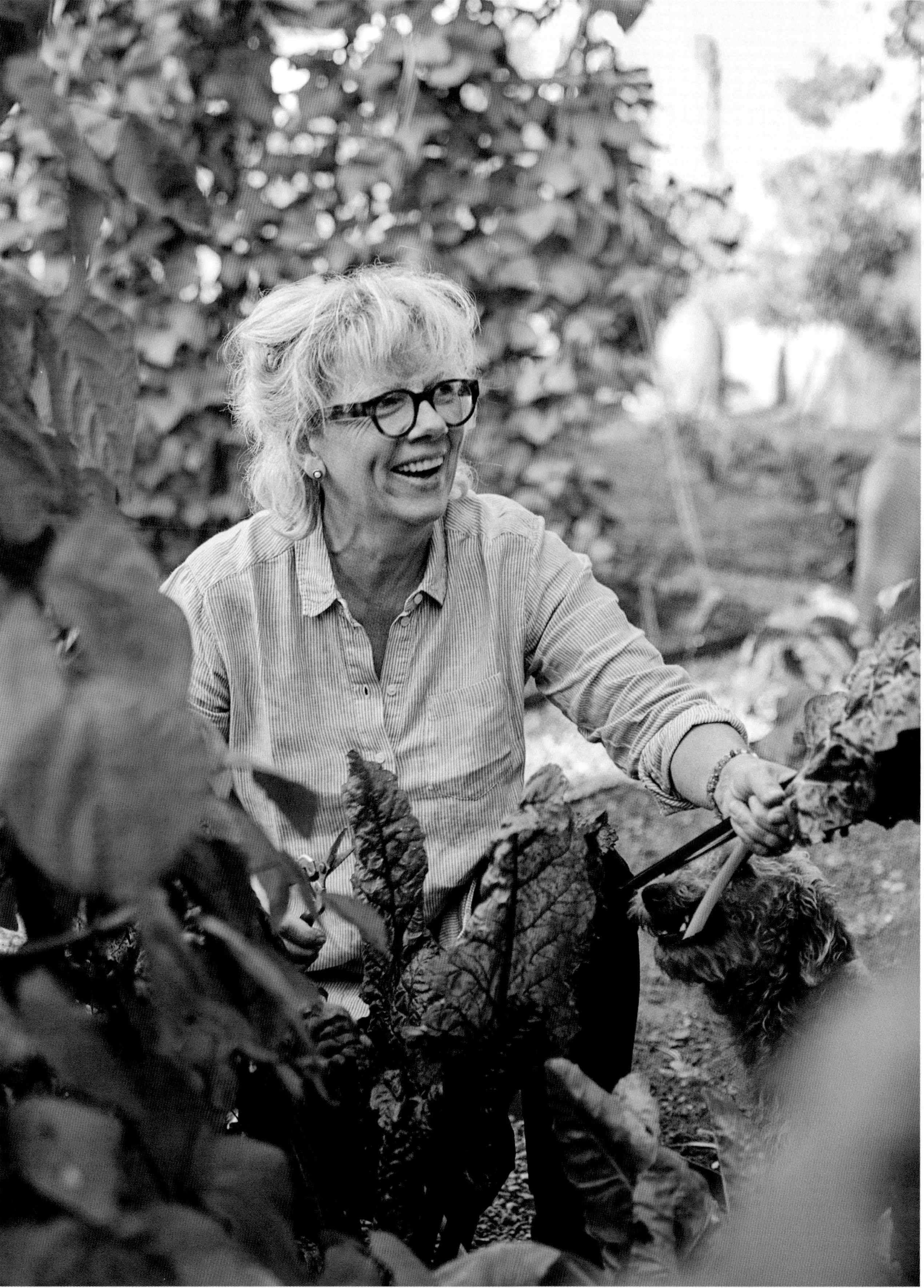

A Few General Pointers

Who doesn't love a speedy aid? I have used some speedy store cupboard aids, such as pouches of ready-cooked grains and tinned pulses, to make things easier. Of course, it's always nice to use the base, dry ingredients, but let's be kind to ourselves, we are trying to save time and, in my book ('scuse the pun!), they are perfectly acceptable substitutes and serve a purpose. However, having said that, one person's cheat is another's modus operandi. If you're less of a fan of the shortcuts, you can always adapt the recipes to suit your own style of cooking.

Many of the recipes use some store cupboard ingredients, but all other ingredients are readily available from larger supermarkets. For fresh food, I would recommend buying from butchers, fishmongers, greengrocers, delis and bakers and, where possible, shop as locally as you can.

It's good to have an open mind! I have included swaps and substitutes in many of the recipes. You may simply want to swap an ingredient to use it up or perhaps someone isn't keen on something, or you may want to make a recipe vegetarian or vegan. If you don't have one ingredient, it can often be substituted, or sometimes omitted entirely. Or if a prescribed herb is just for garnishing rather than key to the flavour of a recipe, use whatever herbs you have to hand. Be brave and try not to get too wound up about ingredients, etc, as these recipes are meant to be both time- and stress-saving.

Which pan? Try to match the size of cooking vessel as closely as you can to the one I recommend in each recipe, but don't worry too much. Be creative and remember that when a large roasting tin is called for it's generally because the base ingredients need to be in (roughly) one single layer and the uppermost ones (e.g. pieces of chicken or fish) need to fit in a single layer, too, without being hugger-mugger. I have gone into more detail about useful one pan equipment on pages 22–4.

Stay calm! Remember also that a recipe isn't going to fail because nuts and seeds aren't browned (they'll just taste better if they are) or that you haven't got any basil or coriander to scatter over the top to garnish. Don't get too caught up in the small detail – it's only cooking! And don't mention to guests if you think you've messed up a recipe or you've forgotten to add an ingredient – it only draws attention to something that would otherwise probably go unnoticed.

Cooking around the world – a quick reminder here that where I have ascribed recipes to particular cultures or cuisines, these are my take on those recipes, and, with one-pan cooking in mind, where easy availability of ingredients and getting ahead are important, in some cases the recipes have been simplified. I don't claim them to be an authentic representation, but they are what I consider to be a delicious 'spin' nonetheless.

Always read through a recipe fully before going shopping for it or before getting started.

Seasoning is imperative to good-tasting food. Season as you go along rather than as an afterthought, and season each component or step of a recipe, as directed.

Use the best quality ingredients you can afford – this and good seasoning both contribute to creating the tastiest meals.

Remember, piping hot food has little or no taste or flavour, so it's always advisable to allow a finished hot dish to cool down for a few minutes before serving. If steam is in evidence when the dish is cut or spooned into, this is a good indicator that the food is too hot. This is particularly true of eggy recipes (frittatas, tortillas), gratins, pies and vegetable-heavy dishes that often create lots of steam.

KNOW YOUR OVEN

Always preheat the oven first (except where some longer prep needs to be completed before the cooking begins, such as soaking or marinating). It may sound obvious, but it's the first fence to fall at when trying to make a speedy one-pot-wonder in the oven for supper.

I also advise setting the oven a little higher than indicated for big trays with lots of food to cook properly, as laden trays sap the heat when going into the oven. Turn it down to the given temperature once the food goes in.

When roasting or browning, always put food at the very top of a hot oven. Hot air rises so it will always be hotter at the top (except in a fan oven where the heat is distributed more evenly around the oven). And if you want to cook something more slowly, or if something is cooking too fast, move it lower down in the oven.

All ovens are different – so be vigilant. You'll know your oven well, but do keep checking as sometimes things need turning around or over to ensure even cooking or browning. I always recommend checking progress before the recommended cooking time is up, too. An oven thermometer is useful to have as well (and isn't very expensive) for occasionally checking that your oven is operating at the correct temperature.

GET AHEAD

The essence of one-pan cooking is that it is inherently more 'real-time' cooking, the kind of recipes you use for 'in the moment' cooking. However, just one pan doesn't preclude you from getting ahead, and if you do want to get ahead, occasionally it may require using more than one pan, which I think is a small price to pay. In most recipes, I have included useful tips on how to get ahead at various stages when making the recipes. This may simply mean some preparation here and there in a spare moment to lighten the final load on the day, or other preparation and cooking a couple or so days ahead.

LOVE YOUR LEFTOVERS

I'm very keen on using up leftovers and rarely throw any food away. One-pan cooking is ideal for this – perhaps as simple as frying up leftovers on the stove or cooking them in the oven. Ready-cooked pouches of grains are ideal for transforming a few leftover bits and bobs into a delicious meal with very little effort. All that's required is your imagination and a bit of confidence. I encourage you to mix and match and play around, as very little can really go wrong, then perhaps choose a sauce or dressing from chapter 7 (see pages 191–209) to bring it all together or add that final flourish.

STORAGE INFO

The recommended storage time for many 'get ahead' sections of the recipes is up to 3 days in the fridge, but some will keep for a little longer, so do use your common sense when preparing and storing food. When reheating food, always ensure it is reheated until hot throughout. If making cooked rice dishes in advance, they should be cooled and chilled quickly, reheated thoroughly and used within 24 hours of making.

Many of the recipes in this book can be frozen (and this is indicated on individual recipes). Freezing times will vary but ensure you either wrap them well or freeze in airtight containers or sealed freezer bags, and defrost before use.

INGREDIENT TIPS

Olive oil. For Mediterranean-style food, use either a good-quality everyday (mild) olive oil or an extra-virgin one for cooking – or just whatever you have to hand. You may also like to have a special, top-quality extra-virgin olive oil for salads and dressings and finishing off recipes.

Vegetable and other flavourless oils. Use these for non-Mediterranean-style cooking, such as Indian or Asian, where a flavourless oil is required.

Chillies. All the red and green chillies used in the book are the 'un-named' everyday mild- to medium-heat chillies, commonly available in packets in all supermarkets. If using other chillies, the general rule is, the smaller they are, the hotter they will be.

MY GET AHEAD TIME-SAVING INGREDIENT TOP TIPS AND SHORTCUTS

Time-saving tips and shortcuts are so useful to have in your cooking arsenal. I go to great lengths to save time (and washing-up!) and these are a few of the useful tips that I've accumulated throughout my cooking career. I might be repeating myself, but as I wend my way around the country demonstrating, these are the tips I'm told over and over again that are the top time-saving, useful or handy ones.

There are small ways in which you can get ahead and save time with repeatedly used ingredients. These tips are so well worth doing and save time when cooking a recipe. I know they pay dividends, as I'm constantly told as much by attendees at my demonstrations who have now adopted them as a matter of course.

PARMESAN CHEESE

Cut a large block (or two, or more) into smallish chunks and grate using the grater blade of a food-processor. Remove the grater, replace with the general chopping blade and whizz until the cheese is very fine. Alternatively, you can use a hand grater or Microplane to finely grate the cheese. Store in a sealed bag in the fridge or freezer, where the cheese stays crumbly and won't set/clog up, allowing you to spoon it out and use it when required (you can use it straight from the freezer, too).

NUTS AND SEEDS

Nuts and seeds are full of oil and as a result go rancid quite quickly once a packet is opened (some more quickly than others, such as walnuts and sesame seeds), so I recommend storing them in the freezer in their original packaging.

Some of the one-pan recipes in this book require toasted nuts and seeds (to enhance their flavour or appearance), which are mostly toasted in the 'vessel' before embarking on the main body of the recipe. However, if you'd like to get ahead, I recommend toasting batches of (individual) nuts and seeds in a dry frying pan on a medium heat for a few minutes, then freezing them (as above), ready to be pulled out and used, without defrosting, as and when required. Or, if you are short of time, ready-toasted nuts are readily available to buy.

STOCK CUBES AND STOCK

Firstly, it should be said that stock cubes don't always need reconstituting first. For example, when making soup, just crumble them into the pan of ingredients and top up with the given amount of water. If a cube does need to be dissolved first, I find it easiest to put it into a measuring jug with a very small amount of boiling water and whisk until the cube has dissolved, before adding the rest of the water – far easier than chasing the undissolved cube around in a jugful of water. Fresh stock can also be used in the recipes, and it's easy to make your own in a batch, then keep individual portions in the freezer to use as required (defrost before use). Pouches of (long-life) liquid stock are also readily available in many supermarkets.

BREADCRUMBS

Whizz up a 2–3 days-old loaf of crustless bread (or a few slices) in a food-processor to make breadcrumbs, then store in a sealed bag in the freezer, ready to spoon out when required (no need to defrost first).

For dried breadcrumbs, dry out (but don't brown) old leftover or stale bits of bread and/or rolls in a low (or cooling) oven, until pale in colour, then cool and whizz into fine breadcrumbs. Stored in an airtight container, they will last for ages.

FRESH GINGER

Fresh ginger can be frozen (peeled or left unpeeled) and then simply grated from frozen.

Everyday Handy Tips

PASTRY

1. Stack up trimmings of puff pastry before re-rolling, therefore retaining its fundamental layers. Scrunched up into a ball, the layers are lost, thus precluding it from rising.

2. Avoid brushing egg wash onto the cut edges of puff pastry. The egg sets firm immediately on contact with heat, gluing the pastry layers together and preventing them from rising.

3. Save pastry trimmings in case they're needed for running repairs later on.

4. When cutting out pastry shapes or biscuits, roll out the pastry on silicone or baking parchment. Having cut out the shapes, remove the surplus trimmings rather than the other way round, then carefully transfer the shapes/biscuits to a baking sheet (still on the silicone or baking parchment) ready for baking (or chilling, then baking).

5. When re-rolling, don't overwork the pastry as this will toughen it.

AVOCADOS

1. Ripen at room temperature, then store in the fridge where they will last for weeks (as long as they're not squidgy and overripe when going into the fridge).

2. Halve, remove the stone, then slice or dice avocado in its skin and remove the flesh with a tablespoon. It's almost impossible to cut an avocado neatly and without it becoming mushy once it's peeled.

EGGS

1. Adding a pinch of salt to egg wash breaks it down, producing a smoother wash.

2. Salt breaks down egg whites, which is why a pinch is added when whisking whites. For this reason, add salt to scrambled eggs at the very end, thus producing lovely large curds. If added at the outset, the whites are broken down, changing the egg structure and producing less volume.

3. Adding salt to egg poaching water breaks the whites down, separating them from the yolk, so poach eggs in unsalted water.

General Hints & Tips

CREAM

Always under-whip cream. Spooning out and spreading cream thickens it more. If whipped in advance, it will thicken up more while standing in the fridge.

FRESH HERBS

Wrap fresh herbs in damp kitchen paper or newspaper, then return them to their bag or wrap in clingfilm (to retain dampness) as this will prolong their life considerably.

RESTING MEAT AND POULTRY

Roast meat and poultry needs resting (uncovered) somewhere warm, such as in a low or cooling oven, warming drawer or hot cupboard, for a minimum of 30 minutes to allow the juices to redistribute throughout, rendering it juicy and tender.

KEEPING FOOD WARM

Always ensure steam can escape when keeping food warm in the oven by leaving the oven door or drawer slightly ajar, otherwise food becomes soggy and loses its colour and crispness.

1. Cut potatoes and other root vegetables the same size for mashing and roasting so they cook evenly.

2. When softening onions, adding a pinch of salt speeds up the process.

3. Roughly halve or quarter garlic cloves before adding to a food-processor. Whole cloves will stubbornly remain in a bruised lump, but with cut edges will process properly.

4. Cook bags of fresh spinach to free-up more fridge space. It also prolongs its life. The quickest way to do this is to put the spinach into a colander in the sink and pour over a kettleful of boiling water, then rinse under cold running water, squeeze out the excess juice and cool before storing in the fridge. Alternatively, wilt bags of spinach in a microwave. Prick the top of each bag several times with a fork, place the bag (one at a time) in the microwave and heat on high for 2–4 minutes or until wilted. Drain into a colander and continue as above.

5. Salting both sides of a steak before cooking creates the difference between a 'good enough' and a fantastic steak. The salt caramelises with the juices when it hits the hot pan/rack, producing a wonderful umami flavour. Use pouring salt.

6. Adding a splash of water to French dressing helps it to emulsify – a French trick!

7. To soften rock-hard sugar, put it into a bowl draped with a clean, damp cloth, towel or tea towel.

8. Break chocolate up in its wrapper and tip out, to save it melting in your hands.

Store Cupboard & Ingredient Tips

Many of the recipes in this book are made using some store cupboard ingredients. I realise that one person's store cupboard is another one's nightmare, but whatever form your store cupboard takes, I'm confident there will be recipes that anyone will be able to make without the need for a big shop, or a trip for a more unusual ingredient. Having said that, all the recipe ingredients are available from larger supermarkets and, of course, just about anything is obtainable online.

Store cupboard ingredients are your friend and saviour when one-pan cooking, so are well worth stocking up on, and some just need reconstituting and no cooking, which is a huge bonus.

Pouches of ready-to-eat grains have a very long shelf life (often up to 2 years), so I think they are invaluable store cupboard staples. You can literally pull together a meal out of almost nowhere within minutes. The addition of eggs, vegetables, meat, fish or poultry, either in a pan on the stove or in a tin in the oven, means you can tailor them to suit all tastes.

On the following pages you'll find plenty of ideas for cheats and speedy aids, all from the store cupboard. This isn't a definitive list of ingredients, merely items that help back up one-pan cooking.

JARS

- anchovy fillets in oil (or use tinned)
- tomato purée (or from a tube)
- 'Very Lazy Chilli' (handy for adding a quick hint of heat to recipes)
- ginger paste
- lemon grass paste
- harissa paste (I like Belazu Rose Harissa Paste)
- tahini paste
- hot creamed horseradish sauce
- roasted red peppers (in oil or brine)
- capers (the smallest possible)
- gherkins (cocktail size)
- honey
- artichoke hearts (in oil)
- mayonnaise (fresh or a good-quality jar, if you must!)
- pesto sauce (fresh or a good-quality jar, if you must!)
- mustards – Dijon, whole grain (seedy), English, dried powder
- pitted olives, black and green (or in pouches)
- stem ginger
- preserved lemons

TINS

- tinned tomatoes (I like chopped)
- tinned beans and pulses, such as chickpeas, and butter, cannellini, borlotti, flageolet and haricot beans
- coconut milk and coconut cream
- artichoke hearts in brine

BOTTLES

- olive oil – mild for everyday cooking and a special top-quality extra-virgin olive oil for finishing off salads and platters
- flavourless oils, such as vegetable oil
- specialist oils, such as hazelnut, walnut and toasted sesame oils
- bottled Asian sauces, such as Hoisin, dark soy (I like Kikkoman), fish, sweet chilli, sriracha and oyster sauces
- vinegars – white wine and red wine, sherry, dark and white balsamic
- Worcestershire sauce
- Tabasco® sauce

POUCHES

- straight-to-wok noodles – these have a long shelf life, can be egg or rice, come in various sizes and, as the name suggests, are ready to heat and eat
- pouches of ready-cooked rice, grains and pulses, such as freekeh, Puy lentils, smoky Spanish-style grains and rice (I like Merchant Gourmet)
- stock liquid pouches (vegetable, fish, chicken, beef and lamb)

DRY INGREDIENTS	PERISHABLE INGREDIENTS
• dried pasta, rice, grains and pulses, such as spaghetti, Basmati rice, Carnaroli or Arborio risotto rice, red Camargue and wild rice, pearl barley, bulgur wheat, couscous, giant couscous (maftoul/ Mograbiah), mung beans and Puy lentils • flours (plain white, self-raising white, plain wholemeal), sugars (granulated, caster, demerara, light and dark muscovado, icing), semolina, baking powder, bicarbonate of soda, cream of tartar • spices (ground) – basics, such as ground cumin (and seeds), turmeric, ground coriander (and seeds), ground cinnamon (and sticks), ginger; hot smoked paprika, curry powder, hot chilli powder, garam masala; spice mixes, such as dukkah • whole spices and seeds – star anise, nutmeg, green cardamom pods (or ground), dried chilli flakes, saffron strands, lime leaves, curry leaves; mustard, fennel, onion and/or nigella seeds • dried herbs – oregano, thyme, tarragon, bay leaves • stock cubes • dried mushrooms • dried breadcrumbs, such as panko • nuts, seeds and dried fruit, such as walnuts, blanched hazelnuts, pine nuts, pistachios, flaked and ground almonds; pumpkin and sunflower seeds, black and white sesame seeds; semi-dried prunes and apricots, raisins • dried noodles – these come in varying sizes, have a long shelf life, can be egg or rice (gluten-free) and mostly require no actual cooking – simply reconstituting in boiled water for a few minutes • poppadoms (also ready-cooked in pouches)	• chilled fresh ready-made pastry, including ready-rolled puff and shortcrust pastry sheets and blocks • natural or thick Greek-style yoghurt (or coconut milk yoghurt for a plant-based vegan, dairy-free and gluten-free alternative) • fresh gnocchi (has a long shelf life) • fresh root ginger • onions • garlic • lemons, limes • potatoes • eggs (free-range) • milk **FREEZER** • Parmesan cheese, pre-grated • breadcrumbs – fresh • seeds and nuts, toasted • frozen chopped onions (for real emergencies!) • frozen ready-made pastry, including ready-rolled puff and shortcrust pastry sheets and blocks • prawns, raw and cooked

Useful One-pan Equipment

Pans, Pots, Tins, Trays & Dishes

THE WIDER PICTURE

From the outset, I wanted the recipes in this book to be more than just 'tray bakes'. Delicious (not to mention labour-saving) as those are, there is so much more scope than using just the stereotypical roasting tin or casserole dish. For example, using stove-top pans, particularly for suppers, widens the range of one-pan recipes considerably.

One-pan cooking is a wide-ranging and versatile theme for cooking, as demonstrated by the range of cooking vessels used throughout the book – from saucepans to a wok; frying pans to sauté pans; roasting tins to baking trays and sheets; tart tins to cake tins; casseroles to other ovenproof dishes.

Where it matters more (and particularly with oven-cooked recipes), I have indicated the recommended size of the vessel to use at the beginning of each recipe. Having said that, don't worry too much as these are only a guide – just use whatever pans, pots, dishes and tins you already have. I have used a mixture of round, oval and rectangular ovenproof dishes and tins, but the shape is generally irrelevant, so adapt with what you have, roughly matching them up to the measurements given in the recipe. If food is to be brown and crispy on top, it mustn't be overcrowded and touching its neighbours in the tin or dish (it would be better to use two smaller tins or dishes, if necessary).

In some recipes, the tin can be lined with baking parchment, which saves on washing-up, too. Marvellous! However, in some recipes, the ingredients need to be in direct contact with the tin to cook evenly, brown or caramelise and wouldn't work so well on baking parchment. I have indicated in the recipes where baking parchment is suitable and recommended.

POINTERS FOR BUYING PANS AND TINS

Obviously, you want to avoid having to buy new pots, pans and tins, but if yours need an upgrade and you're thinking of splashing out, here are a few pointers.

Always buy the best you can afford. This will reap huge rewards and they will last a lifetime if looked after properly, as well as produce the best possible results. Generally, the heavier the pan or tin, the better quality it is, food is less likely to burn and it will cook more evenly.

Think about the finish you want on pans – cast iron, anodised or hard anodised (non-stick, easy to clean and scratch-resistant) or stainless steel are just some of the choices. It's useful to have at least one pan that can be used on the stove as well as in the oven and possibly one with a metal or a removable handle for both forms of cooking, too. Food slides off non-stick-style finishes more easily and doesn't stick, plus it also requires less oil. The same applies to baking tins.

Consider how many people you feed on a regular basis, do some research and buy sizes accordingly.

Many of my good-quality (heavier/thicker) baking/roasting/cake tins are old and battered favourites but still produce excellent results. The thinner, inferior-quality ones are buckled and do not, so are rarely used. Non-stick ones vary enormously in quality, too, so do buy the best that your budget will allow for if you choose this style.

I prefer shallow, rather than deep, roasting tins as they let out steam and therefore the food roasts and crisps up better. Buy the biggest baking tray/sheet you can find which ideally will just fit in your oven, as it saves fiddling around with two smaller trays/sheets.

If you like serving food straight from the oven or stove, think about how the container looks. The more rustic the better for me, but your taste may be more refined.

Sizes & Dimensions of Pans & Tins

I have pretty much used the same-sized pans and tins repeatedly throughout the book. If your pans are not exactly the right size, be inventive. A bit of leeway is fine.

For stove cooking, as well as regular small/medium/large saucepans, I have mainly used the following pans and pots in recipes:

- Sauté pan, 24cm diameter (that's ideally about 6cm deep) with a lid
- Large frying pan, 28cm diameter
- Medium frying pan, 25cm diameter
- Small frying pan, 20cm diameter
- Wok, 28 x 9cm (non-stick)
- Large, oval, cast iron (lidded) casserole dish, 30 x 24 x 11.5cm (also used for oven-cooking)
- Deep, round, cast iron (lidded) casserole dish, 23 x 10cm (also used for oven-cooking)

For oven-cooked or baked recipes, I have mainly used the following tins in recipes:

- Large, shallow roasting tin, 41 x 26cm and ideally no deeper than 4cm, or a large (lipped) baking tray of same size (I use this and the next medium size the most)
- Medium, shallow roasting tin, 35 x 26cm and ideally no deeper than 4cm, or a medium (lipped) baking tray of same size
- Large (lipped) baking tray, 44 x 34 x 2.5cm (41 x 31 x 2.5cm excluding lip)

For other oven-cooked recipes, I have mainly used the following ovenproof dishes in recipes:

- Large, shallow, oval ovenproof dish, 33 x 26 x 6cm
- Round ovenproof dish, 27 x 6cm

Useful Electrical Kitchen Equipment

I regularly use and wouldn't be without these:

- food-processor (preferably including a very small additional bowl and blade for making spice pastes and chopping herbs and small quantities – or a similar individual small grinder)
- blender and/or a stick blender
- stand mixer or hand-held electric whisk

Brunching & Snacking

Being a lover of all things savoury, this chapter is right up my street! Savoury snacking for any time of the day, with a quick and easy throw-together feel. I also like to cook two, three or more dishes together for a slap-up sharing feast or a lazy weekend brunch spread. Joy of joy, many components, and indeed a few whole recipes, can be prepared entirely in advance.

Warm Baked Artichoke & Parmesan Pâté

SERVES 6–8

For the pâté
1 jar or 1 x 400g tin artichoke hearts, drained (approx. 240g drained weight)
1 garlic clove, crushed
3 tablespoons grated Parmesan cheese
3 tablespoons mayonnaise
a good handful of parsley leaves
sea salt and freshly ground black pepper

To serve
smoked paprika (optional)
olive oil, for drizzling (optional)
sourdough toast or a selection of crudités, such as: radishes (with smaller leaves intact); watermelon radishes, cut into batons; carrots (with leafy tops if possible); celery sticks; chicory leaves; fennel sticks; cucumber sticks; breadsticks

This tasty pâté always conjures intrigue and surprise. Firstly, few people can guess what the main ingredient is, and secondly, when served as a dip, the fact that it's warm is an unexpected delight.

1. Preheat the oven to 220°C/200°C fan/gas 7.

2. Whizz all the pâté ingredients together in a food-processor to make a textured purée – it won't be completely smooth. Check the seasoning – it should be well seasoned.

3. Spoon the pâté into a small, shallow, ovenproof dish. Bake for 15 minutes until bubbling and turning golden.

4. Remove from the oven and leave to stand for 10 minutes or so to cool a little before serving.

5. Scatter with a light dusting of smoked paprika and a drizzle of olive oil (if using). Serve the pâté spread onto toast, or with crudités and/or breadsticks for dipping.

GET AHEAD

- Prepare to the end of step 2 up to 3 days in advance, then cover and chill.

HINTS & TIPS

- To make this pâté vegetarian, simply swap the Parmesan for a vegetarian Italian-style hard cheese.

Ham, Egg & 'Chips'

SERVES 2

good glug of olive oil, plus extra for drizzling
150–200g celeriac (or 2 slices), peeled and cut into 'frite'-sized batons
4 waxy new/salad potatoes, halved, sliced and cut into 'frite'-sized batons
pinch of dried oregano
¼ teaspoon white or black mustard seeds
sea salt and freshly ground black pepper
170g cooked ham cut into thin batons, or cooked pulled ham hock
2–4 eggs (serving 1 or 2 eggs per person)

To serve
a selection of the following: roughly chopped parsley; sliced spring onions; snipped chives; sriracha or Tabasco® sauce; knob of butter atop the eggs; dried chilli flakes or Aleppo pepper (pul biber)

Fuss- and frill-free, this has 'brunch' written all over it! Good honest comfort food or leftover 'hash', this is a very quick, rustic and tasty way of using up bits and bobs from the fridge. Use the recipe as a guide only, quantity-wise, and substitute or add whatever you have to hand. See the *Hints & Tips* for ingredient variations and additions. Just leave out the meat for vegetarians, as well as the eggs (and butter, to serve) for vegans.

1. Heat a glug of olive oil in a 24cm sauté pan (that's ideally about 6cm deep) or a frying pan with a lid. Add the celeriac and potato batons, the oregano, mustard seeds and some salt and pepper and cook on a high heat, stirring, until everything is coated with oil, sizzling and beginning to caramelise around the edges, about 5–10 minutes.

2. Lower the heat, cover with a lid and cook very slowly until tender, about 10 minutes, stirring occasionally and scraping any caramelised bits off the bottom of the pan. Some of the vegetables will be soft, possibly falling apart a little, and some will be crispy and crunchy. Gently stir in the ham, then check the seasoning.

3. Make two or four small hollows in the mixture and break an egg into each one. Drizzle a little olive oil over everything in the pan, season the eggs, cover with a lid and cook on a medium heat for 5 minutes or so until the whites are just set and the yolks still runny.

4. Serve scattered/topped with any of the serving suggestions. Ketchup or brown sauce served alongside is good, too.

GET AHEAD

- Make to the end of step 2 any time on the day, then leave the mixture in the pan, allow to cool, then cover loosely. Reheat gently on the stove until hot throughout, then add and cook the eggs as above.

HINTS & TIPS

- Focus on the seasoning for this recipe.

TRY THESE INGREDIENT VARIATIONS:

- Step 1 – sliced fennel/celery and/or onion, or cherry tomatoes.

- Step 2 – cooked pork, chicken, sausages, chorizo or a mixture of any cooked meats. (Green vegetables like kale, spinach, chard, petit pois, etc, stirred in at the same time as the meat are a delicious addition.)

Cheesey Smoked Haddock & Spinach Stuffed Baked Potatoes

SERVES 4

4 medium potatoes (around 225–255g each), scrubbed
150g baby spinach leaves (or use frozen spinach – 55g cooked and squeezed weight)
55g butter, plus extra for serving
85g mature Cheddar cheese, grated
2 egg yolks
1 teaspoon sea salt
freshly ground black pepper
freshly grated nutmeg
1 skinless un-dyed smoked haddock fillet (about 255g), finely diced (I snip it with scissors)

GET AHEAD

- Prepare to the end of step 5 up to 2 days in advance, then cool, cover and chill (or wrap and freeze, then defrost). Reheat in the oven (temp as in step 1) for about 15 minutes or until hot throughout.

HINTS & TIPS

- Swap the Cheddar for Gruyère cheese, and try smoked cod in place of the smoked haddock, if you like.

Deliciously savoury, these baked potatoes are perfect for brunch, lunch or even a light supper. Who doesn't love a baked potato? Do try to get un-dyed smoked haddock fillets rather than the inferior and ubiquitous bright yellow, day-glow ones, if you can. Don't worry too much about the potato, haddock and spinach quantities being exact – a little flexibility either way is fine.

1. Preheat the oven to 200°C/180°C fan/gas 6. Put a kettleful of water on to boil and line a baking sheet with silicone or baking parchment.

2. Cut a deep criss-cross through the top of each potato, being careful not to cut quite all the way down to the bottom. Bake directly on the oven shelf for 1 hour or until crisp on the outside and soft in the middle.

3. While the potatoes are baking, put a colander or large sieve into the sink, add the spinach and pour over the boiling water from the kettle, which will wilt the spinach. Cool under the running cold tap, squeeze out all the liquid with your hands, then roughly chop (I snip it with scissors in a mug or small bowl).

4. Remove the potatoes from the oven and while still hot, but cool enough to handle, cut down through the scored edges and scoop out the soft flesh into a heatproof bowl, keeping the skins intact as best you can. Reserve the skins, which will look unpromising and disconcertingly floppy.

5. Mash the flesh (the odd lump doesn't matter!), then add the butter, cheese, egg yolks and salt with a grinding each of pepper and nutmeg and mash again. Stir in the spinach followed by the smoked haddock, then check the seasoning. Pile the mixture back into the potato skins, reforming the potatoes. Flatten and slightly splay out the criss-cross on top of each to reveal the green filling.

6. Transfer to the lined baking sheet and bake for 15 minutes or until heated through. Just before serving, make an indent in the filling in the middle of each potato and press in a generous knob of butter.

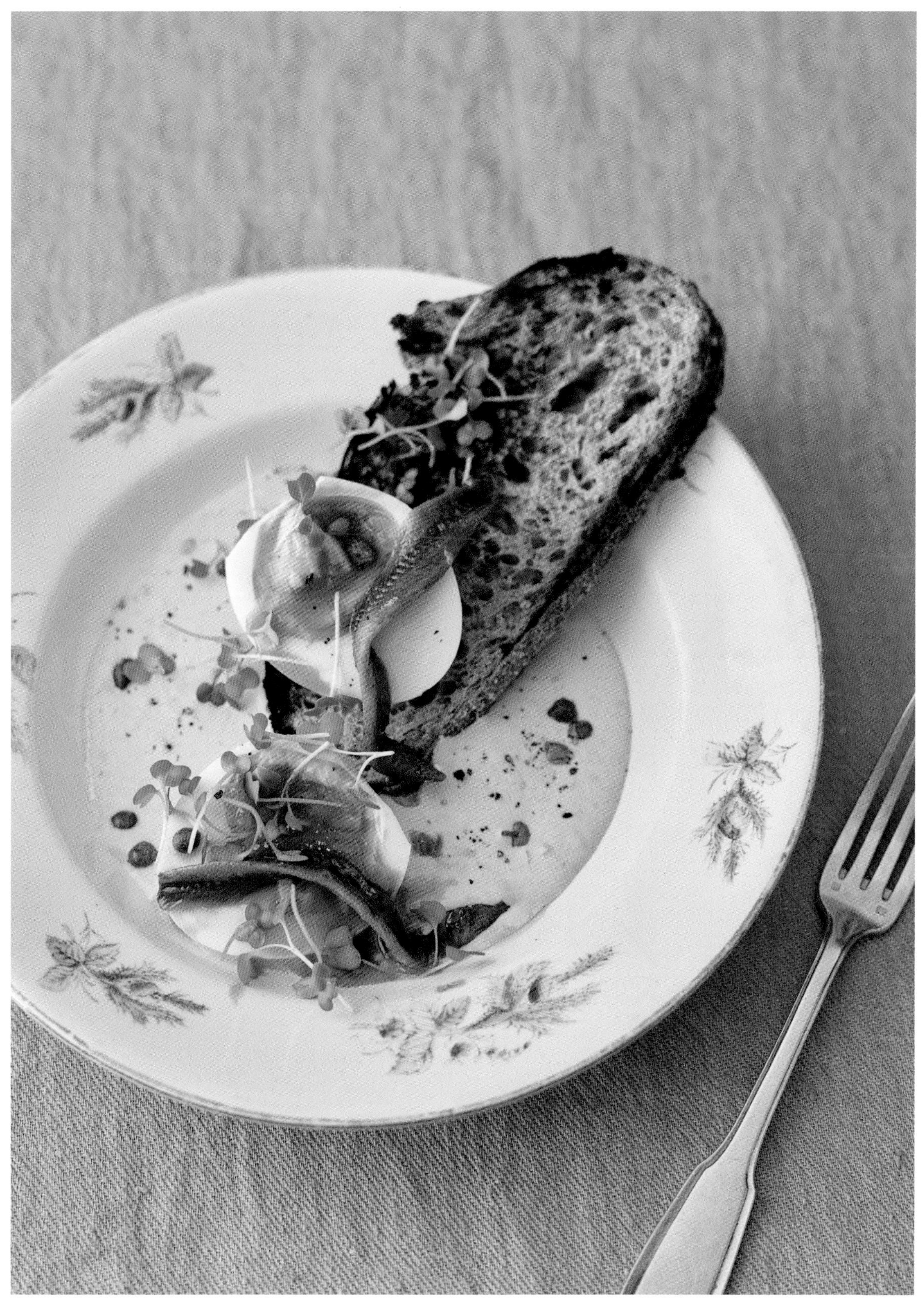

Eggs Tonnato

SERVES 4

2 heaped tablespoons thick Mayonnaise (see page 198)
80g tin tuna, in oil or brine, drained
4–8 anchovy fillets in oil (from a jar), drained
1 teaspoon small capers in brine, drained, plus a few extra to garnish
freshly ground black pepper
a squeeze of fresh lemon juice
4 eggs

To serve (optional)
a selection of:
chopped spring onions; pitted black olives, halved or chopped; tapenade; chervil; cress or micro leaves; watercress; snipped chives

Veal (or pork) Tonnato is one of my favourite Italian recipes, and here I have rung the changes, using eggs instead of meat. Snuggled into this scrumptious velvety tuna mayonnaise, the perfectly soft boiled eggs become delectable, with the anchovies and capers being the savoury 'icing on the cake'. Scoop up and enjoy with bread, toast, crackers or warm flatbreads.

1. Using a stick blender, small food-processor, or elbow grease and a fork, whizz/mix the mayonnaise, tuna, 1 anchovy (roughly snipped), the capers and some pepper into a smooth sauce. Add a squeeze of lemon juice to taste. If the sauce is too thick, whizz/mix in a little warm water to thin it to a double cream consistency (be careful, as it's easy to add too much in one go). Check and adjust the seasoning with pepper.

2. Lower the eggs into a small saucepan of boiling water and simmer for 6 ½ minutes. Drain, cool under cold running water until just cool enough to peel, if serving warm, or cool completely if serving cold and then peel. Set aside.

3. Spread the sauce over the bottom of a pretty serving plate or platter or between four individual plates. Halve or quarter the eggs, then arrange randomly, yolk-side up, over the sauce. Drape the anchovies over the eggs and scatter the capers over.

4. Scatter over any of the serving suggestions, if you like (including one of the green leafy options), then finish with a grinding of pepper.

GET AHEAD

- Step 1 can be completed up to 3 days ahead, then covered and chilled.
- If serving cold, the eggs can be cooked 2–3 days ahead, cooled, peeled and kept submerged in a bowl of water, covered, in the fridge.

HINTS & TIPS

- Replacing the tonnato sauce with Watercress Mayonnaise (see page 199) is a delicious (and bright green!) alternative. Save a few watercress sprigs for garnish.

Full-English-Breakfast-in-the-Oven

SERVES (this varies; see recipe introduction)

vegetable oil
tomatoes, halved
sea salt and freshly ground black pepper
sausages
bacon rashers
black pudding, cut into roughly 1cm-thick slices
very fresh eggs
mustard of your choice, to serve (optional)

Frying is my least favourite way of cooking, largely because I can't bear the splattery, greasy mess. Cooked breakfast is one of the worst offenders, and for this reason, I always cook it in the oven. No mess and everything is added to one baking tray – marvellous! Better still, I line the tray with foil, which leaves no washing-up whatsoever. A gift at any time, but particularly at the beginning of the day!

I haven't suggested quantities here because cooked breakfast (or brunch) is such a personal thing – some like sausages, some don't; some devour several rashers of bacon, some fewer; the same with eggs – one or sometimes two each. So, I have listed the ingredients in the order of adding them to the baking tray, which remains the same whatever quantity you're cooking. Just remember the more you're cooking, the larger the baking tray you will need and some of the ingredients may take a little longer to cook. The tomatoes should be falling apart.

1. Preheat the oven to 220°C/200°C fan/gas 7.

2. Choose a (lipped) baking tray that will fit your chosen amount of ingredients comfortably in one layer, line it with foil and lightly grease with vegetable oil.

3. Put the halved tomatoes onto the prepared baking tray, season generously and drizzle with vegetable oil. Place the sausages next to them, leaving space on the remainder of the tray for the other ingredients later. Bake at the top of the oven for 10 minutes. Add the bacon and black pudding and bake for a further 10 minutes or until the bacon is crisp (the time will depend on the type and quality of bacon – watery bacon will take longer).

4. Remove from the oven, then break the eggs into spaces on the tray (making spaces, if necessary) or, if the tray is crowded, transfer all the cooked ingredients to a large platter or individual plates and keep warm, before breaking the eggs onto the tray. Bake the eggs for 3–4 minutes until the whites are set and the yolks runny (or cook for longer if you prefer a firmer yolk). Serve for breakfast or brunch.

GET AHEAD

- Step 3 can be cooked up to 1 hour in advance and kept warm in a low oven (with the door ajar) on a plate/plates until the eggs are required. Heat the baking tray up again in the oven before adding and cooking the eggs.

HINTS & TIPS

- The eggs need to be very fresh, otherwise the whites will run all over the tin. The whites of fresh eggs stand proud and cling to the yolks, whereas older whites become more liquified and spread out away from the yolks (but they're still perfectly fine to eat and will take less time to cook).

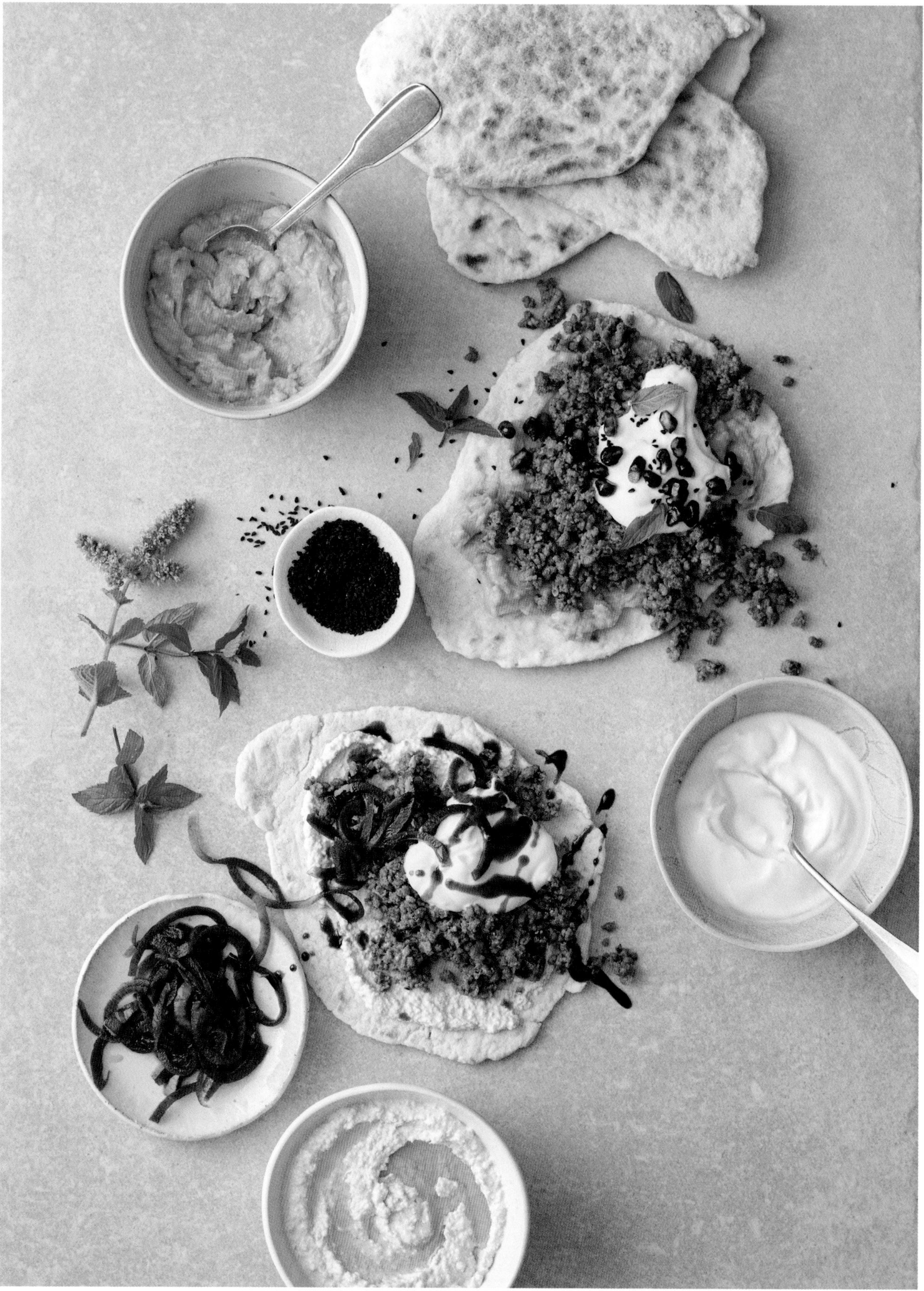

Lebanese-style Spicy Lamb Flatbreads

SERVES 4–6

1 x quantity Ridiculously Easy Flatbreads recipe (see page 159) or 6–8 ready-made flatbreads, soft flour tortillas or pitta breads
2 tablespoons pine nuts (optional)
splash of olive oil
1 onion, finely chopped
1 garlic clove, crushed
good pinch of dried oregano
1 teaspoon rose harissa paste, or more to taste
500g raw (or cooked) minced lamb
1 teaspoon sea salt
freshly ground black pepper

To serve (for topping and filling)
a selection of the following:
200g thick Greek-style yoghurt or Cucumber Raita (see page 207); Quick Pickled Red Onions (see page 203); hummus; avocado flesh, mashed or sliced; rocket or other salad leaves; extra rose harissa paste; fresh pomegranate seeds; dried barberries or other small dried fruits; date syrup or pomegranate molasses; tinned chickpeas, drained and rinsed; olive oil; dried chilli flakes or Aleppo pepper (pul biber); nigella or onion seeds; mint leaves

These lamb flatbreads are equally as tasty made with minced beef as they are with cooked, leftover minced lamb or beef. A delicious brunch recipe that's really just an assembly job once the minced meat is cooked. Make your own Ridiculously Easy Flatbreads (see page 159) or use ready-made shop-bought ones. Either way, all that's needed is one frying pan.

1. If you are making your own flatbreads, follow the recipe on page 159 and keep them warm. If you are using ready-made flatbreads, just before serving, warm them through according to the packet instructions.

2. If using put the pine nuts into a medium, dry frying pan and cook on a medium heat, shaking the pan occasionally until they are beginning to brown, about 5 minutes. Tip onto a plate and leave to cool, then transfer to a small serving bowl and set aside.

3. Heat the olive oil in the same frying pan, add the onion and cook on a medium heat until soft, about 10 minutes. Add the garlic, oregano and harissa paste and cook for a minute or two, then add the raw minced meat, the salt and some pepper and cook on a high heat for 8–10 minutes or until cooked, breaking up the clumps as best you can with a wooden spoon. For ready-cooked minced meat, cook for 5 minutes or until heated through. Check the seasoning, bearing in mind it should be well seasoned.

4. Organise a selection of the serving suggestions imaginatively into and onto appropriate bowls and plates ready for everyone to help themselves and concoct their own flatbread or tortilla topping or pitta bread filling – not forgetting the toasted pine nuts, if using.

GET AHEAD

- The flatbreads can be made the day before and warmed through in a medium oven (180°C/160°C fan/gas 4) for a few minutes or in a dry frying pan.
- Cook the minced meat mixture up to 3 days in advance, then cool, cover and chill. Reheat in the frying pan on a low heat until hot throughout.

HINTS & TIPS

- Add a pinch of chilli powder or dried chilli flakes if you prefer the lamb spicier. A little ground cumin added to taste, at the same time as the harissa paste, is good, too.

All-in-one Chicken Liver Pâté with Green Peppercorns

SERVES 8–10 (generously)

500g chicken livers
1 onion, finely chopped
2 garlic cloves, quartered
good pinch of dried thyme
1 teaspoon sea salt
freshly ground black pepper, to taste
1 bay leaf
1 x 250g packet butter, roughly diced, plus an extra 55g if using clarified butter at the end (see *Hints & Tips*)
2 tablespoons brandy
1 tablespoon green peppercorns in brine, drained

To finish (optional)
clarified butter; dried pink or black peppercorns and/or green peppercorns in brine (drained); bay leaves; dill sprigs

You can't beat a classic! Satisfyingly luscious and smooth, this pâté makes quite a sizeable quantity, but is easily halved. However, it's worth getting ahead by making the full recipe and freezing half for another time. Having said that, a bowl of this in the fridge rarely lasts very long . . .

1. Preheat the oven to 190°C/170°C fan/gas 5. Find a shallow roasting tin around 35 x 26cm. A smaller tin is fine but the pâté might take a little longer to cook.

2. Tip the chicken livers into a sieve and pick them over, snipping off and discarding any bits you don't like the look of. Leave to drain while you prepare the other ingredients.

3. Put all the remaining ingredients, except the brandy and green peppercorns, into the roasting tin. Add the chicken livers, then mix and spread everything out. Flame the brandy by heating it in a metal ladle (at arm's length) over a naked gas flame. Tilt the ladle slightly until it ignites, then immediately pour into the tin. (Alternatively, warm the brandy in a small pan and light with a match, then pour into the tin.) Cover the tin tightly with foil and bake for 35 minutes. At this stage, the livers may still be a little pink in the middle.

4. Remove from the oven, remove the foil and discard the bay leaf, then leave for 5–10 minutes to let the butter settle and cool a little, before blitzing in a blender or food-processor until very smooth. Stir in the green peppercorns, then pour into one serving dish or several individual ones. If using clarified butter (which acts as a preservative), pour a thin layer over the top and garnish with any of the remaining suggestions to finish, before the butter sets.

GET AHEAD

- The pâté will keep (covered) for up to 3 days in the fridge without clarified butter (or for a couple more days with). It also freezes beautifully (defrost before serving).

HINTS & TIPS

- To make clarified butter, gently melt 55g (2oz) butter in a small saucepan. Skim the white scum off the top (I find a bit of kitchen paper is handy for this) and then carefully pour the butter over the pâté, leaving behind the milky sediment in the bottom. The depth of the butter seal will depend on the size of the surface area of the bowl/pots.

- Packets of chicken livers are widely available in supermarkets, often frozen (defrost them before use), as well as from butcher's shops.

OPINEL
SAVOIE FRANCE
OPINEL
INOX

Roasted Red Pepper Hummus

SERVES 6

2 tablespoons mixed nuts and seeds (such as hazelnuts and/or cashew nuts, roughly chopped; pumpkin, sunflower and/or sesame seeds)
1 x 400g tin chickpeas, drained and rinsed
3 tablespoons tahini paste
2 whole roasted red peppers from a jar, drained
2 garlic cloves, crushed
juice of ½ lemon
3 tablespoons olive oil, plus a little extra to serve
large pinch of ground cumin
large pinch of smoked paprika
½ teaspoon sea salt
freshly ground black pepper, to taste
2 tablespoons iced water

To garnish (optional)
reserved chickpeas; mint leaves; rose harissa paste; fresh pomegranate seeds; ground sumac; smoked sea salt

Gorgeously smooth, this Middle Eastern-style hummus has a slight twist with the addition of roasted red peppers and gentle spices, and it's suitable for vegetarians and vegans, too. Serve as a snack with warm Ridiculously Easy Flatbreads (see page 159) or pitta bread, or serve as part of a mezze, or with the Lebanese-style Spicy Lamb (see page 39) if you are not veggie or vegan, or as a dip for crudités.

1. Toast the mixed nuts and seeds in a small, dry frying pan on a medium heat for 3–5 minutes, stirring, until they are turning golden and fragrant. Tip onto a plate and set aside to cool.

2. Reserve a few chickpeas for garnish, if you like, then place the remainder in a food-processor and process into a thick paste. Add all the remaining ingredients, except the iced water, and process again until smooth. Taste, and if necessary add more of anything that you think is required. It should be well seasoned.

3. Add the iced water and process for 5 minutes, during which time the hummus will become paler and very smooth. Transfer the hummus to a pretty serving dish, plate or bowl.

4. Just before serving, swirl a little olive oil over the top, scatter with the toasted nuts and seeds and garnish with any of the suggestions (if using).

GET AHEAD

- The hummus will keep in a covered container in the fridge for up to 3 days.

HINTS & TIPS

- Tahini paste tends to separate out in the jar but careful mixing with a spoon (in the jar) will bring it back together again. Be patient, it will take a minute or two!
- If the finished hummus is too thick, add a little more iced water.
- A thinly sliced shallot fried in a little olive oil until caramelised and crispy is a tasty alternative topping to the toasted nuts and seeds.

Spanish Squid & Chorizo

SERVES 2

2 good glugs of olive oil
110g raw squid, cleaned, cut into thin rings, any tentacles left intact
5cm piece of cured 'salami-style' chorizo (preferably spicy), halved and cut into ½cm-thick slices
8 cherry tomatoes, halved
2 garlic cloves, chopped
large pinch of dried oregano
¼ teaspoon smoked paprika ('hot' if possible), or more to taste
1 teaspoon sherry vinegar, or more to taste
sea salt and freshly ground black pepper

To serve
toasted sourdough or rustic bread (optional)
a few parsley leaves, roughly chopped

An unbelievably quick Spanish-style snack, which takes no time to cook once all the ingredients are assembled (ensure you prep them all in advance, so they are to hand when you are ready to cook). Eat as it is, or piled onto toasted bread – hearty, rustic and chewy bread, rather than the flimsy, processed type. The tasty juices seep pleasingly into the toasted bread, creating an irresistibly flavoursome mouthful.

1. Heat a good glug of olive oil in a small frying pan, then add the squid and cook on a high heat very quickly, just until it turns from transparent to opaque – this will take less than a minute. Remove from the pan to a plate and set aside.

2. Add the chorizo to the pan and fry on a high heat until its oil begins to run, then add the tomatoes, garlic, oregano, smoked paprika, vinegar and some salt and pepper. Cook for a few minutes, until the tomatoes are just beginning to soften around the edges.

3. Return the squid to the pan along with another good glug of olive oil, allow the mixture to bubble up and then check the seasoning.

4. Serve in individual dishes, with toasted bread for mopping up or piled onto toasted bread, if you like, scattered with the chopped parsley.

GET AHEAD

- Steps 1 and 2 can be completed any time on the day and then left in the pan (step 2) until required. Reheat on a high heat and then continue with step 3 until hot throughout.

HINTS & TIPS

- Squid is readily available from fishmongers or (usually) frozen from supermarkets (defrost before use). Pre-cut rings are often thickly sliced, so halve them with scissors, keeping the 'ring' intact.
- This is very good (if a little messy) served on toast, then cut up into small pieces and served with drinks, tapas-style.

Spinach, Parma Ham & Taleggio Frittata

SERVES 4–6

about 250g spinach leaves, washed
splash of olive oil, plus extra for drizzling
good grating of nutmeg
sea salt and freshly ground black pepper
1 garlic clove, crushed
8 eggs
knob of butter
150g Taleggio cheese, thinly sliced
5 slices Parma ham, each cut in half lengthways
freshly chopped herbs, such as chives or basil leaves, to garnish (optional)

GET AHEAD

- Complete steps 2 and 3 up to 2 days ahead, then cool, cover and chill. Bring back to room temperature (or reheat gently until hot throughout), then continue with step 4 as above.
- The whole recipe can be made up to 1 day in advance (chilled overnight) and eaten warm or cold.

I cook frittatas for brunch (or lunch) when there seems to be very little on offer apart from eggs. Practically anything can be added to the egg mixture, leftovers or otherwise. This delicious version is one of our favourites.

1. Preheat the oven to 200°C/180°C fan/gas 6. Find a deep-ish, preferably ovenproof, frying pan, ideally 20 x 4.5cm. (See *Hints & Tips* for non-ovenproof frying pan guidelines.)

2. Cook the spinach in the frying pan with a splash of water until just wilted (or microwave in a heatproof bowl on high for about 4 minutes until wilted). Drain, cool under cold water, then squeeze out all the excess moisture (hands are best for this) and chop roughly (I snip it with scissors).

3. Heat a splash of olive oil in the same frying pan, then add the spinach, nutmeg and some salt and pepper. Stir for a minute or so on a high heat, then add the garlic and cook for another minute. Remove from the heat.

4. Whisk the eggs and some seasoning together in a large measuring jug or bowl. Tip in the spinach mixture and stir together well to combine.

5. Wipe out the frying pan, then melt the butter, swirling it up the sides of the pan to grease it. Pour in the egg mixture, then cook on a low heat until the bottom is golden and the egg is set around the edges and about halfway up through its depth, about 7–10 minutes, depending on the depth of the pan. After 5 minutes or so, arrange the cheese slices over the top, tearing them into pieces if necessary, then drape the Parma ham strips over the cheese in a wavy, undulating pattern.

6. Drizzle with a little olive oil, then transfer to the oven and cook for about 12 minutes or until barely set in the middle. Serve warm or at room temperature (not piping hot) scattered with the fresh herbs (if using).

HINTS & TIPS

- For non-ovenproof frying pans, finish off the final step under the grill. Preheat the grill (well in advance) to its highest setting and slide the pan underneath to finish off cooking.
- Cut the warm or cold cooked frittata into bite-sized squares for tasty canapés. It's great served cold for a picnic, too.

Sticky Chinese Slow-cooked Pork Belly Bao Buns

SERVES 5

For the marinade
2 tablespoons dark muscovado sugar
1 tablespoon hot sweet chilli sauce
1 tablespoon sesame oil
1 tablespoon vegetable oil
2 tablespoons dark soy sauce
thumb-sized piece of fresh root ginger, peeled and finely chopped (or use 2 teaspoons ginger paste from a jar)
2 garlic cloves, crushed

For the pork belly and buns
1.3kg piece of pork belly, bones and skin removed, but fat left on
15–20 ready-made bao buns (3–4 per person)

For the accompaniments and fillings (optional)
⅓ cucumber, cut into thin batons
4–5 spring onions, halved lengthways and cut into long, thin strips
a handful of salted peanuts, roughly chopped
Hoisin sauce, to taste
salad leaves
Quick Pickled Red Onions (see page 203) or other pickles
toasted sesame seeds

Scrumptious sticky pork belly is stuffed into light-as-air steamed bao buns, with lots of tasty bits and bobs. Think Peking Duck but with pork and bao buns instead of duck and pancakes. This succulent (if messy!) Chinese street food is perfect for brunch as it can be prepared the day before, or even a couple of days ahead. It's a great snack, too. You might be pleased to hear that the bao buns are shop-bought and ready-made! Use pitta pockets if you prefer.

1. Preheat the oven to 180°C/160°C fan/gas 4.

2. Cut a long piece of baking parchment large enough to enclose the pork and seal into a tent-like package. Find a shallow roasting tin a little bit larger than the piece of pork and line it with the baking parchment. Sit the pork on the parchment in the tin.

3. Mix all the marinade ingredients together, then pour over the pork, turning to coat it all over, but being careful not to tear the parchment. With the pork sitting fat-side up, bring the parchment up and over the pork and seal it tightly, rolling over the top and sides to create an airtight 'tent'.

4. Cook in the oven for 1½ hours, then remove from the oven, open the parcel and baste the pork with the juices, which should be syrupy, sticky and caramelised. Transfer the pork to a chopping board and slice. Decant the syrupy cooking juices into a small, heatproof bowl, skimming the fat off the top with a spoon or piece of kitchen paper, and keep warm (if using and serving them alongside the Hoisin sauce.)

5. Meanwhile, heat the bao buns according to the packet instructions and then serve with the pork, accompaniments and fillings of your choice (if using) for everyone to make up their own buns. Napkins are essential!

GET AHEAD

- Make the recipe to the middle of step 4 (before the pork is transferred to a board and sliced) up to 3 days in advance, then cool, cover and chill. Reheat the pork in the baking parchment 'tent' in the oven at 200°C/180°C fan/gas 6 for 20–30 minutes until hot throughout.
- The accompaniments can be prepared up to 1 day in advance. Keep the prepped cucumber and spring onions in the fridge.

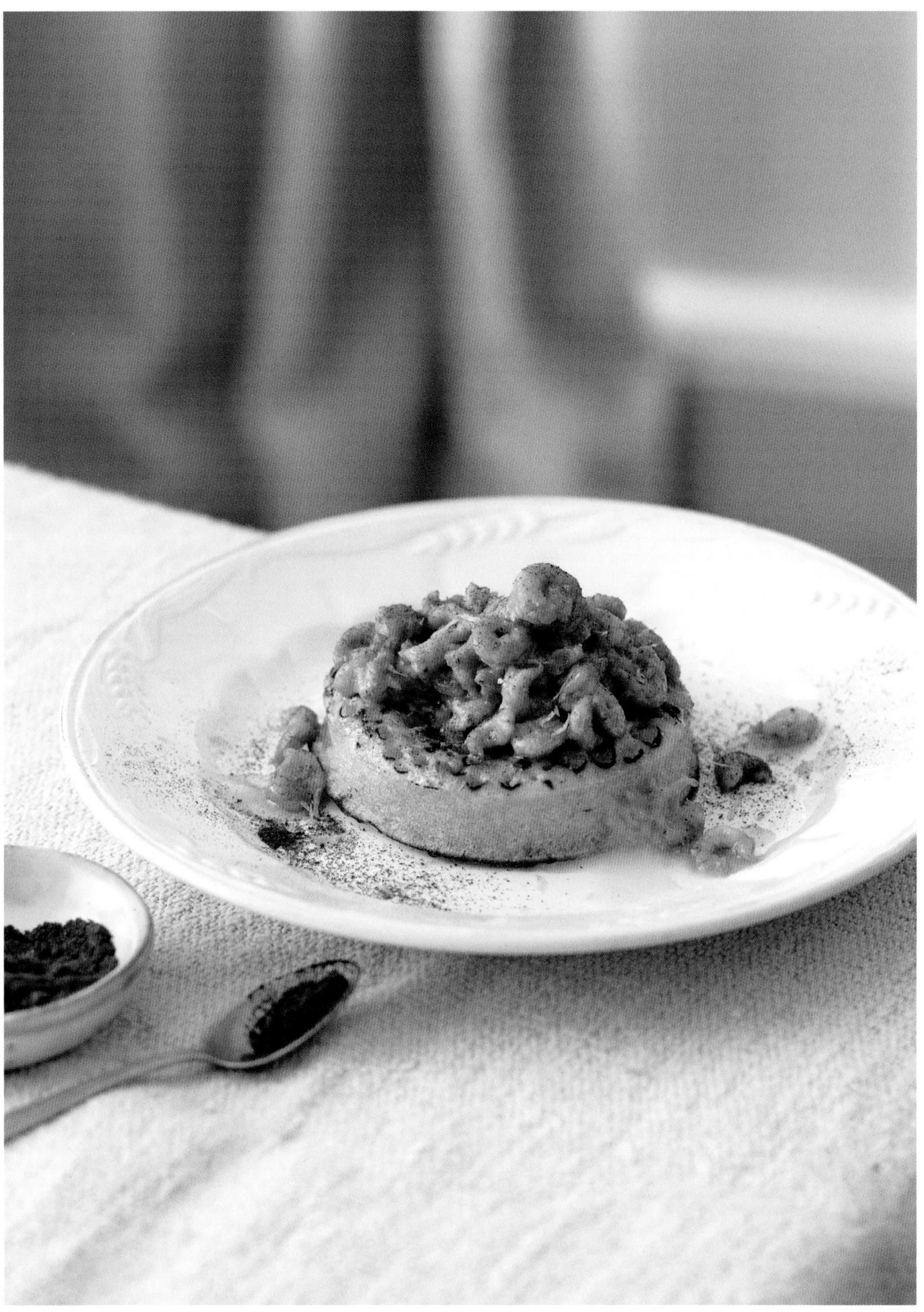

Hot Smoked Paprika Potted Shrimp Crumpets

SERVES 2

70g cooked, peeled brown shrimps
85g butter
1/8 teaspoon hot smoked paprika
1/8 teaspoon shrimp paste
1/8 teaspoon sea salt
2 crumpets
a little grated lemon zest (optional)

GET AHEAD

- Once potted, the shrimps will keep for up to 3 days in the fridge and they freeze beautifully, too (defrost before serving).

HINTS & TIPS

- The texture of the butter for potted shrimps is a very personal thing – some like the butter hard straight from the fridge, others like it a soft, spreadable consistency, and others slightly melted. It's up to you!

- Shrimp paste is available in small jars from large supermarkets or Asian shops. Replace with an extra pinch of hot smoked paprika, if you prefer.

A favourite for supper on Sunday evenings in our house, especially after a full-blown Sunday lunch! These tasty, shrimp-topped toasted crumpets are also delicious served as a light brunch or weekday snack.

1. Wrap the shrimps in some kitchen paper to soak up the excess liquid.

2. Clarify the butter by melting it gently in a small saucepan. Skim the white scum off the top (I find a piece of kitchen paper is handy for this) and then carefully pour the butter into a small, heatproof jug, leaving the milky sediment behind in the bottom of the pan.

3. In a small bowl, mix about half the clarified butter with the hot smoked paprika, shrimp paste and salt. Add the shrimps and mix together, ensuring they are evenly coated. Pack tightly into two very small containers/bowls (such as ramekins or mini metal moulds), or one slightly larger one. Press down to level the top and then spoon over the remaining clarified butter. Chill in the fridge until set.

4. Bring the potted shrimps back to room temperature an hour or so before serving.

5. Toast the crumpets on both sides – they should be well toasted and crunchy rather than soft and chewy.

6. Top each piping hot crumpet with a turned-out pot of shrimps, either as they are, or, if you prefer the butter softer or even partly melted, warm them slightly in a low oven, briefly (a few seconds) in a microwave or sitting in a bowl of boiling water. Dust with a fine grating of lemon zest, if you like, and serve.

One-pan Whole Feta in Spicy Tomato Sauce

SERVES 2–3

good glug of olive oil
1 onion, finely chopped
sea salt and freshly ground black pepper
2 garlic cloves, crushed
pinch of dried oregano
1 teaspoon rose harissa paste, or more to taste
1 x 400g tin chopped tomatoes
250g cherry tomatoes
pinch of caster sugar
1 roasted red pepper from a jar, drained and cut into thin slivers
1 x 200g block of feta cheese (see *Hints & Tips*)
4 pitted black olives, roughly chopped (or a blob of tapenade if you have an opened jar)

To serve (optional)
thick Greek-style yoghurt
basil or oregano leaves or dried oregano

Exceptionally quick to throw together, versatile and similar to the ever-popular Middle Eastern dish, shakshuka, this is a brilliant pick-me-up and a super-tasty brunch or snack. The flavours are quite intense, so a little goes a long way, too. All manner of things can be substituted to ring the changes (cubed tofu or eggs), but the base ingredients are largely store cupboard items.

1. Heat the olive oil in a 24cm sauté pan (that's ideally about 6cm deep), then add the onion and a pinch of salt and cook slowly until soft but not coloured, about 10 minutes. Add the garlic, oregano and harissa paste and cook for a minute or two more. Add the tinned tomatoes, then half-fill the empty tin with water, swirl it around and add this to the pan, along with the cherry tomatoes, sugar, red pepper and some salt and pepper, bearing in mind that feta is salty.

2. Bring to the boil and bubble fast for 10–15 minutes, giving it an occasional stir, until most of the liquid has evaporated and it has become jammy (but not totally dry). (As tomato sauce splatters everywhere, I recommend using a splatter guard over the pan.) Check the seasoning and add a splash of water for a slightly sloppier mixture or less intense flavour, if necessary.

3. Drain the feta of its excess milky liquid and then nestle it into the middle of the tomato sauce. Cook gently, uncovered, for 5–10 minutes until the cheese has warmed through and softened a little.

4. Heap the olives on top of the feta, and (if using) blob some yoghurt over the sauce, then dot with basil or oregano leaves (or sprinkle over a little dried oregano) and serve. Or, you can serve the yoghurt separately, if you like.

GET AHEAD

- Make to the end of step 2 up to 2 days in advance, then cool, cover and chill. When you are ready to serve, reheat the sauce gently in the pan until hot throughout, then add the cheese and continue as above.
- The tomato sauce also freezes well (defrost before use, then reheat).

HINTS & TIPS

- Buy feta cheese that carries the round orange and yellow PDO symbol. Brands without this are best avoided.
- If you have vegetarian guests, ensure the feta you use is suitable.
- A little clear honey drizzled over the warm feta just before serving adds a pleasing sweet touch.

OVENEX
MADE IN ENGLAND

Ready-steady Quick Suppers

For me, one-pan cooking is a gift at the end of a long, busy day when the vigour I woke up with is beginning to flag. Supper has to be as easy and fuss-free as possible.

Most of these recipes are on the table in under an hour and some of them within 30 minutes. Some are cooked on the stove and others in the oven. A few can be made in advance and reheated. A mixture of meat, fish, vegetarian and vegan options, there is something for everyone. You might also like to accompany some of them with one of the adaptable sauces in chapter 7 (see pages 191–209).

Aubergine-chickpea Mélange with Chard & Ricotta

SERVES 4–5

2 good glugs of olive oil
1 onion, finely chopped
1 small–medium aubergine, sliced, then cut into 2cm dice
2 celery sticks, stringy bits removed with a peeler, cut into roughly 1cm slices
2 garlic cloves, crushed
4 baby courgettes or 1 medium courgette, quartered lengthways, and cut into roughly 1cm chunks
2 thyme sprigs, leaves picked, or generous pinch of dried thyme
sea salt and freshly ground black pepper
1 x 400g tin chickpeas, drained and rinsed
150ml fresh vegetable or chicken stock (or use ½ stock cube)
100g chard, stems and leaves separately cut into 1cm pieces/ ribbons respectively (halve any extra-wide stalks lengthways)
juice of ½ lemon
100g ricotta cheese
a small handful of parsley or basil leaves, roughly chopped or torn

My inspiration for this 'no bells and whistles' yet wonderful plant-based mélange, comes from our veg patch and changes depending on what's ready and when. Apart from celery, we grow pretty much all the ingredients at some point during the year. A tin of chickpeas bulks up the vegetables, and some delicious soft ricotta nestled into the mixture at the end lends a creamy texture. The final result is a little bit soft, a little bit crunchy and rather comforting.

1. Heat a good glug of olive oil in a 24cm sauté pan (that's ideally about 6cm deep), then add the onion, aubergine and celery and cook on a medium heat until soft but not coloured, about 10 minutes. Add the garlic, courgettes, thyme and some salt and pepper and cook for a few minutes more. The courgettes should be tender yet still retain some crunch. Stir in the chickpeas.

2. Add the stock and chard stems and bring to a simmer, then gradually stir in and wilt the chard leaves, a handful at a time, about 2–3 minutes. If you think it needs more liquid at any time, splash in a little water. Add the lemon juice and check the seasoning – be generous with both salt and pepper.

3. Just before serving, nestle little teaspoonfuls of the ricotta into the top of the mixture, spreading it out slightly with the back of a spoon, then swirl with another good glug of olive oil and scatter with the fresh herbs.

GET AHEAD

- Make to the end of step 1 any time on the day, leave in the pan, cool and cover, then reheat gently when required.
- The chard can be prepared (but not cooked) up to 3 days ahead and chilled.

HINTS & TIPS

- Almost any soft summer herbs can be used. We grow summer savory, which is delicious with summer vegetables – and with eggs, too.
- This is very good spread out attractively on a pretty serving platter, drizzled with olive oil and served as a salad.

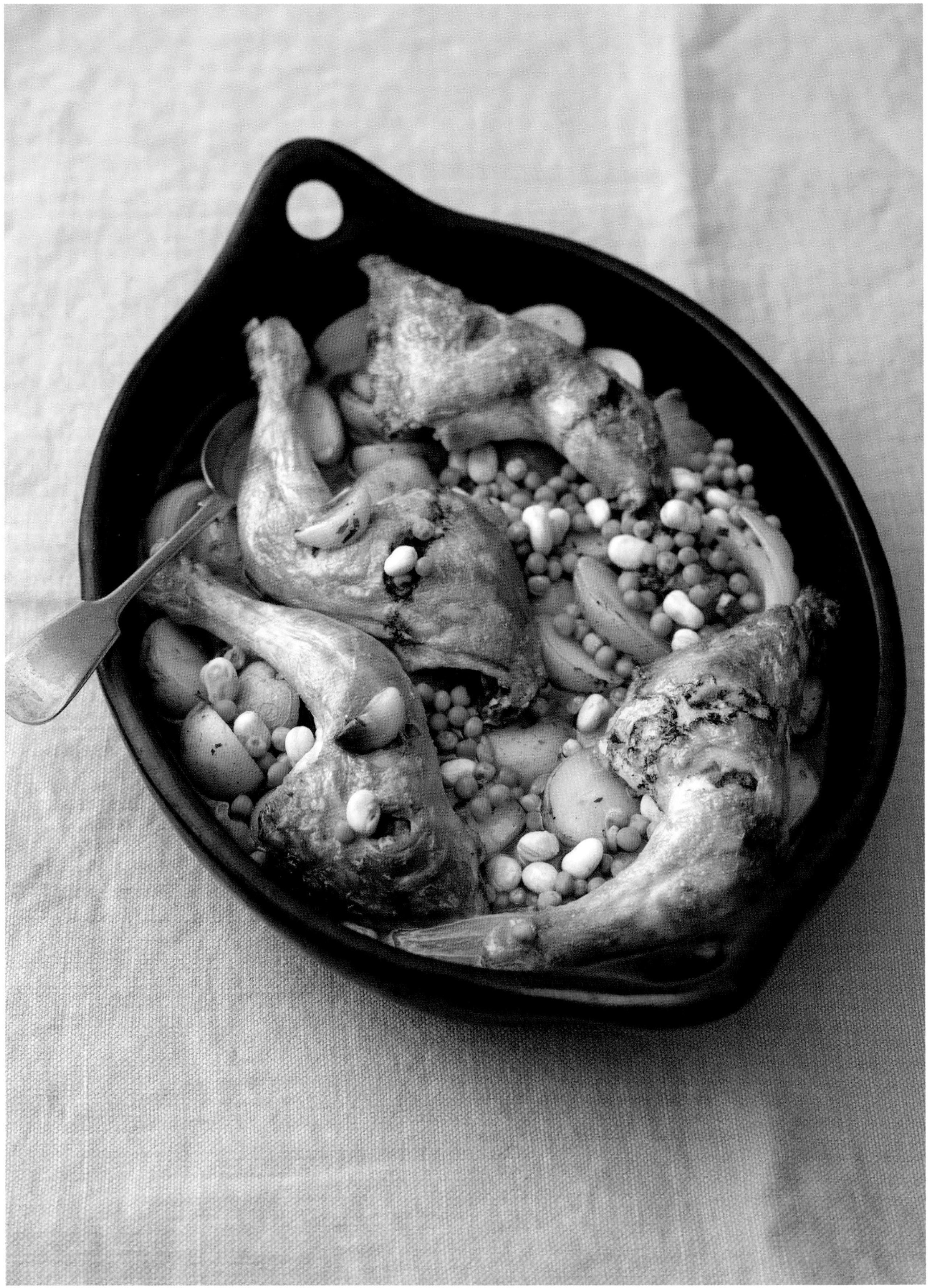

All-in-One Braised Chicken Legs

SERVES 4

1 large onion, cut into 8 wedges
500g waxy new/salad potatoes, cut in half lengthways (quartered if large)
1 head of garlic, cloves separated and left unpeeled
good pinch of dried tarragon, rosemary or oregano
sea salt and freshly ground black pepper
4 chicken legs, skin-on, trimmed and slashed twice through the skin and flesh with scissors
olive oil, for drizzling
200g frozen broad beans
200g frozen petit pois
1 x quantity Lucy's Green Sauce (see page 195), to serve (optional)
coriander sprigs or roughly chopped mint and/or parsley, to garnish (optional)

One of our family favourites and definitely one of those recipes that's far better than the sum of its parts! A cinch to make, with lots of variations for every season, this is a very easy supper. Leave out the green sauce, if you like, as the braise juices are delicious in their plainness, but it's a lovely addition. If there's one recipe in this book that you return to time and again, I bet it's this one.

1. Preheat the oven to 220°C/200°C fan/gas 7.

2. Find a large, shallow, oval, ovenproof dish around 33 x 26 x 6cm (or a similar-sized roasting tin) that will hold the chicken legs comfortably in one layer. Spread the onion wedges over the bottom of the dish/tin, followed by the potatoes, garlic cloves, herbs and some salt and pepper. Pour over 175ml water and then sit the chicken legs, skin-side up, on top.

3. Drizzle the legs with a little olive oil and a light sprinkling of salt. Cook at the top of the oven for 50 minutes, turning the dish/tin halfway through the cooking time, or until the chicken is cooked through and the skin is golden brown and crispy. Stir in the broad beans and petit pois and cook for a further 10 minutes.

4. Remove from the oven, then just before serving, dot spoonfuls of green sauce over the top (if using) and serve the remainder separately. Swirl over a little olive oil and scatter with the herbs (if using).

GET AHEAD

- Prepare to the end of step 2, 2–3 hours ahead.
- Or cook entirely up to 2 days in advance, omitting the broad beans and petit pois, cool, cover and chill, then reheat in the oven at 200°C/180°C fan/gas 6 for about 30 minutes or until hot throughout, and then add the broad beans and petit pois as above. If adding extra green vegetables (see *Hints & Tips*), add them after reheating and just before serving.

HINTS & TIPS

- Adjust the vegetables according to the season. For example, for a winter version, cut raw celery and root vegetables (carrots, parsnips, celeriac) into chunky dice and add with the potatoes.
- Whole spinach leaves or shredded kale or chard leaves can be added by the handful just before serving. The leaves will wilt in the hot liquid almost instantly.

Chinese Duck Breast & Pak Choi Stir-fry

SERVES 4

3 boneless duck breasts (approx. 400g in total)
1 teaspoon Chinese five-spice powder
2 splashes of vegetable oil
2 pak choi bulbs, leaves and stems separated (keep them separate) and cut into 2cm-thick slices on a diagonal
600g cooked fresh egg noodles

For the sauce
2 tablespoons toasted sesame oil
3 tablespoons dark soy sauce
2 tablespoons sweet chilli sauce
2 tablespoons oyster sauce

To serve (optional)
½ red chilli, de-seeded and very thinly sliced
2 spring onions, trimmed and thinly sliced lengthways or diagonally
toasted sesame seeds (toast them in the dry wok/pan on a medium heat for 2–3 minutes)
a few coriander sprigs, if you have them

GET AHEAD

- Prepare the sauce up to 3 days in advance, cover and keep at room temperature.
- Prepare step 1 and slice the pak choi up to 1 day ahead, cover and store both separately in the fridge.

As with most stir-fries, I would recommend preparing everything in advance before you begin, then all's set to go for a very tasty, quick supper. The sauce ingredient list seems quite long, but they're mostly store cupboard items from bottles. The duck is extraordinarily tender.

1. Pull the skin off the duck breasts and discard, then with the palm of one hand laid on top of a breast, slice each breast in half horizontally lengthways to make two pieces exactly the same breast shape, but half the thickness. Slice each one into roughly 1cm strips. Put the strips in a bowl, add the five-spice powder and stir to coat.

2. Mix the sauce ingredients together, adding 1 tablespoon of water, then set aside. Boil a kettleful of water.

3. Heat a splash of vegetable oil in a wok or large frying pan until hot, add the pak choi stems and stir-fry on a high heat for a few minutes until beginning to soften, yet retaining a little bite, then add the leaves. Stir-fry until just wilted, but still bright green. Transfer to a plate and keep warm.

4. Heat a splash more vegetable oil in the pan, add a small handful of the duck strips and stir-fry on a high heat for a few minutes until just beginning to take on some colour. Remove from the pan onto a separate plate and repeat with the remaining duck.

5. Meanwhile, put the noodles into a large, heatproof bowl. Pour the boiling water over to cover and leave for a few minutes to heat through.

6. Add the sauce to the wok or pan, allow it to bubble up and then scrape the tasty sediment off the bottom. Return the duck to the wok/pan, plus any escaped juices.

7. Drain the hot noodles and divide between four bowls or plates. Spoon over the duck and sauce mixture, followed by the pak choi, then sprinkle over any/all of the serving suggestions (if using) to finish, and serve.

HINTS & TIPS

- Shredded Savoy cabbage is a good alternative to pak choi, as are spinach leaves.

Fried Sausagemeat Gnocchi Three-ways

EACH VARIATION SERVES 2–3

For the basic tomato version
splash of olive oil
225g best quality sausagemeat (or use your favourite sausages and slit their skins lengthways with a sharp knife to release the sausagemeat)
500g fresh ready-made gnocchi
pinch of dried oregano
2 garlic cloves, crushed
1 x 400g tin chopped tomatoes
sea salt and freshly ground black pepper
grated Parmesan cheese, a little chopped parsley or a few basil leaves, to garnish (optional)

GET AHEAD

- The main recipe and Variation 2 can be made the day before, cooled, covered and chilled. Reheat in the pan on a low heat until hot throughout. The former will need a little extra water stirred in.
- Variation 1 can be made the day before (apart from adding the cream; stir this in when reheating), cooled, covered and chilled. Reheat gently as above.

Fried gnocchi is very different from that which is cooked in boiling water. Less doughy, it crisps up, browns into a very appealing golden colour and tastes like fried potato – which it is really! This recipe is so simple, yet so tasty and versatile, too. The sausagemeat contributes oodles of flavour to the gnocchi, producing a very delicious supper. It's inexpensive and nice and quick, too.

1. Heat the olive oil in a 24cm sauté pan (that's ideally about 6cm deep), preferably non-stick, so the gnocchi will fit in roughly one layer. Add the sausagemeat and fry on a high heat for 5–10 minutes, breaking it up with a wooden spoon, until it is crumbly, still a tad lumpy and brown. Transfer to a plate using a slotted spoon, leaving the fat behind.

2. Add the gnocchi to the same pan and fry in the residual fat (adding a little more oil, if necessary) on a high heat for 5–10 minutes until golden brown and crispy.

3. Return the sausagemeat to the pan with the oregano, garlic, tomatoes and some salt and pepper. Rinse the tomato tin out with a little water and add that, too. Bring to a simmer and then bubble gently for a few minutes until the gnocchi is heated through (you may need to add a little more water as it thickens up). Check the seasoning and serve scattered with grated Parmesan cheese, chopped parsley or a few basil leaves (if using).

Variation 1 – Creamy
Cook the sausagemeat and gnocchi as above. Mix 1 teaspoon of Dijon mustard with 100ml double cream or crème fraîche. Return the sausagemeat to the pan with the cream, plus some seasoning. Turn everything over very gently to coat with a wooden spoon and warm through on a low heat. You may need to thin it with a little water. Add a little more cream, if you'd like an even creamier sauce.

Variation 2 – Au Naturel with Fennel & Cherry Tomatoes
Remove and discard the tough outer layer and stems of a fennel bulb and reserve the green ferny fronds (roughly chop them). Halve and thinly slice the fennel. Cook the fennel with the sausagemeat as above until the fennel is soft and a little charred and the sausagemeat is browned. Remove from the pan, as in the main recipe, and fry the gnocchi until golden brown. Return the sausagemeat and fennel to the pan with 12 small cherry tomatoes, halved, and some seasoning. Heat through until the tomatoes are beginning to collapse. Scatter with the reserved chopped fennel fronds.

Gigot Lamb Steaks with Flageolet Beans & Spinach

SERVES 2

2 lamb gigot steaks (leg steaks, also known as gigot chops)
olive oil
sea salt and freshly ground black pepper
a sprig of rosemary, leaves picked and roughly chopped
1 x 400g tin flageolet beans, drained and rinsed
2–3 tablespoons crème fraîche or double cream
2–3 generous handfuls of baby spinach leaves
2 teaspoons redcurrant jelly

Possibly the quickest recipe in the book, this takes less than 10 minutes from start to finish. Hurrah for that at the end of a busy day!

1. Snip the steaks at two or three intervals through the fat – this stops them curling up when cooking (see *Hints & Tips*). Heat a dry frying pan or sauté pan (into which they fit comfortably, allowing a little extra space around the edges) on a high heat until very hot. Rub the steaks with a little olive oil followed by a little salt, then add them to the hot pan and cook until well browned on the underside and almost cooked through. Turn them over (little beads of blood appearing on the top is a good indicator of when to turn over) and repeat, but for less time this side.

2. Add the rosemary and flageolet beans and nestle around and under the steaks. Add the crème fraîche or cream and some salt and pepper and bring to a gentle simmer, just to heat everything through. Add a splash or two of water at any time if the consistency becomes too 'gluggy'.

3. Nestle in the spinach and nudge around for a minute or two until it's beginning to wilt. Top each steak with a little redcurrant jelly (or serve it separately) and serve straight from the pan.

HINTS & TIPS

- When snipping through the lamb fat, ensure you cut through the membrane running between the fat and the meat as well, as this is the bit that contracts upon heating and causes steaks and chops to curl up.
- When in season, I like to swap the spinach for wild garlic leaves.

Parma Ham-wrapped Salmon Fillets with Creamy Spinach & Puy Lentils

SERVES 2

2 salmon fillets, skinned
2 slices Parma ham
good glug of olive oil
sea salt and freshly ground black pepper
150g spinach leaves, washed and coarse leaves sliced into thick ribbons
1 x 250g pouch of ready-cooked Puy lentils
1 garlic clove, crushed
1 teaspoon Dijon mustard
3 tablespoons crème fraîche or double cream
juice of ½ lemon

Another one of the quickest recipes in the book, this can be on the table in around 10 minutes. It involves a little bit of cheating in the form of a pouch of ready-cooked Puy lentils, which have a very long shelf life and are so handy to have on standby in the store cupboard. The remaining ingredients are easily picked up.

1. Find a small–medium frying pan, no bigger than 24cm.

2. If the salmon fillets are much thinner at one end, tuck this underneath so they become a more even thickness. Wrap a slice of Parma ham around the middle of each one, ensuring the seam is underneath.

3. Heat the olive oil in the frying pan on a medium–high heat, sprinkle a good pinch of salt over the bottom of the pan, then add the salmon fillets and lightly brown the salmon on all four sides (top, bottom and two edges of each fillet), starting with the seam-side down to seal it. This will take around 2 minutes per side, by which time the salmon will be just cooked in the middle. Transfer to a plate and keep warm.

4. Add the spinach to the pan and stir around on a high heat until just wilting. Add the lentils, garlic and some salt and pepper, reduce the heat to medium and warm through for a few minutes. Mix together the mustard and crème fraîche or cream, add to the pan and bubble up. You may need to thin the mixture to your liking with a little water. Check the seasoning – it should be well seasoned.

5. Return the salmon to the pan, plus any escaped juices, squeeze the lemon juice over the top and serve straight away.

HINTS & TIPS

- The spinach can be swapped for frozen petit pois, if you like, and the salmon for white fish fillets, such as haddock or cod.
- Any leftover Parma ham can be wrapped and chilled for several days, or frozen for use in another recipe (defrost before use).

Plaice with Butter Bean & Tahini Purée & Cherry Tomatoes

SERVES 2

1 x 400g tin butter beans, drained and rinsed
1 tablespoon tahini paste
4 tablespoons olive oil, plus extra for frying and serving
juice of ½ lemon
sea salt and freshly ground black pepper
1 small garlic clove, crushed
12 baby cherry tomatoes, halved
pinch of dried oregano
2 handfuls of baby spinach leaves (optional), left whole and washed
knob of butter
2 plaice fillets, trimmed of any lacy edges, skin-on or skinless
Pistachio, Parsley & Green Chilli Pesto (see page 202), to serve

GET AHEAD

- The purée can be made up to 3 days in advance – keep it covered in the fridge.
- The pesto can be made a few days in advance and kept in a covered jar in the fridge. You won't need it all for this recipe.

HINTS & TIPS

- Add a small pinch of dried chilli flakes to the purée for a bit of spice, and add a couple of knobs of butter to the warm purée for some richness.

This supper is in and out of the frying pan in around 10 minutes or so. The light, soft and lemony butter bean purée makes a tasty alternative to potatoes alongside all sorts of other recipes, too, and is also very good served as a dip. The plaice can be substituted with almost any white fish or salmon fillets. Brill is a particular favourite of mine.

1. To make the butter bean purée, put the butter beans, tahini, olive oil, lemon juice, 2 tablespoons of water and some salt and pepper into a food-processor and whizz together, adding some extra water, if needed, to make a smooth, soft, velvety purée. Set aside.

2. In a frying pan, into which the fish fillets will fit comfortably side-by-side, heat a splash of olive oil and cook the garlic on a medium heat for 1 minute. Add the purée and heat through, stirring all the time, thinning it with a little extra water, if necessary. Check the seasoning. Divide the mixture between serving plates and spread it out, then keep warm. Wipe out the pan with kitchen paper, if necessary.

3. Heat a splash more olive oil in the pan, then add the tomatoes, oregano and some seasoning and cook on a high heat for a few minutes until the tomatoes are just beginning to soften and 'give'. Add the spinach to the pan (if using) and swish round for a minute or two until just wilted. Spoon this mixture on top of the purée, scraping out all the tasty sticky bits from the pan as well. Keep warm. Wipe out the pan.

4. Heat another splash of olive oil and the butter in the pan, then scatter a good pinch of salt over the base. Add the plaice fillets, top side down, and cook on a high heat until they are turning golden brown, about 5 minutes, then turn over and cook for a further minute.

5. Arrange the plaice on top of the tomatoes, then spoon over a little of the pesto (thin it with some olive oil, if you prefer a looser sauce). Finish with a grinding of pepper and a swirl of olive oil.

Posh Fish & (Chunky) Chips

SERVES 4

500g small–medium good-quality potatoes (such as Maris Piper – about 2–3 potatoes), unpeeled and scrubbed
splash of olive oil
large pinch of dried oregano or thyme
sea salt
4 white fish fillets (around 140g each), such as cod, haddock, coley or hake, skinned (or use 1 larger whole fillet, around 450g)
200g samphire, any tough 'spiny' pieces removed
knob of butter (optional)

For the Parmesan crust
4 heaped tablespoons fresh white breadcrumbs
3 tablespoons grated Parmesan cheese
2 tablespoons olive oil
¼ teaspoon sea salt
freshly ground black pepper, to taste

To serve (optional)
Tartare Sauce (see page 200)
Vinegar (of your choice)

This one-pan, oven-baked take on the classic British 'fish and chips' is an unbelievably quick and easy family supper, popular with all age groups, plus it's a lot healthier, too. For me the home-made tartare sauce is non-negotiable, but for others it's the vinegar that's a must.

1. Preheat the oven to 220°C/200°C fan/gas 7. Find a large (lipped) baking tray around 41 x 31cm (or use a large, shallow roasting tin of a similar size).

2. Cut the potatoes in half lengthways, then cut each half into three or four wedges, depending on their size. Place in a bowl, add the olive oil and dried oregano or thyme, season with salt and toss to coat the wedges. Spread out in a single layer, with a cut-side down, on the baking tray. Bake for 15–18 minutes until crisp and golden all over, turning after 10 minutes.

3. Meanwhile, mix or whizz the Parmesan crust ingredients together. Boil a kettleful of water.

4. If using one larger fillet of fish, cut it into manageable pieces, then tuck any thin ends of the fillets/pieces underneath so they are a more even thickness. Divide and spread the Parmesan crust mixture evenly over the top of the fish, then place them in between the potato wedges on the baking tray, moving the wedges to make space, but keeping everything in one layer. Return to the top of the oven for a further 5–7 minutes, depending on the thickness of the fillets (see *Hints & Tips*), until the fish is just cooked through.

5. Meanwhile, whilst the fish is cooking put the samphire into a heatproof bowl and pour over enough boiling water to just cover it. Leave for 5 minutes, then drain and stir in the butter (if using). Add the samphire to the baking tray when the fish is cooked, then serve.

GET AHEAD

- Complete to the end of step 2 any time on the day. Leave on the baking tray at room temperature. Reheat the potatoes for a few minutes until sizzling, before continuing.
- Make the crust (step 3) up to 1 day in advance, cover and chill.

HINTS & TIPS

- Fish cooking times depend on the thickness of the fillets. 2.5cm-thick fillets will take 7–8 minutes, thinner fillets will take about 5 minutes and thicker ones up to 10 minutes.

Prawn Laksa

SERVES 4

For the paste

2 mild red chillies, cut into small chunks (remove seeds and membrane if you like less heat, but this isn't very hot)
5 garlic cloves, roughly chopped
2 thumb-sized pieces of fresh root ginger, peeled and chopped (or use 6 teaspoons ginger paste from a jar)
4 small round shallots, quartered
1 stick of lemon grass, woody outer layers removed and soft bottom section cut into chunks (or use 1 teaspoon lemon grass paste from a jar)
½ tablespoon ground coriander
1 teaspoon ground cumin
2 teaspoons shrimp paste
½ teaspoon ground cinnamon
1 tablespoon vegetable oil

For the laksa

1 tablespoon vegetable oil
1 x 400g tin coconut milk
1 litre fresh fish or chicken stock (or use 2 stock cubes)
sea salt and freshly ground black pepper
300g (frozen weight) raw shelled tiger or king prawns (around 8 per person), defrosted
a good handful of baby spinach leaves
juice of 1 lime, to taste
a little dark soy sauce, to taste
600g 'straight-to-wok' ribbon rice noodles (or similar) (or see *Hints & Tips*)
a handful of coriander, leaves picked and roughly chopped
1 lime, cut into quarters, to serve (optional)

As with most Asian recipes requiring spices, the list of ingredients for this aromatic, refreshing, spicy Malaysian noodle soup might look dauntingly long – but don't be put off as they're mainly just store cupboard items whizzed into a paste and cooked all in one go. It's then plain sailing with rice noodles and raw prawns added to stock and coconut milk, creating a meal in itself in a bowl. It's delicious! To ring the changes, swap the prawns for 400g of firm tofu, cubed.

1. Blitz all the paste ingredients together to make a very smooth, fine paste using a herb chopper, stick blender in its beaker or a small food-processor.

2. For the laksa, heat the vegetable oil in a deep saucepan or wok on a medium heat. Add the paste and cook for 5 minutes, stirring, until it becomes aromatic and begins to turn a darker colour.

3. Stir in the coconut milk and stock (if using cubes, crumble them into the pan and add 2½ empty coconut milk tins full of water) and bring to the boil. Add some salt and pepper to taste, bearing in mind it will taste a bit raw at this stage. Reduce the heat and simmer very gently for 20 minutes, giving it the odd stir.

4. When you are ready to eat, add the prawns and baby spinach to the hot soup, then immediately remove from the heat, allowing the prawns to cook in the indirect heat for a few minutes. As soon as they turn pink, they are cooked. Add some lime juice and soy sauce to taste.

5. Distribute the (unheated) noodles between four serving bowls, untangling them, if necessary. Ladle the laksa over the noodles, scatter with the chopped coriander, nestle in the lime wedges (if using) and serve.

GET AHEAD

- The paste can be made up to 3 days in advance, but keep it well covered in the fridge to avoid the strong smell escaping.
- Or, make the recipe to the end of step 3 up to 3 days in advance, then cool, cover and chill. Reheat gently in the pan until hot throughout before adding the prawns and spinach as above.

HINTS & TIPS

- For the noodles, alternatively, you can use 200g dried flat rice noodles, cooked according to the packet instructions (place the noodles in a bowl, cover with boiling water, leave for 3 minutes, then drain). Boil the kettle before you're ready to add the prawns to the laksa.

Baked Chinese Chicken & Rice

SERVES 6

20g dried mushrooms (preferably shiitake)
100ml boiling water
vegetable oil, for greasing
1 onion, finely chopped
250g white Basmati rice
700ml hot fresh chicken stock (or use 2 stock cubes)
3 tablespoons dry sherry
3 tablespoons dark soy sauce, plus a little extra for spooning over the chicken
1 teaspoon sesame oil
3 garlic cloves, crushed
thumb-sized piece of fresh root ginger, peeled and chopped (or use 1 teaspoon ginger paste from a jar)
12 chicken drumsticks, bone-in, skin-on, well-trimmed
fine sea salt
Cucumber Raita, to serve (see page 207) (optional)

Despite possibly not winning a beauty contest, I think this recipe is fairly high up there in the taste stakes. Redolent of a Chinese takeaway, according to my children, it really couldn't be easier, with all the ingredients going into the dish raw, leaving the oven to do the work, then, hey presto, supper's ready!

1. Place the mushrooms in a small, heatproof measuring jug or bowl, cover with the boiling water and set aside for 30 minutes to allow them to rehydrate. Drain in a sieve, retaining the soaking liquid, then snip the mushrooms into small pieces using scissors. Set aside.

2. Preheat the oven to 220°C/200°C fan/gas 7. Find a large, shallow, oval, ovenproof dish around 33 x 26 x 6cm (or a similar-sized roasting tin), and grease lightly with vegetable oil.

3. Distribute the onion, rice and snipped mushrooms in the bottom of the dish/tin. Pour the reserved mushroom liquid through a fine sieve (to catch any gritty sediment) into the hot stock in a jug, stir in the sherry, soy sauce, sesame oil, garlic and ginger, then pour into the dish/tin. Arrange the chicken drumsticks on top, then drizzle a little extra soy sauce over the chicken skin and dust with a sprinkling of salt.

4. Bake at the top of the oven for 1 hour or until the chicken is cooked through and the skin is golden brown and crispy and all the stock is absorbed. Remove from the oven and leave to sit for 10 minutes before serving. Serve with the raita, if you like.

GET AHEAD

- All the ingredients can be prepared (but not cooked) up to 1 day in advance and stored individually in covered containers in the fridge.
- I mix the sherry, soy sauce, sesame oil, garlic and ginger together 1 day in advance. This soy mixture can also be added to the stock any time on the day and reheated with the stock when required.

HINTS & TIPS

- Use chicken thighs (skin-on), if you prefer. However, if allowing two thighs per person, you may need to use a slightly larger dish so they aren't hugger-mugger.

Smoked Haddock & Sweetcorn Chowder

SERVES 4–5

30g butter
1 onion, finely chopped
2 rashers smoked streaky bacon, snipped into fine strips
1 large potato (approx. 225g), peeled and cut into 1cm dice
1 leek, trimmed, washed and finely sliced
½ teaspoon ground turmeric
1 rounded tablespoon plain flour
300ml fresh fish or chicken stock (or use a stock cube)
600ml full-fat milk
2 tablespoons double cream, or more to taste
1 bay leaf
sea salt and freshly ground black pepper
400–450g un-dyed, smoked haddock fillets, skinned and snipped into bite-sized dice
1 x 198g tin sweetcorn, drained and rinsed
a squeeze or two of fresh lemon juice (optional)
a handful of parsley leaves, chopped
a pinch of black mustard seeds (optional)

A quick, easy, sustaining and delicious one-pot warming supper (or lunch), made even better with a good wedge of Seedy Soda Bread (see page 163). A meal in itself!

1. Melt the butter in a medium saucepan, add the onion and bacon and cook slowly until beginning to soften, about 10 minutes. Add the potato, leek and turmeric and cook gently for a further 5 minutes, stirring occasionally.

2. Stir in the flour, cook for a minute or two, then gradually stir in the stock, followed by the milk and cream, keeping the sauce smooth. Add the bay leaf and some salt and pepper, then bring to just below boiling point and simmer very gently for 5 minutes, giving it the odd stir.

3. Add the smoked haddock and sweetcorn and bring up to just below boiling point (the fish will cook/heat through in this time).

4. Just before serving, remove the bay leaf, then stir in a squeeze or two of lemon juice to taste (if using) and check the seasoning. Scatter with the parsley and mustard seeds (if using).

GET AHEAD

- Make to the end of step 3 up to 2 days in advance, then cool, cover and chill. Reheat gently in the saucepan to just under boiling point before serving.

HINTS & TIPS

- Be careful not to boil the soup, otherwise it may curdle slightly (but should it do so, it doesn't really matter, it just won't look quite so nice!).

- To spice it up, add ½ teaspoon garam masala or curry powder at the same time as the turmeric. Slices of crispy fried chorizo also make a tasty topping (but this does require another pan!).

- All manner of things can be added to the chowder instead of, or as well as the smoked haddock, such as raw peeled prawns or any white fish, cooked shelled mussels or crab meat, baby spinach leaves, kale, chard, warm 6-minute soft-boiled eggs (halved and nestled on top just before serving). Except for the eggs, they should all be added towards the end just before serving and simmered for no more than a few minutes until cooked in the chowder.

Sri Lankan Cashew Nut, Cauliflower & Potato Curry

SERVES 4

150g unsalted cashew nuts
good glug of vegetable oil
1 large onion, sliced
a small handful of dried curry leaves, roughly crushed in your hands
1 medium cauliflower (approx. 600–700g)
4 medium waxy new/salad potatoes, skin on
2 garlic cloves, crushed
1 teaspoon ground turmeric
1 teaspoon medium curry powder
½ teaspoon ground cinnamon
⅛ teaspoon hot chilli powder (or ¼ teaspoon if you like more heat)
1 teaspoon sea salt
freshly ground black pepper
1 green chilli, halved
1 x 400g tin coconut milk

To serve (optional)
natural yoghurt
a good handful of roughly chopped coriander leaves
onion seeds
warm flatbreads
poppadoms

HINTS & TIPS

- A handful or two of green leafy vegetables, such as baby spinach, can be wilted into the curry at the last minute, or you can add a handful of frozen petit pois. Regular white potatoes could be used but may break up a little during cooking.

On holiday in Sri Lanka I spent considerable time in the kitchen, notepad in hand, watching and learning about new ingredients and how to make the wide range of curries, sambals and chutneys being prepared. Lovely Lahiru, the Singhalese chef, showed me this delicious vegetarian curry (which can be vegan, too, if using vegan yoghurt).

1. Put the cashews into a bowl, cover with cold water and leave to soak for 2–3 hours.

2. Heat the vegetable oil in a large saucepan, add the onion and curry leaves and cook slowly until soft, about 10 minutes.

3. Meanwhile, discard the tough outer leaves from the cauliflower, then cut off and reserve all the fresh inside leaves, leaving them whole (halve them lengthways if they're very big). Snap off or cut the head into small-ish, even-sized florets. Discard the tough bits of the core/stem and cut the fleshy parts into bite-sized pieces. Cut the potatoes in half and then each half into three even-sized chunks (or just halve, if small).

4. When the onion is cooked, add the garlic, spices, salt and some pepper and continue to cook, stirring, for a few minutes until they become fragrant. Add the green chilli halves and the coconut milk. Fill the coconut tin with water and add half of this (reserve the remainder for possible use later). Bring to the boil, then add the potatoes, bring back to the boil and simmer gently for 10 minutes. Add the cauliflower and simmer for another 10 minutes.

5. Drain the cashews, add these to the pan and simmer for a further 10 minutes, adding the reserved cauliflower leaves 5 minutes before the end of the cooking time. If the sauce is becoming too thick at any stage, add a little more of the reserved coconut tin water. The finished curry should be the consistency of double cream. Check the seasoning.

6. Remove from the heat and cool slightly for 5–10 minutes before serving. Serve either from the pan or in individual bowls, topped with generous dollops of yoghurt and a scattering of chopped coriander and onion seeds, with flatbreads alongside for mopping up, and poppadoms, too, if you like.

Toad in the Veg Patch

SERVES 4–5
(depending on the size of the sausages)

125g carrots, peeled, halved and cut into wedges
1 red onion, cut into 8 wedges
good glug of olive oil
sea salt and freshly ground black pepper
8 good-quality sausages (I use fat ones)
125g tenderstem broccoli, tough bottom stalks peeled off, then split lengthways into 'trees' of equal breadth
16 small cherry tomatoes

For the batter
150ml milk
110g plain flour
1 teaspoon English mustard powder
pinch of sea salt
2 eggs
a sprig of rosemary, leaves picked and roughly chopped

To serve (optional)
sea salt flakes
2 rosemary sprigs
mustard

This recipe can be varied in so many ways. Any combinations of veg – just whatever you like or have to hand, and the same for the sausages – fat, thin, flavoured or even possibly wrapped with rashers of streaky bacon. It creates a lovely, quick, all-in-one 'meat and (more than) two veg' supper!

1. Preheat the oven to 220°C/200°C fan/gas 7. Find a large, shallow roasting tin around 41 x 26cm and ideally no deeper than 4cm.

2. First, make the batter. Add the milk, flour, mustard powder, salt, eggs and 150ml water to a blender (this won't work in a food-processor) and briefly blend together until just combined. Stir in the rosemary and set aside.

3. Put the carrots and red onion into the roasting tin with the olive oil and some salt and pepper and swirl around to coat. Spread out in a single layer, then slot in the sausages. Cook at the top of the oven for 15 minutes.

4. Turn the vegetables and sausages over with a fish slice, add the broccoli and cook for a further 5 minutes. Remove from the oven and scatter over the cherry tomatoes.

5. Give the batter a quick stir and pour it over the sizzling hot vegetables, then return to the oven for a further 25–30 minutes or until risen and deep golden brown.

6. Serve straight away, scattered with a few sea salt flakes and sprigs of rosemary, if you like. Some mustard alongside is good, too.

GET AHEAD

- Make the recipe to the end of step 4 up to 1 day in advance, then cool, cover and chill (storing the batter separately). Reheat the veg and sausages in the oven (temp as above) until sizzling hot again (5–10 minutes) before continuing with the batter.

HINTS & TIPS

- All vegetable quantities given are approximate. Just ensure the vegetables and sausages sit in a single layer in the tin.

- Other veg suggestions include chunks of courgettes, aubergine, butternut squash, sweet potato or red pepper, or frozen petit pois or broad beans.

Turmeric Roasted Cauliflower & Chickpeas

SERVES 4–6
(depending on the size of the cauliflower)

1 medium cauliflower
1 tablespoon ground turmeric
1 teaspoon ground cumin
1 teaspoon ground coriander
1 teaspoon garam masala
1 teaspoon sea salt
freshly ground black pepper
75ml olive oil, plus extra for greasing and serving
1 x 400g tin chickpeas, drained and rinsed
1 tablespoon pumpkin seeds
2 teaspoons white sesame seeds
1 teaspoon black sesame seeds (optional)

To serve (optional)
thick Greek-style yoghurt (use vegan yoghurt, if you prefer)
a handful of coriander, leaves and thin stalks roughly chopped
nigella or onion seeds

This quick and versatile recipe can be eaten hot as a main course or at room temperature as a salad. It's worth cooking for the smell alone! Healthy, vegetarian – and vegan, too, if using vegan yoghurt.

1. Preheat the oven to 220°C/200°C fan/gas 7. Find a large, shallow roasting tin, around 41 x 26cm and ideally no deeper than 4cm (or use a large, lipped baking tray) and grease it very lightly with a smidgen of olive oil.

2. Discard the tough outer leaves from the cauliflower, then cut off and reserve all the fresh inside leaves, leaving them whole (halve them lengthways if they're very big). Snap off or cut the head into small-ish, even-sized florets. Discard the tough bits of the core/stem, and cut the fleshy parts into bite-sized pieces. Put into a large bowl.

3. Mix the ground spices, salt and some pepper with the olive oil, pour over the cauliflower and mix well to coat evenly – (gloved!) hands are easiest for this. Spread out in a single layer in the roasting tin – the cauliflower shouldn't be too overcrowded.

4. Roast for 20 minutes, turning the cauliflower over and adding the chickpeas, pumpkin seeds and white and black (if using) sesame seeds after 10 minutes. When it's ready, the cauliflower should be just tender and charred in places, but still retain a little bite.

5. Serve from the tin (when the steam has subsided) or transfer to a serving platter. Garnish with swirled blobs of yoghurt, a drizzle of olive oil, the chopped coriander and a scattering of nigella or onion seeds. Serve some extra yoghurt separately, too, if you like.

GET AHEAD

- Make up to 1 day in advance, then cool, cover and chill. Reheat in the oven (temp as above) until sizzling hot, about 5–10 minutes.

HINTS & TIPS

- Choose a cauliflower with fresh green leaves and crispy stems. It's important to make the florets roughly the same size, so they cook evenly.

Traffic Light Chicken

SERVES 4

olive oil, for drizzling
8 chicken thighs, skin-on and bone-in, well trimmed and snipped twice through the skin and flesh with scissors
4 small–medium (around 300g) raw beetroots, peeled, halved and each cut into 6 wedges
350g carrots, peeled, halved lengthways, larger ones cut into quarters lengthways
1 head of garlic, cloves separated and peeled (halve any larger cloves)
1 teaspoon dried tarragon
sea salt and freshly ground black pepper
250g dried orzo
500ml well-seasoned fresh chicken or vegetable stock (or use 2 stock cubes)
3 medium courgettes (around 250g), cut diagonally into 2cm triangular chunks

A lovely, silky-soft and colourful mélange, that was originally created when I had a glut of vegetables in the garden. The name came about when my friend Georgie exclaimed, 'Ooh, traffic light chicken,' upon seeing the bright red, amber and green colours! Use the recipe as a guide and swap around any vegetables that you have to hand, bearing in mind that root vegetables need to go in with the chicken, and green ones (that grow above the ground) should be added with the orzo. For a vegetarian version, simply leave out the chicken and use vegetable stock.

1. Preheat the oven to 230°C/210°C fan/gas 8. Find a large, shallow roasting tin around 41 x 26cm and ideally no deeper than 4cm, and line it with a large piece of baking parchment (including up and above the sides).

2. Drizzle the paper with a little olive oil and arrange the chicken thighs, beetroot and carrots in the tin, spaced out in a single layer. Scatter over the garlic cloves. Drizzle with a little more olive oil, scatter over the tarragon and season everything generously with salt and pepper. Put into the top of the oven, turn the oven down to 220°C/200°C fan/gas 7 and cook for 30 minutes.

3. Remove from the oven, baste the chicken with the juices and turn the beetroot over (the point of a knife is best for this). Add the orzo, avoiding the chicken as you do so. Pour the stock into the tin around the chicken, ensuring all the orzo is submerged in the liquid and not sitting on top of the chicken, otherwise it won't cook. Scatter over the courgettes, then return to the oven for a further 10 minutes.

4. Remove from the oven and stir the orzo around a little with a teaspoon to ensure it's all submerged and cooking evenly. Turn the vegetables over and nestle them in, too, if necessary. Cook for a final 10 minutes, then remove and leave to stand for 10 minutes (or a little longer) before eating.

GET AHEAD

- Make to the end of step 2 any time on the day, then cool, cover and chill, if necessary. Reheat the ingredients in the oven until sizzling and hot throughout (about 5–10 minutes) before continuing with steps 3 and 4.

HINTS & TIPS

- If the beetroot comes complete with leaves and stems, these are delicious washed, sliced and cooked in salted water (or steamed) for a few minutes until tender, then served alongside the chicken.
- Sliced courgette flowers, rinsed out and the stamens removed, are good scattered over the top at the same time as the courgettes.

Chorizo Sausage, Red Pepper & Mixed Grain Bake

SERVES 4

olive oil, for drizzling
8 raw chorizo cooking sausages (I like picante, the spicy ones)
1 large onion, cut into 8 wedges
2 red peppers, de-seeded and cut into chunks
1 head of garlic, cloves separated and peeled
a good pinch of dried oregano
sea salt and freshly ground black pepper
2 x 250g pouches of ready-to-eat smoky Spanish-style mixed grains and rice
10 black olives, pitted and halved
a few basil leaves or oregano sprigs, to garnish

This smoky sausage bake really couldn't be easier, or tastier, for that matter! Ensure you buy raw cooking chorizo sausages rather than the cured 'salami-style' ones. I have allowed two sausages per person in the recipe as their denseness makes them quite filling. However, you might like to up the total quantity to 12 depending on who you are feeding.

1. Preheat the oven to 220°C/200°C fan/gas 7. Find a large, shallow roasting tin around 41 x 26cm and ideally no deeper than 4cm and line it with a large piece of baking parchment (including up and above the sides).

2. Drizzle the paper with a little olive oil, then arrange the sausages, onion, red peppers and garlic cloves in the tin, spaced out in a single layer. Drizzle with a little more olive oil and scatter with the oregano and some salt and pepper. Cook at the top of the oven for 30 minutes.

3. Remove from the oven, then turn the sausages and vegetables over. Add the grains (having first broken them up in the un-opened pouches) and black olives, distributing, coating and nestling them in between everything in the tin. Return to the oven for a final 10 minutes. Scatter with basil leaves or oregano sprigs and serve.

GET AHEAD

- The vegetables can be prepared (but not cooked) up to 1 day in advance, covered and stored in the fridge.
- Make to the end of step 2 any time on the day, then cool, cover and chill, if necessary. Reheat the ingredients in the tin (temp as above) until sizzling and hot throughout (about 5–10 minutes) before continuing with step 3.

HINTS & TIPS

- Raw cooking chorizo sausages are available either 'picante' (spicy) or 'dulce' (gentler/less spicy), or use your favourite regular sausages, if you prefer.
- Use drained roasted red peppers from a jar if you're in a hurry, added at the same time as the grains.
- Stir in a few handfuls of baby spinach leaves with the grains, if you like.

LODGE

Rice, Pasta & Grains

The recipes in this chapter are speedy to prepare and suitable for varied occasions, including lunch, supper or for entertaining. By the very nature of the base elements (rice, pasta and grains) they're comforting and built around store cupboard ingredients, so are handy standbys to have up your sleeve.

A couple of things to remember when cooking pasta – always use a pan bigger than you think you need to allow the pasta plenty of space for movement during cooking, and add far more salt than you might think is necessary or decent, bearing in mind the Italian phrase that pasta water should be 'as salty as the sea'.

Baked Mackerel, Fennel & Freekeh with Horseradish & Coriander Sauce

SERVES 4

olive oil, for drizzling and greasing
2 fennel bulbs, tough outer layers and stems discarded, fronds roughly chopped and reserved
sea salt and freshly ground black pepper
2 x 250g pouches of ready-cooked freekeh
2 tablespoons preserved lemon (rind only), drained and chopped, plus 2 tablespoons liquid from the jar
4 spring onions, finely sliced diagonally
8 fresh mackerel fillets, skin-on
1 lemon, cut in half

For the horseradish and coriander sauce
200g thick Greek-style yoghurt
1 teaspoon hot or creamy horseradish sauce, or more to taste
a handful of coriander, leaves and thin stems roughly chopped (reserve a few sprigs for serving)
½ teaspoon Dijon mustard

Healthy, tasty and inexpensive, as well as robust and earthy, sums up this recipe nicely. If you're up for the trouble of working for your supper (as we are as a family), swap the fillets for whole mackerel, but do remember to ask the fishmonger to gut and clean them for you.

1. Preheat the oven to 200°C/180°C fan/gas 6. Lightly grease a large, shallow roasting tin around 41 x 26cm and ideally no deeper than 4cm (or use a large, lipped baking tray) with olive oil.

2. Halve the fennel bulbs through the root and cut each half into thin slices, through the root. Spread out in the tin in one layer, trickle over a little olive oil, season with salt and pepper and bake for 12 minutes, turning once, until cooked and caramelising around the edges.

3. Meanwhile, mix all the sauce ingredients together in a small bowl and season. If you prefer a slightly runnier sauce, thin it with a little water. Set aside.

4. Break the freekeh up in its unopened pouches and add to the fennel in the tin, along with the preserved lemon rind plus juice, spring onions and some seasoning. Mix everything together and level it out.

5. Lay the mackerel fillets, some skin-side down and some skin-side up, over the freekeh mixture, leaving a little space between each one. Cut one lemon half into eight thin, half-moon slices. Arrange a slice on each fish fillet, trickle with a little olive oil, season and return to the oven for 5 minutes or until the mackerel is just cooked.

6. Just before serving, squeeze the juice from the remaining lemon half over the fish, then scatter with the chopped fennel fronds and reserved coriander sprigs. Serve the sauce separately, although you might like to trickle or dot a little over the fish and freekeh as well.

GET AHEAD

- Steps 1–4 can be completed anytime on the day. Leave the freekeh mixture in the tin at room temperature and keep the sauce chilled. Reheat in the oven (temp as above) for 5–10 minutes until hot throughout before adding the mackerel.

HINTS & TIPS

- If using whole mackerel, follow the recipe as for fillets, allowing one fish per person (about 275–300g pre-gutted weight), gutted and cleaned (with or without the head – it's up to you). Slash the top of each three times with a sharp knife and slip a thin, half-moon sliver of lemon into each slash. Cut the remainder of the lemon into chunks and stuff into the cavities. Bake on top of the freekeh mixture for 10–15 minutes until just cooked through.

OPINEL

Baked Spanish-style Sea Bream Fillets with Pearl Barley & Romesco Sauce

SERVES 4

300g pearl barley
1.2 litres fresh fish or chicken stock (or use 2 stock cubes)
1 teaspoon hot smoked paprika
1 teaspoon sea salt, plus extra for general seasoning
140g cured 'salami-style' chorizo, halved and cut into ½cm-thick half-moon slices
around 200g baby cherry tomatoes on the vine, vines snipped into smaller sections
freshly ground black pepper
4 sea bream fillets (or use sea bass fillets), skin-on
olive oil, for drizzling
16 black olives, preferably pitted
1 x quantity Romesco Sauce (see page 206)
2 basil sprigs, leaves picked

As well as being nutritious, I love pearl barley for its chewy texture and nutty taste. Here, it absorbs the smoky flavours it's cooked with beautifully, creating a delicious base for the fish.

1. Preheat the oven to 170°C/150°C fan/gas 3. Find a large, shallow roasting tin, around 41 x 26cm and ideally no deeper than 4cm.

2. Put the pearl barley into the tin, stir in the stock, hot smoked paprika and measured salt, then bake for 45 minutes.

3. Stir in the chorizo, then add the tomato vines, spreading them out on top of the other ingredients. Bake for a further 15 minutes, by which time the pearl barley will have absorbed all the stock and be cooked, and the tomatoes will be soft, with the skins partially burst but still retaining their shape. Turn the oven up to 200°C/180°C fan/gas 6. Check and adjust the seasoning, adding some pepper (and a little more salt, if needed).

4. Arrange the fish fillets over the top of the pearl barley and between the tomato vines and sprinkle them with a little salt, then drizzle with a swirl of olive oil. Scatter over the olives and then bake for a further 5–7 minutes or until the fish is just cooked through.

5. Serve with a little romesco sauce spooned over and a scattering of basil leaves. Serve the remaining sauce separately.

GET AHEAD

- Steps 2 and 3 can be completed the day before, then cooled and kept covered in the fridge overnight. Reheat the pearl barley mixture in the oven (temp as above) until sizzling (about 5–10 minutes), before continuing with the recipe as above.

HINTS & TIPS

- I like to use hot smoked paprika, but regular smoked paprika is fine if you prefer the lovely smoky flavour without the spicy heat. Conversely, add an extra ½ teaspoon, if you like it a bit hotter.

Beetroot, Goats' Cheese, Hazelnut & Mint Spaghetti

SERVES 4

30g whole (shelled) hazelnuts, blanched
sea salt and freshly ground black pepper
350g dried spaghetti
115g cooked beetroot (not in vinegar), peeled and cut into chunks
125g soft goats' cheese
10 mint leaves, plus a few extra to garnish
good glug of olive oil, plus extra to serve
120g soft goats' cheese log, rind discarded from each end and cut into ½cm-thick slices

---

GET AHEAD

- Steps 2 and 4 can be completed up to 3 days in advance. Keep the nuts in a covered dish and transfer the beetroot purée to a bowl, cover and chill.

HINTS & TIPS

- The beetroot purée makes a delicious dip for dunking strips of warm flatbreads or vegetable crudités into.

This recipe creates the most strikingly coloured spaghetti, thanks to the beetroot, and it's extremely tasty as well. People will ask if you actually made the beetroot spaghetti, they always do – it's up to you whether or not to own up!

1. Put a kettleful of water on to boil.

2. Find a large saucepan, big enough for cooking the pasta. Heat the dry saucepan on a medium heat, add the hazelnuts and toast them until brown and fragrant, about 5 minutes, swirling them around so they brown evenly and don't burn. Tip onto a board and roughly chop, then set aside.

3. Pour the water from the kettle into the pan, bring back to the boil, add plenty of salt and then the spaghetti. Cook according to the packet instructions.

4. While the spaghetti is cooking, put the beetroot, soft goats' cheese, mint leaves and some seasoning into a small food-processor and whizz together into a smooth-ish purée. Check and adjust the seasoning accordingly. It needs to be well seasoned.

5. Drain the pasta in a colander (reserving a mugful of its cooking water first) and set aside.

6. Heat the olive oil in the pasta pan and add the beetroot purée, followed by the pasta, plus a tablespoon or so of the reserved pasta water. Mix together well and add a little more pasta water to achieve a looser, or your required, consistency, if necessary.

7. Divide the pasta between four serving bowls, dot with the goats' cheese log slices broken up into smaller pieces, the chopped hazelnuts, a few mint leaves and a good swirl of olive oil. Serve.

Cheesey Mushroom & Kale Orzotto

SERVES 4

good glug of olive oil, plus extra for drizzling
1 onion, finely chopped
250g shiitake mushrooms, large ones halved or quartered
sea salt and freshly ground black pepper
300g dried orzo
1 litre fresh chicken or vegetable stock (or use 2 stock cubes)
3 tablespoons double cream
2 good handfuls of kale leaves, finely shredded, or several handfuls of spinach leaves
150g Vacherin, Taleggio or Pié D'Angloys cheese, or more if you like

This is a very speedy meat-free supper. The meatiness of the mushrooms would fool even the most ardent meat-eater! For a vegetarian version, use a creamy vegetarian cheese and vegetable stock.

1. Heat the olive oil in a large saucepan, add the onion and cook on a low–medium heat until softened, about 10 minutes. Add the mushrooms and some salt and pepper and cook on a high heat until all the liquid has evaporated and the mushrooms are cooked, about 5 minutes. Add the orzo and stir until lightly coated in the oil, adding a splash more oil, if necessary.

2. Add the stock and bring to the boil, then simmer gently for 9 minutes until the orzo is tender. Add the cream, then gradually add the kale or spinach in batches, letting each batch wilt before adding the next. The mixture will be sloppy. Check the seasoning, then remove from the heat and leave to stand for a few minutes before eating, during which time it will have thickened up a little.

3. Spoon the orzotto into individual bowls and dot generous blobs of your chosen creamy cheese over the top, nestling it in a little. It will start oozing and melting into the orzotto immediately. Finish with a drizzle/swirl of olive oil. This is best eaten warm rather than piping hot.

GET AHEAD

- Complete step 1 up to 2 days in advance, then cool, cover and chill until required. Reheat gently in the pan until warmed throughout, then continue as above.

HINTS & TIPS

- If the kale is ready-sliced, pick it over before using as there are invariably unappealing tough stalks included with the leaves. For this reason, it's best to use whole leaves if possible and remove the stalks yourself before slicing.

- Enjoy this risotto-style, as above, or transform it into a gratin. Up to 3 days in advance, once fully made, transfer to an ovenproof dish, scatter with grated cheese and a few breadcrumbs and bake at the top of a hot oven for around 15 minutes or until golden and bubbling.

Crab & Chilli Linguine

SERVES 4

sea salt and freshly ground black pepper
350g dried linguine
2 good glugs of olive oil, plus extra to serve
2 shallots, finely chopped
2 garlic cloves, chopped
2 small (regular heat) red chillies, de-seeded and finely chopped (or use dried chilli flakes, to taste)
grated zest and juice of 1 lime
a large handful of parsley, leaves picked and finely chopped
200g cooked fresh white crab meat

Crab is one of my favourite things to eat and would definitely be one of my desert island food choices. This quick and easy pasta recipe makes a lovely, fresh and tasty lunch or supper.

1. Bring a large pan of very well salted water to the boil and cook the linguine according to the packet instructions. Scoop out and reserve a mugful of the cooking water before draining the pasta in a colander or sieve.

2. Heat a good glug of olive oil in the same pan and cook the shallots and garlic on a gentle heat for a few minutes, until softening but not coloured. Stir in the chillies, lime zest and juice, parsley and crab meat.

3. Return the linguine to the pan with another good glug of olive oil, stirring and tossing gently to combine. Check the seasoning and loosen with some of the reserved pasta water, if necessary.

4. Divide the pasta between four serving bowls and finish each with a swirl of olive oil and a grinding of pepper.

GET AHEAD

- All the fresh ingredients can be prepared any time on the day. Keep covered (keep the crab meat in the fridge).

HINTS & TIPS

- If you're using whole dressed crab, add the brown meat, too – either mixed in with the white meat, or spooned over the top of each bowl.

Quick & Creamy Bacon, Pea & Mushroom Risotto

SERVES 4–6

1 tablespoon olive oil
1 onion, finely chopped
10 rashers smoked, streaky bacon, snipped into thin strips
125g shiitake mushrooms, roughly chopped
2 garlic cloves, crushed
400g risotto rice (such as Carnaroli or Arborio)
150ml white wine
1.2 litres hot fresh chicken stock (or use 3 stock cubes)
225g frozen petit pois
sea salt and freshly ground black pepper
125g mascarpone cheese
2 tablespoons grated Parmesan cheese
freshly chopped parsley or basil, to garnish

This is a very tasty, quick and easy supper, with endless possible variations! Use these quantities as a guide, substituting whatever ingredients you feel like eating or have to hand.

1. Heat the olive oil in a large saucepan, then add the onion, bacon, mushrooms and garlic and cook gently, without browning, until the onion is soft, about 10 minutes.

2. Stir in the rice and cook for a few minutes to coat the grains in oil. Add the white wine and stir on a high heat until it has all evaporated. Stir in half the hot stock and then leave to bubble gently for 5–10 minutes or until all the stock is absorbed, giving it the odd stir.

3. Add the remaining stock, cook for 5 minutes, then add the petit pois and cook for another 5 minutes. By this time, the stock should all be absorbed and the rice just cooked.

4. Check the seasoning, adding salt and pepper to taste, then gently stir in the mascarpone and Parmesan. Garnish with chopped parsley or basil and spoon into bowls to serve.

GET AHEAD

- Make to the end of step 2 up to 1 day ahead, then cool, cover and set aside, or chill if leaving overnight. Gently reheat the rice mixture in the pan, then continue with step 3, add the stock (don't worry it not being hot) and bring to a simmer before adding the petit pois.

HINTS & TIPS

- Replace the bacon with cooked ham.
- For a vegetarian version, omit the bacon, use vegetable stock and swap the Parmesan for a vegetarian Italian-style hard cheese.

Sausage Balls with Fennel, Tomato, Orzo & Mozzarella

SERVES 4

500g sausagemeat
splash of olive oil, plus a little more if needed
1 onion, finely chopped
1 fennel bulb, tough outer layers removed and stems discarded, then bulbs thinly sliced horizontally (fronds roughly chopped and reserved – optional)
250g dried orzo
1 garlic clove, crushed
1 teaspoon fennel seeds, roughly ground/crushed
½ teaspoon dried thyme (or use 2 fresh thyme sprigs)
1 chicken stock cube, crumbled
1 x 400g tin chopped tomatoes
sea salt and freshly ground black pepper
1 ball of buffalo mozzarella (or burrata), drained and thinly sliced
a few thyme sprigs, to garnish (optional)

A very tasty supper, served from the sauté pan in which it's made. Rather than sausagemeat, use your favourite sausages, if you prefer – just slit their skins lengthways with a sharp knife to release the sausage meat.

1. Shape the sausagemeat into 12–14 ping-pong-sized balls. This is easiest done with wet hands to form a better shape.

2. Heat the olive oil in a lidded 24cm sauté pan (that's ideally about 6cm deep) and fry the sausage balls on a high heat until deep brown all over, about 10–15 minutes. Don't be tempted to turn them until a good dark crust has formed underneath and they release willingly from the pan with no resistance, otherwise they will stick, leaving the crust behind in the pan. They may become a little misshapen, but that's fine. Remove from the pan and set aside.

3. Add the onion and fennel to the pan and cook in the residual fat (adding a splash more oil, if necessary) on a medium heat until soft, about 5–10 minutes.

4. Drain off all but one tablespoon of fat from the pan (if necessary) and then add the orzo, garlic, fennel seeds and thyme. Cook, stirring, for a minute or so, then add the crumbled stock cube, followed by the tomatoes. Fill the empty tomato tin with water and add this, then season generously. Bring to the boil, check the seasoning and then return the sausage balls to the pan along with any leaked juices. Cover and simmer very gently for 15 minutes.

5. Remove the lid and ruffle up the orzo. Dot the mozzarella (or burrata) over the top, breaking it up as necessary, then cover and cook for a few more minutes until the cheese is just melting and oozy. Remove the lid and leave to sit, off the heat, for 5–10 minutes, before scattering with either the thyme sprigs or the chopped fennel fronds (if using) and serving.

GET AHEAD

- Make to the end of step 3 any time on the day, then cool and cover with the lid until required. Reheat gently in the pan until sizzling before continuing as above.

HINTS & TIPS

- The meat from Toulouse or fennel sausages are favourites of mine to use for this recipe.

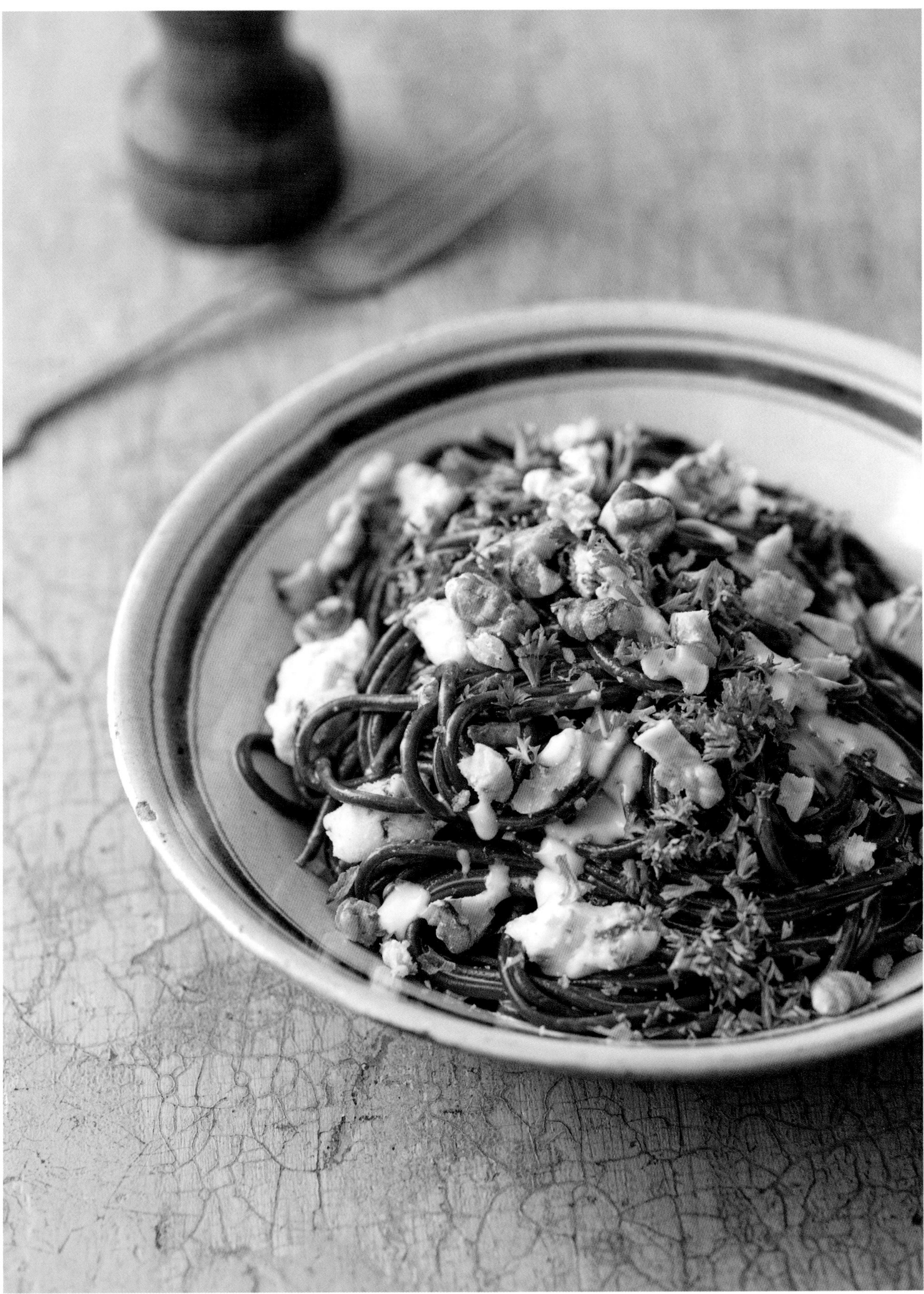

Spaghetti with Gorgonzola Sauce & Toasted Walnuts

SERVES 2

a handful of walnut pieces
sea salt and freshly ground black pepper
180g dried black cuttlefish or squid ink spaghetti (or you can use regular spaghetti)
85g Gorgonzola cheese (plus a little extra to serve, optional), cut into small chunks or crumbled
2 tablespoons milk
2 tablespoons crème fraîche
a little roughly chopped parsley or a few snipped chives, to garnish (optional)

Spaghetti with Gorgonzola sauce has long been one of our favourites. It couldn't be a tastier, quicker or easier supper (or lunch). It's worth seeking out black cuttlefish or squid ink spaghetti from Italian delis (or, of course, online) for its briny, faintly fishy flavour, not to mention its dramatic appearance!

1. Put a kettleful of water on to boil.

2. In a dry saucepan, large enough for cooking the spaghetti in, toss the walnuts on a medium heat until fragrant and beginning to brown, about 5 minutes. Tip onto a plate and set aside.

3. Pour the boiling water into the pan, bring back to the boil and add a generous amount of salt, followed by the spaghetti. Cook according to the packet instructions, then drain and leave in the colander.

4. Melt the Gorgonzola, milk and crème fraîche together in the same pan on a low heat, stirring until it forms a sauce. Taste for seasoning, but it is unlikely to need salt. Return the pasta to the pan and stir gently with a wooden spoon to distribute the sauce evenly.

5. Divide the pasta mixture between two bowls, scatter over the toasted walnuts, plus the herbs (if using), and add a few extra little blobs of oozy Gorgonzola, too, if you like.

HINTS & TIPS

- Other blue cheese can be used but it needs to be creamy (such as Dolcelatte).
- To make this vegetarian, use regular spaghetti and swap the Gorgonzola for a vegetarian soft and creamy blue cheese.
- Swap the walnuts for pine nuts and the crème fraîche for double cream.

Spiced Lamb & Couscous with Cucumber Raita

SERVES 4

3 lamb shoulder fillets (550–600g in total), trimmed of excess fat and membrane and cut into 1.5cm slices
2 teaspoons rose harissa paste
1 teaspoon ground cumin
sea salt and freshly ground black pepper
a good handful of unsalted cashew nuts
good glug of vegetable oil
200g couscous
200g frozen petit pois or edamame beans
a good handful of sultanas or raisins
425ml fresh lamb or chicken stock (or use 1 stock cube)
2 tablespoons freshly chopped mint and/or coriander leaves (1 tablespoon of each, if using both)
1–2 tablespoons fresh pomegranate seeds (optional)

Along the lines of a grainy pilaf, this nice and easy, very tasty, mid-week supper takes no time at all to make. It's served with Cucumber Raita (see page 207), but if time is short, just natural yoghurt seasoned and flavoured with chopped mint is also good. The Ridiculously Easy Flatbreads (see page 159), served warm alongside, would be good, too.

1. Put the lamb into a bowl and mix with the harissa paste, cumin and some salt and pepper.

2. Heat a dry 24cm sauté pan (that's ideally about 6cm deep) and preferably with a lid, then add the cashews and toss in the pan on a medium heat until pale brown and toasted, about 5 minutes. Tip onto a plate and set aside.

3. Heat the vegetable oil in the same pan, then add the lamb and cook on a high heat for 10–15 minutes, stirring from time to time, until the lamb is brown and cooked through.

4. Add the couscous, frozen vegetables, cashews, sultanas or raisins, stock and some seasoning. Bring to the boil, then remove from the heat, cover with the lid (or a cloth) and leave for 10 minutes (by which time the couscous will be cooked through).

5. Fluff up the couscous with a fork and check the seasoning. Scatter over the herbs and the pomegranate seeds (if using). Serve with cucumber raita and warmed flatbreads, if you like.

GET AHEAD

- The lamb can be cooked any time on the day and set aside in the pan (cover, once cool), then reheat gently until hot before adding the couscous, etc, and continuing as above.
- The cashew nuts can be toasted up to 2 days ahead and kept in a covered dish.

HINTS & TIPS

- To ring the changes, complete steps 1 and 3 and stuff the lamb into warmed flatbreads or pitta pockets with some cucumber raita, fresh herbs, crisp salad leaves and pomegranate seeds. If you have any hummus to hand, that would be good, too.

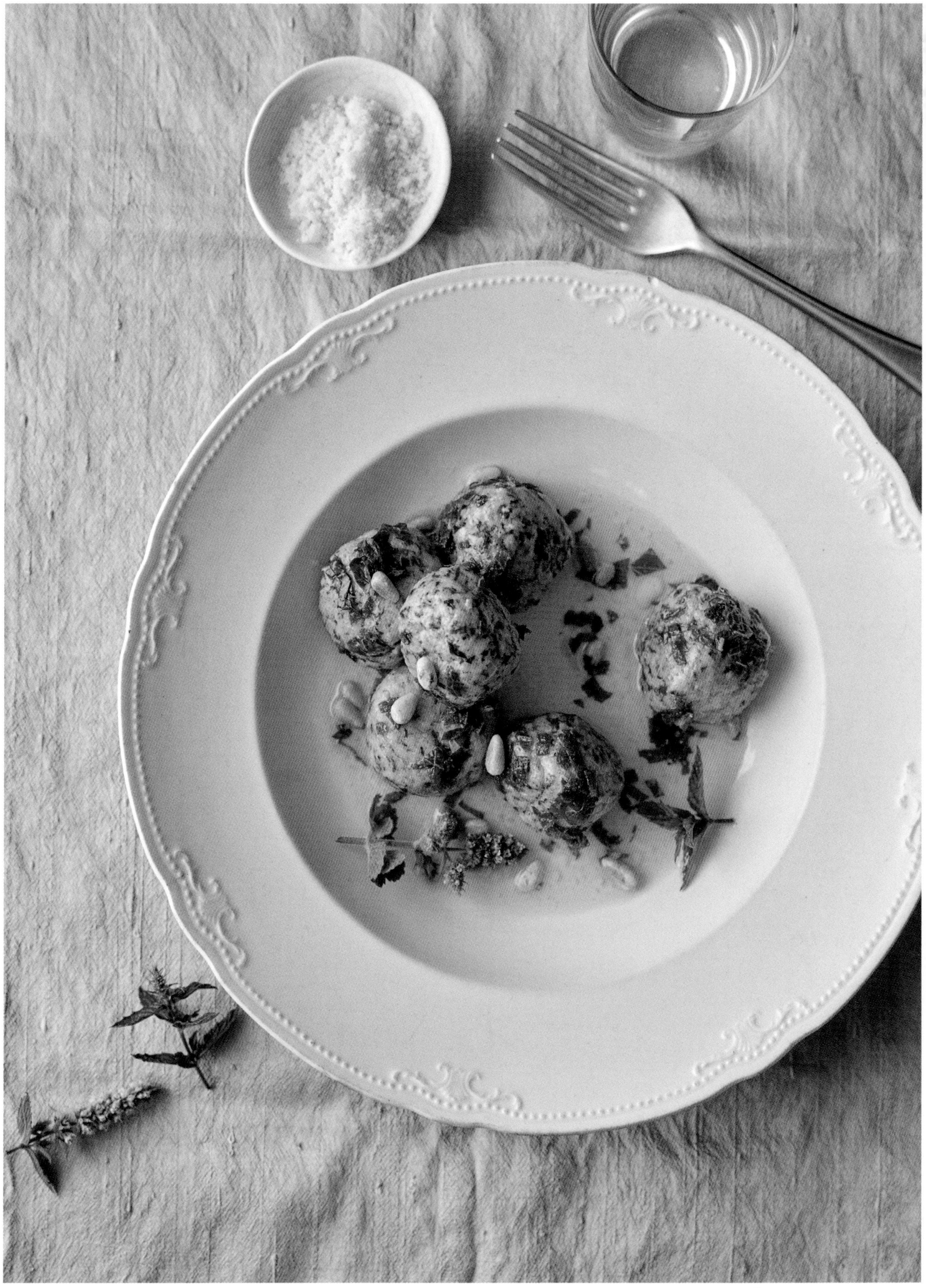

Spinach Malfatti with Mint Butter

SERVES 4–6
(makes 40–45 malfatti)

500g spinach leaves (250g cooked weight)
sea salt and freshly ground black pepper
500g ricotta cheese (excess liquid drained off)
3 egg yolks
125g semolina
140g Parmesan cheese, grated (or use half Parmesan and half pecorino cheese), plus extra for serving
1 large garlic clove, crushed
2 teaspoons sea salt
freshly grated nutmeg
plain flour, for dusting
50g butter
3–4 mint sprigs, leaves picked and roughly chopped

To serve (optional)
a few toasted pine nuts and/or rocket leaves
olive oil, for drizzling

These spinach and ricotta dumplings (roughly translated as 'badly formed' in Italian) are very savoury. Though similar to gnocchi, they are made with semolina and ricotta, so they are lighter. Serve as a light lunch or supper.

1. Cook the spinach in a large saucepan with a splash of water for a few minutes or until just wilted. Alternatively, wilt in a microwave (use 2 x 250g bags of spinach, prick the top of each bag several times, then wilt the spinach in each bag in turn, on high for 2–4 minutes). Drain, cool under cold running water, then squeeze out all the excess moisture. Put the cooked spinach into a mixing bowl and chop quite finely (I use scissors to do this).

2. Fill the same pan with water, add a generous amount of salt and bring to the boil.

3. Add the ricotta, egg yolks, semolina, Parmesan, garlic, the measured salt, plus some pepper and a grating of nutmeg to the spinach and mix to a fairly stiff paste. The malfatti need to be very well seasoned, so check before cooking. Flour your hands and roll the mixture into 40–45 walnut-sized balls, then put onto a plate. They don't need to be perfectly formed.

4. Drop the malfatti into the boiling water, roughly 10–12 at a time. After a few minutes, when cooked, they will helpfully bob to the top of the pan. Immediately remove with a slotted spoon and place in a serving dish. Keep warm and continue cooking the remainder in the same way.

5. Once all the malfatti are cooked, discard the water and melt the butter in the same pan. Add the chopped mint, then spoon the mint butter over the malfatti. Scatter with a little extra cheese, then scatter with toasted pine nuts and/or rocket and a drizzle of olive oil (if using), then serve.

GET AHEAD

- Make to the end of step 4 up to 3 days in advance, then cool, cover and chill, or freeze (defrost before use). Reheat in the oven at 200°C/180°C fan/gas 6 for about 15 minutes until hot throughout, with a swirl of olive oil and some grated Parmesan or pecorino scattered over the top. Spoon over the mint butter just before serving.

HINTS & TIPS

- To make this suitable for vegetarians, swap the Parmesan (and pecorino) for a vegetarian Italian-style hard cheese.

- Made into smaller, bite-sized balls, these malfatti make delicious (warm) canapés, too.

Zesty Courgette & Ricotta Spaghetti with Pine Nuts & Mint

SERVES 2

a small handful of pine nuts
sea salt and freshly ground black pepper
180g dried spaghetti
2 medium courgettes
good glug of olive oil, plus extra to serve
knob of butter
1 garlic clove, crushed
grated zest of ½ lemon
100g ricotta cheese
2 mint sprigs, leaves picked and shredded
1–2 tablespoons grated Parmesan cheese

A fresh and simple yet very tasty pasta recipe that we enjoy in the summer months, particularly when we have courgettes in abundance. We usually have fresh peas on offer, too, and I like to scatter a few over the top, freshly podded and raw.

1. Put a kettleful of water on to boil and find a saucepan large enough for cooking the spaghetti in.

2. Add the pine nuts to the pan and cook on a medium heat, stirring, until pale brown and toasted, about 5 minutes. Tip onto a plate and set aside.

3. Pour the boiling water into the same pan, bring back to the boil and add a generous amount of salt, followed by the spaghetti. Cook according to the packet instructions.

4. Meanwhile, shave the courgettes into ribbons using a swivel peeler: firstly, peel and discard three strips of skin off the courgettes, leaving a gap between each one and thus producing a stripy effect. Then peel off long ribbons, working around the outside of each courgette and turning after each strip. Most ribbons should have a strip of green skin along the edges. Stop at the core of seeds in the middle and discard.

5. Reserve a mugful of pasta cooking water, then drain the spaghetti and leave in the colander.

6. Heat the olive oil and butter in the same pan, add the courgette ribbons and garlic and fry on a high heat very quickly and briefly (a couple of minutes), gently moving the ribbons around the pan, until only just beginning to wilt. Remove from the heat, season with salt and pepper, then add the spaghetti and lemon zest and toss to mix. Put the pan back on the heat and mix everything together gently – I find tongs easiest for this – and loosen with a little reserved pasta water, if necessary. Divide between two bowls.

7. Dot the pasta mixture with blobs of ricotta, nestling it into the pasta with the back of a spoon so that it melts a little. Season, then scatter over the toasted pine nuts, the mint, a good swirl of olive oil, and lastly, the Parmesan cheese. Tuck in and enjoy.

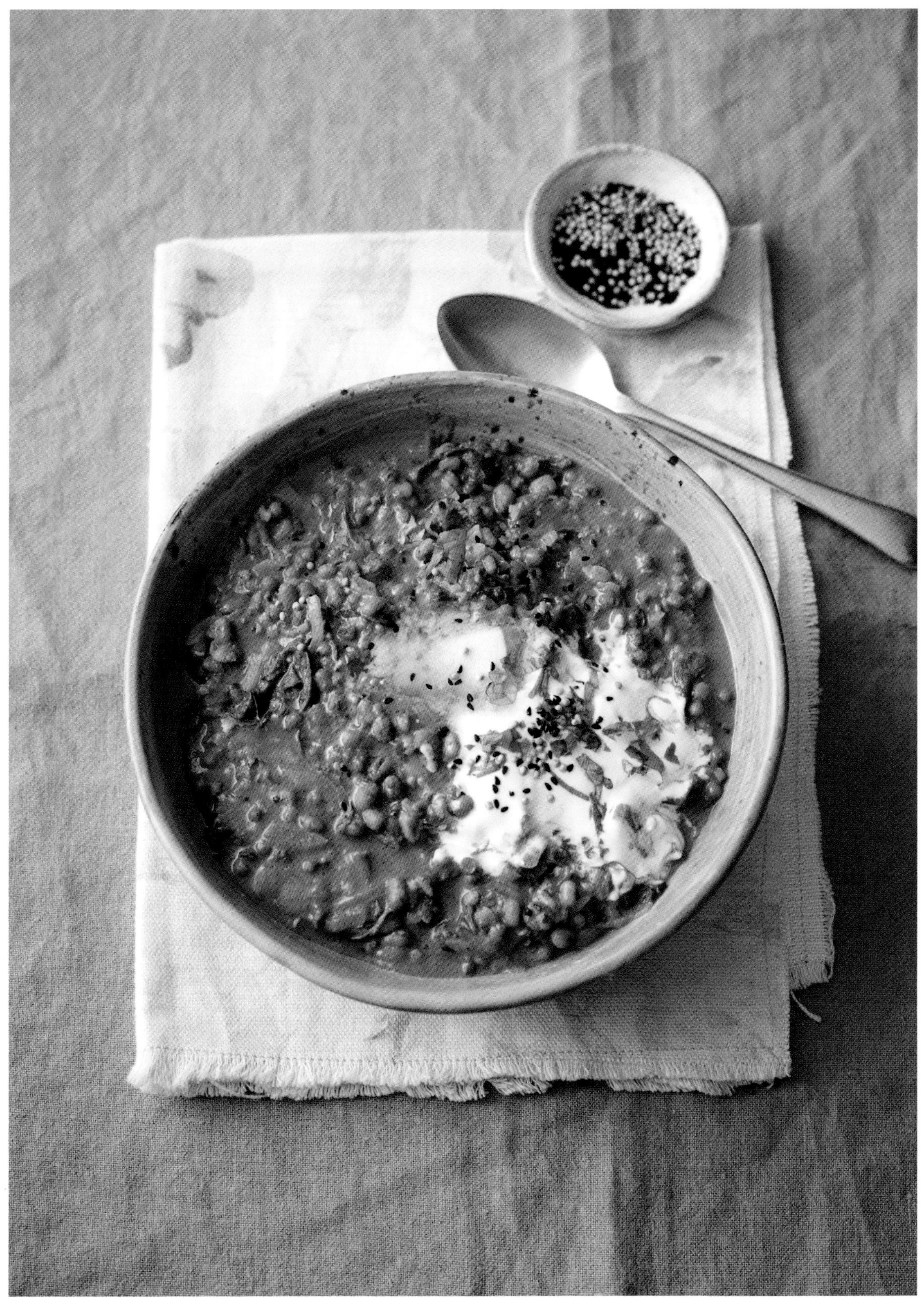

Mung Bean, Coconut & Spinach Dhal

SERVES 3–4

For the dhal
250g dried mung beans
1 large onion, thinly sliced
3 tomatoes, roughly chopped
6 garlic cloves, crushed
2 teaspoons black mustard seeds
3 teaspoons medium curry powder
1 teaspoon ground turmeric
2.5cm piece of fresh root ginger, peeled and finely chopped or grated (or use 1 teaspoon ginger paste from a jar)
good pinch of ground cinnamon
¼ teaspoon hot chilli powder
a good handful of dried curry leaves, roughly crushed (I use the palm of my hand)
1 x 400g tin coconut milk
1 teaspoon sea salt
250g spinach leaves (left whole), washed

To serve
a knob of butter per person
a handful of coriander, leaves and fine stems roughly chopped
3–4 tablespoons thick Greek-style yoghurt
nigella or onion seeds, or a few extra black mustard seeds for scattering (optional)
poppadoms (see *Hints & Tips*)

A cross between dhal and a curry, this is a lovely warming supper that I was taught how to make by a chef in Sri Lanka. Simple to prepare, it's very healthy, providing fibre, protein and many important minerals and nutrients, as well as being vegetarian (to make it vegan, simply omit the butter and yoghurt). Don't be put off by the seemingly long list of ingredients – they're all pretty much store cupboard staples. The mung beans need soaking overnight, so start the recipe the day before.

1. The night before, put the mung beans into a large bowl, cover with twice their volume of cold water and leave to soak overnight.

2. When you are ready to cook, drain and rinse the beans, then add them to a large saucepan with all the remaining dhal ingredients, except the salt and spinach. Fill the empty coconut milk tin with water and add just under half of this to the pan as well. Reserve the remainder in case the dhal needs thinning while it's cooking.

3. Bring to the boil, then reduce the heat and simmer, uncovered, for 30–35 minutes, giving it a stir every so often, or until soft and the required consistency. The beans should mainly retain their shape and all the liquid will be absorbed, but the mixture will be sloppy. However, if the dhal becomes too thick during cooking, thin with a little of the reserved coconut tin water. Bear in mind it will thicken up as it cools, if not using straight away.

4. Finally, season with the salt, adding a little more, if necessary. Just before serving, stir in the spinach by the handful, allowing each handful to wilt before adding the next, then bring back to a simmer to warm through.

5. Serve in individual bowls with a knob of butter nestled and melting into the middle of each serving, then finish with a scattering of coriander, a blob of yoghurt and a sprinkling of seeds (if using). Serve with poppadoms.

GET AHEAD

- Make up to 3 days in advance, cool, cover and chill. Reheat gently in the pan, stirring, until hot (you may need to thin with a little water).

HINTS & TIPS

- Preferring to avoid frying poppadoms, I cook them in a toaster, the microwave or straight onto a solid hotplate (such as an electric stove with raised, solid rings, or the cooler hot-plate of an Aga).

Oven-to-table

What's not to like about oven-to-table recipes? It's hard to beat bringing a tray of deliciousness, in the form of a whole main course, straight from the oven to the table with a flourish, for people to help themselves.

Lots of these recipes require little effort, some as easy as putting all the ingredients in the tin at the same time, then waiting for the ta-da moment when the cooked dish comes out of the oven. Others simply require the addition of a component or a few finishing elements towards the end.

Either way, the oven does most of the work and it is a laidback and convivial way of feeding people, while also being easier on the cook. Do flick to chapter 7 (see pages 191–209) if you think a sauce might be the perfect enhancement.

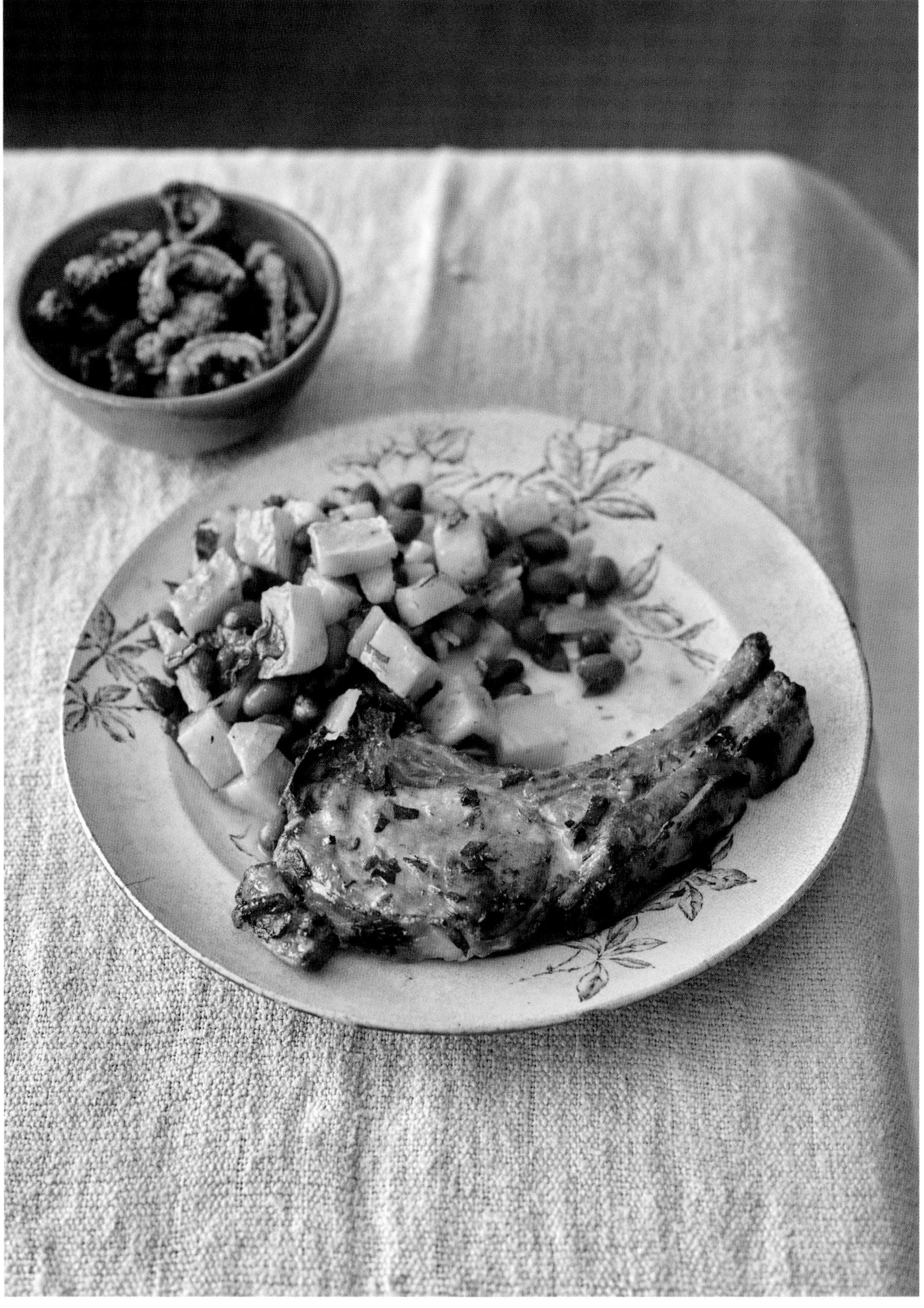

Baked Pork Chops with Fennel, Celeriac & Borlotti Beans

SERVES 4

4 x 325g (cut 2.5cm thick) pork chops (they must be equal in size)
3 garlic cloves, chopped
1 teaspoon fennel seeds, roughly crushed
6 sage leaves, roughly chopped
1 teaspoon sea salt
freshly ground black pepper
generous glug of olive oil, plus extra for greasing and drizzling
2 large fennel bulbs, tough outer layers and stems discarded, fronds roughly chopped and reserved
500g celeriac (unpeeled weight), peeled and cut into 2cm dice
1 x 400g tin borlotti beans, drained and rinsed
100g spinach leaves, cut into thick ribbons

The juiciest of pork chops on a bed of vegetables, marinated in that classic Italian pork pairing – fennel, sage and garlic. There are several options for the pork skin: leave it on the chops, remove it before cooking and discard, or remove and make it into crispy crackling (see *Hints & Tips*) to scatter over the top at the end – it's up to you. We love this with Lucy's Green Sauce (see page 195) or Romesco Sauce (see page 206).

1. Snip the chops at two or three intervals through the rind (if retaining), the fat and just into the flesh with scissors. (To stop the membrane between the fat and meat contracting while cooking, causing the chops to curl.)

2. Put the chops into a bowl with the garlic, fennel seeds, sage, the salt, a good grinding of pepper and a generous glug of olive oil, mix, then cover and leave to marinate at room temperature for 2–3 hours, if possible.

3. Quarter the fennel bulbs through the root and cut into 2.5cm chunks.

4. When required preheat the oven to 220°C/200°C fan/gas 7. Lightly grease a large, shallow roasting tin, around 41 x 26cm and ideally no deeper than 4cm, with olive oil.

5. Scatter the celeriac and fennel over the bottom of the tin. Add a drizzle of olive oil and a little seasoning, then scrape the marinade ingredients from the chops over the vegetables. Swish around to coat, then sit the chops on top and drizzle with a little more olive oil. Cook at the top of the oven for 25–30 minutes, depending on the thickness of the chops. The fat will be a little crisped and golden.

6. Add the borlotti beans and spinach to the tin and nestle in, then return to the oven for 5 minutes to wilt the spinach in the juices and heat the beans through.

7. Serve from the tin, scattered with the reserved fennel fronds and crackling (if using).

HINTS & TIPS

- Thin chops will dry out, so try to stick with the suggested weight (if they seem large, remember the bones are weighty!), and ensure they're even-sized.
- The borlotti beans can be swapped for sliced waxy new potatoes, added at the beginning with the vegetables.
- *Crackling:* While the chops are marinating, snip the rind into 5cm pieces, spread out in the tin, lined with foil, sprinkle with salt and cook at 220°C for 10–15 minutes until crispy. Drain on kitchen paper.

Baked Spiced Aubergines with Feta, Mint, Anchovies & Saffron Yoghurt

SERVES 4

1½ teaspoons white sesame seeds
1 teaspoon black sesame seeds
a handful of pine nuts
olive oil, for greasing and drizzling
small pinch of saffron strands
2 tablespoons boiling water
2 medium aubergines, halved lengthways
sea salt and freshly ground black pepper
200g thick Greek-style yoghurt
100g good-quality feta cheese (see *Hints & Tips* in One-pan Whole Feta recipe on page 52)
4–8 anchovy fillets in oil, drained, or more to taste
2 mint sprigs, leaves picked and roughly torn
a handful of coriander, leaves picked and roughly chopped (optional)

For the paste
3 tablespoons olive oil
5 garlic cloves, crushed
4 teaspoons za'atar
1 teaspoon sea salt

To serve (optional)
a selection of salad cress; micro leaves; a handful of rocket leaves; 1–2 tablespoons fresh pomegranate seeds

Tender, umami and a little bit piquant, this lovely meat-free recipe is deliciously filling and satisfying and can even be made in advance. Ready-toasted sesame seeds and pine nuts are available from larger supermarkets, so if you buy these, skip step 2. If you have vegetarian guests, ensure the feta you use is suitable for vegetarians and omit the anchovies.

1. Preheat the oven to 220°C/200°C fan/gas 7. Find a medium, shallow, roasting tin around 35 x 26cm (or bigger if the aubergines are on the larger side).

2. Spread out the sesame seeds and pine nuts in the tin and cook in the oven until toasted, around 4 minutes. Watch them as they can burn quite quickly! The pine nuts may take a little longer. Tip onto a plate and leave to cool.

3. Lightly grease the roasting tin with olive oil. Put the saffron strands in a ramekin with the boiling water. Set aside to infuse. Mix the paste ingredients together.

4. Score the cut sides of the aubergine halves in a crisscross pattern all over, going as deep as you dare without going through the skin, then divide the paste between the aubergines. Open up the hatching as best you can, smearing the paste deep down inside. Arrange side-by-side (but not touching), in the greased tin. Scatter with some salt and pepper, add a good drizzle of olive oil.

5. Cook at the top of the oven for 45 minutes or until tender and the tops are golden brown. It doesn't matter if they have splayed out a little.

6. Put the yoghurt into a serving bowl, then stir in the infused saffron water (including strands) and season well.

7. Serve from the tin, or transfer to a serving platter, scattered with the crumbled feta, the anchovies, mint, coriander (if using) and toasted sesame seeds and pine nuts. Trickle over some olive oil and any of the serving suggestions (if using). Serve the yoghurt sauce separately (having drizzled a little over the aubergines, if you like).

GET AHEAD

- Make to the end of step 6 up to 2 days in advance. Cool, cover and chill. Reheat at 200°C for 15 minutes until hot.

HINTS & TIPS

- Omit the saffron and serve with the seasoned yoghurt, if you prefer.

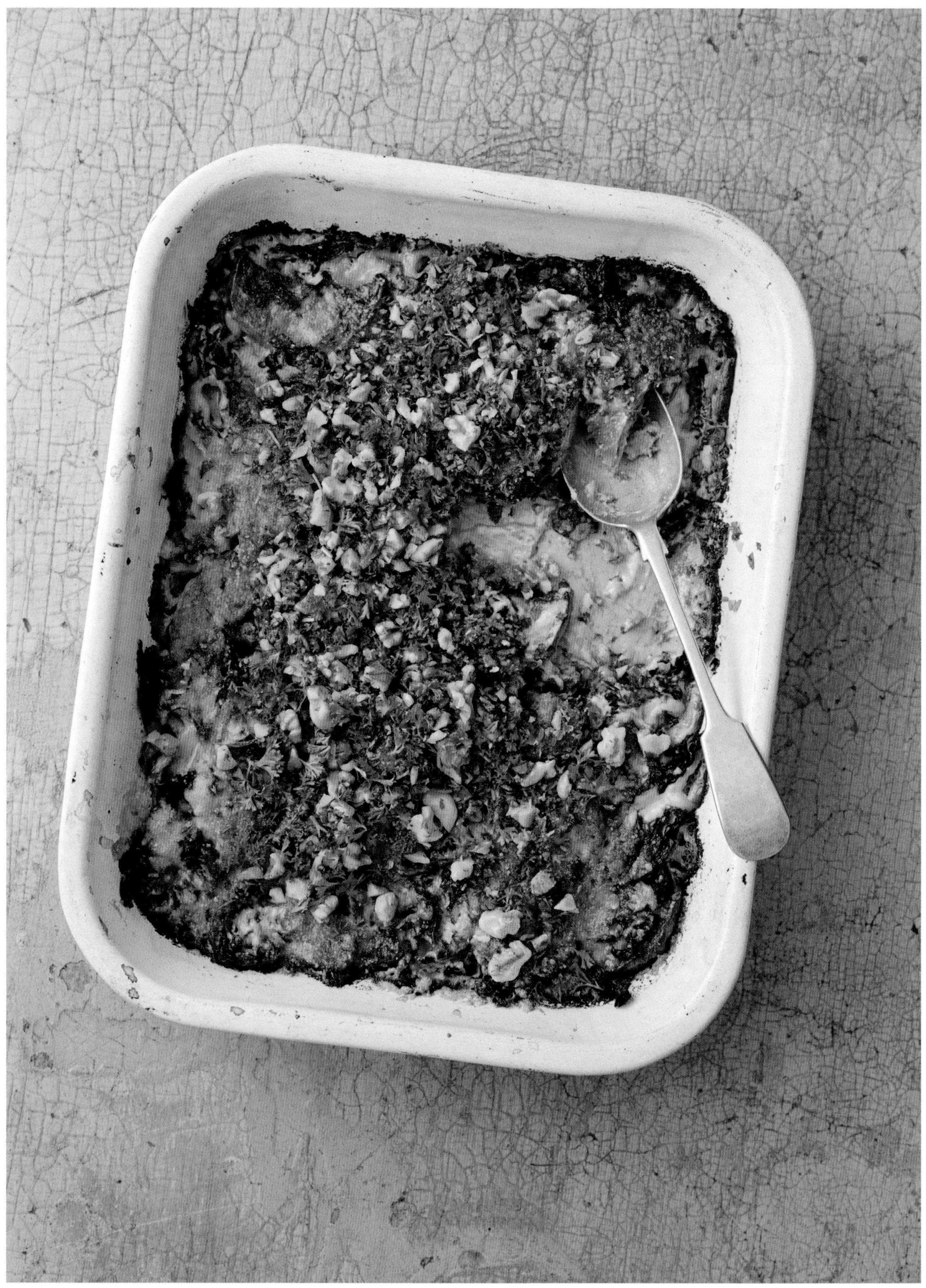

Butternut Squash & Kale Gratin with Walnut & Parsley Crumble

SERVES 4–6 as a main course (or serves 6–8 as a side dish)

olive oil, for greasing and drizzling
1 butternut squash (approx. 1kg)
sea salt and freshly ground black pepper
pinch of dried chilli flakes
200g kale leaves, tough central stalks removed, leaves torn into fat ribbons
3–4 tablespoons grated Parmesan cheese
1–2 tablespoons dried breadcrumbs (such as panko)

For the crumble
a handful of walnut pieces, roughly chopped
a handful of parsley leaves, chopped

For the sauce
300ml whipping cream
2 tablespoons Dijon mustard
1 garlic clove, crushed

Indulgent and comforting on a cold winter's day, this is a delicious meat-free main course, and arguably one of my most popular recipes. For speed, ease and a rustic look, leave the skin on the squash (surprisingly it becomes as soft as butter when cooked). For vegetarians, swap the Parmesan for a vegetarian Italian-style hard cheese.

1. Preheat the oven to 220°C/200°C fan/gas 7. Find a large, shallow, ovenproof dish roughly 33 x 26 x 6cm. Boil a kettleful of water.

2. Put the walnuts for the crumble into the ovenproof dish and toast in the oven for 3–4 minutes or until beginning to brown (but do watch them!). Tip onto a plate, then set aside. Grease the dish with a little olive oil.

3. Cut the squash in half, leave the skin on (or remove it), scoop out the seeds, then cut each half into 1cm-thick slices. Layer up in the ovenproof dish, drizzling the tiniest bit of olive oil, some salt and pepper and a few chilli flakes between the layers. Roast at the top of the oven for 40–45 minutes or until the squash is soft when pierced with a knife.

4. While the squash is cooking, put the kale into a sieve or colander in the sink and pour over the boiling water from the kettle. Cool under cold running water, then squeeze out all the excess liquid with your hands. Set aside.

5. Mix all the sauce ingredients together in a bowl and season well.

6. Remove the squash from the oven, nestle the kale down into it and then spoon the sauce over. Scatter with the Parmesan and breadcrumbs and a drizzle of olive oil, then return to the top of the oven and cook for a further 20–25 minutes or until golden brown and bubbling.

7. Mix the crumble ingredients together and scatter over the top just before serving.

GET AHEAD

- Steps 1–5 can be completed up to 3 days in advance. Cool, cover and chill, keeping each component separate. When required, continue with step 6 as above.

HINTS & TIPS

- This makes a great side dish to accompany roasts, cooked sausages or cold meats.
- To bulk up the recipe for meat lovers, just add a handful or so of cold cooked ham chunks, shredded chicken or snipped bacon, nestled in with the kale. A meal in itself!

Coconut & Chilli Prawns en Papillote

SERVES 4

300g (frozen weight), frozen raw, peeled king or tiger prawns (around 8 per person), defrosted
1 x 300g packet straight-to-wok rice noodles (or similar) (see *Hints & Tips*)
4 baby courgettes, cut into ½cm dice (or use 1 larger courgette, around 175g)
4cm piece of fresh root ginger, peeled and finely chopped (or use 2 teaspoons ginger paste from a jar)
2 sticks of lemon grass, halved lengthways, then each half cut across into 2 chunks
4 kaffir lime leaves, fresh or dried
1 large red chilli, quartered, de-seeded and thinly sliced
1 pak choi bulb, quartered through the root, then cut into 1cm-thick slices on a diagonal
a handful of coriander, leaves and thin stems roughly chopped

For the sauce
8 tablespoons coconut cream (or double cream)
juice of 1 large lime
2 tablespoons fish sauce (gluten-free, if preferred)
1 garlic clove, crushed

Light, fresh and very healthy, these parcels proffer the most wonderful, intoxicating smell when they are opened. Made using rice noodles, they're gluten-free as well (use gluten-free fish sauce). My recipe tester declared this a five-star recipe, so there's no need to say any more than that…

1. Preheat the oven to 200°C/180°C fan/gas 6. Cut four large pieces of baking parchment (roughly 40–43cm square) and lay out on the worktop, turned over so they lie flat.

2. Mix the sauce ingredients together in a small bowl and set aside.

3. Drain and dry the prawns on a kitchen paper.

4. Put a quarter of the noodles in the middle of each piece of paper, separating them, if necessary, as you go, followed by a quarter of the courgettes. Divide all the remaining ingredients, except the coriander, equally between each square, adding the prawns last. Divide and spoon the sauce over the top.

5. Tightly seal each parcel by drawing the paper up over the prawns and then folding the top over and down into small pleats, leaving an airy space above the filling. Twist the ends, forming a sealed, tented parcel. Transfer to a large baking sheet and bake for 10 minutes until cooked.

6. Remove from the oven, then open up each parcel slightly and sprinkle the chopped coriander inside each parcel before serving. Take to the table and remind everyone not to eat their lime leaf and lemon grass. A bowl on the table for empty wrappers is handy, too.

GET AHEAD

- All the ingredients can be prepared up to 1 day in advance. Keep them separate and covered in the fridge. If reconstituting noodles in advance (see *Hints & Tips*), cool and drizzle with a smidgen of vegetable oil to prevent sticking.

HINTS & TIPS

- Straight-to-wok rice noodles are usually available in three sizes. For this recipe, I like the thin or ribbon ones. Each pack contains 2 x 150g sachets; half a sachet per person is plenty. Alternatively, use dried flat rice noodles, which need reconstituting for 3 minutes in a bowl, covered with boiling water. Allow 25g (½ bundle) raw weight (55g reconstituted weight), per person.

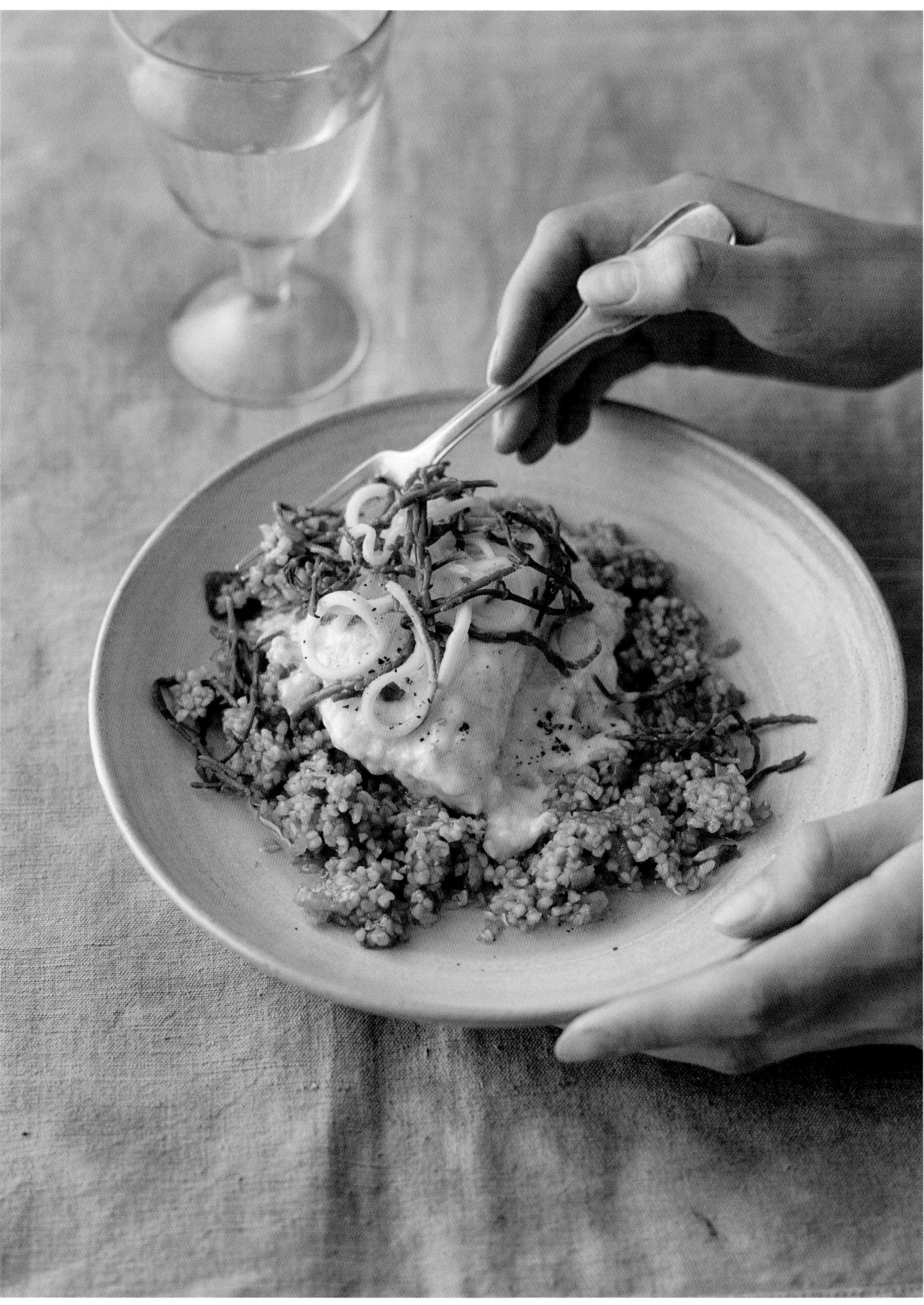

Creamy Cheese-topped Cod & Baked Tomato Bulgur

SERVES 4–5

good glug of olive oil
1 onion, finely chopped
2 garlic cloves, crushed
pinch of dried oregano
sea salt and freshly ground black pepper
1 x 400g tin chopped tomatoes
200g bulgur wheat
400ml fresh fish or chicken stock (or use 1 stock cube)
100–150g samphire, any tough 'spiny' pieces removed
1 large or 2 small courgettes, spiralised or coarsely grated
4 cod fillets (about 140g each), skinned (or use 1 larger fillet, about 500g, skinned) and snipped into fat fish finger-sized pieces

For the topping
100g Gruyère cheese or mature Cheddar cheese, grated
5 tablespoons crème fraîche
1 heaped teaspoon Dijon mustard

An easy tray of deliciousness, where the oven literally does all the work! Any white fish can be substituted for the cod. Samphire, aka 'poor man's asparagus', is widely available now that it's farmed – gone are the mucky, yet enjoyable, days of picking it when in season from the mudflats.

1. Preheat the oven to 200°C/180°C fan/gas 6. Find a medium, shallow roasting tin around 35 x 26cm.

2. Put the olive oil, onion, garlic, oregano and some seasoning into the tin. Add the tomatoes, then half-fill the empty tomato tin with water and add this to the roasting tin. Cook, uncovered, in the oven for 30 minutes, by which time the ingredients will have baked into a thick tomato sauce.

3. Meanwhile, mix the topping ingredients together in a small bowl and set aside.

4. Stir the bulgur wheat and stock into the tomato sauce, check the seasoning and return to the oven for a further 10 minutes. Put a kettleful of water on to boil.

5. Put the samphire and courgettes into two separate, small, heatproof bowls, adding a little salt to the courgette bowl, and then pour over enough boiling water just to cover the vegetables. Leave for 5 minutes, then drain and refresh very briefly under cold running water. Drain again.

6. Remove the tin from the oven and arrange the fish on top, leaving a little space between them. Spread the topping over each piece of fish, then scatter the samphire and courgettes over. Return to the oven for 5–10 minutes or until the fish has become opaque and is just cooked through (thicker pieces may take a little longer), and the topping is melted and creamy. Serve from the tin.

GET AHEAD

- Steps 1–4 can be completed, and the courgettes spiralised/grated, up to 2 days in advance. If not eating on the day, cool, cover and chill, keeping the different components separate. Reheat the tomato bulgur mixture in the oven (temp as above) for 5–10 minutes or until hot throughout, before continuing as above.

HINTS & TIPS

- Swap cod for haddock, coley or hake fillets.
- Tuck under any thin tail end parts of the fish fillets before cooking, so the pieces are the same thickness and will cook evenly.

Creamy Leek, Potato & Parmesan Chicken Thigh Tray Bake

SERVES 4

olive oil, for greasing
4 leeks (around 600–700g in total), trimmed, washed and cut into 2cm-thick slices/rounds
500g waxy new/salad potatoes, unpeeled and cut into 1cm discs
4 garlic cloves, sliced
12 small thyme sprigs (broken up if very long), or use 1 scant teaspoon dried thyme
sea salt and freshly ground black pepper
8 chicken thighs, skin-on, bone-in, well trimmed of fat and excess skin
150ml fresh chicken stock (or use 1 stock cube)
1 teaspoon Dijon mustard
100ml double cream
3 heaped tablespoons grated Parmesan cheese

As well as being a firm family favourite, this is universally popular and always goes down a storm – not just on the eating front, but for the cook as well, as it's unbelievably effortless and produces a delicious lunch or supper way beyond the sum of its parts. The leeks become meltingly tender and sweet and the chicken skin becomes golden and crispy.

1. Preheat the oven to 220°C/200°C fan/gas 7. Find a large, shallow roasting tin around 41 x 26cm and ideally no deeper than 4cm. Grease the tin with a smidgen of olive oil.

2. Put the leeks into the prepared roasting tin with the potatoes, garlic, 6 thyme sprigs or the dried thyme and some salt and pepper. Mix together well, then shake the tin to roughly level everything out into a single layer. Space the chicken thighs out on top and then scatter the skin with a light sprinkling of salt. Pour in the stock, avoiding the chicken. Cook at the top of the oven for 45 minutes until the chicken skin is golden and crispy.

3. Meanwhile, mix the mustard and cream together with a little seasoning (I use the un-washed stock jug for this). The cream may thicken up when mixing, which is fine.

4. Remove the tin from the oven and spoon, or blob, the cream sauce over the vegetables in the tin, avoiding the chicken, and gently nestling it in with a spoon. It won't all be amalgamated at this stage. Scatter the Parmesan over everything in the tin, then return to the oven for a further 10 minutes or until golden and crispy. Some of the cream and stock may not have completely amalgamated, which is fine. Scatter with the remaining thyme sprigs just before serving. Serve from the tin.

GET AHEAD

- Make the recipe up to the end of step 3 up to 2 days in advance, cool, cover and chill, keeping the mustard cream in a separate container. Reheat the chicken mixture in the oven (temp as above) for about 10 minutes or until hot throughout, before continuing as above.

HINTS & TIPS

- Swap the Parmesan for pecorino.

Roast Duck Legs with Celery, Artichokes & Green Olives

SERVES 4

- 1 onion, thinly sliced
- 5 celery sticks, stringy outside bits removed with a potato peeler, cut into 2.5cm-thick slices
- 4 garlic cloves, sliced
- 1 jar or 1 x 400g tin artichoke hearts, drained (approx. 240g drained weight)
- sea salt and freshly ground black pepper
- splash of olive oil, plus extra for drizzling
- 4 duck legs, trimmed of excess fat and skin
- 100g green olives, pitted
- 1 x 400g tin flageolet beans, drained and rinsed

The crispy, salty duck skin here is hard to beat, as is the soft, tender leg meat falling off the bone underneath, creating a lovely contrast to the meltingly soft vegetables below. Although delicious as is, this is also very good with Lucy's Green Sauce (page 195).

1. Preheat the oven to 220°C/200°C fan/gas 7. Find a large, shallow, ovenproof dish, around 33 x 26 x 6cm, that will fit the duck legs comfortably (but not too snugly) in a single layer.

2. Scatter the onion, celery and garlic over the bottom of the ovenproof dish. Halve the artichoke hearts through their roots and add them to the dish. Season with salt and pepper, then add 100ml water and the splash of olive oil and gently mix everything together.

3. Sit the duck legs on top of the vegetables, then sprinkle them with a little salt and a drizzle of olive oil. Roast for 40 minutes.

4. Remove the dish from the oven and reduce the temperature to 200°C/180°C fan/gas 6. Add the olives, nestling them into the vegetables and under the legs as best you can, then return to the oven to roast for a further 50 minutes until the duck skin is golden brown and crispy.

5. Remove from the oven and add the flageolet beans, gently nestling them into the juices, just before serving – they will heat through in the hot juices. Serve from the tin.

GET AHEAD

- The onion, celery, garlic and artichokes can be prepared and the duck legs trimmed up to 1 day in advance and all kept individually covered in the fridge.

HINTS & TIPS

- Other tinned pulses, such as borlotti, cannellini or haricot beans, can be added in place of the flageolet beans.
- Or add 450g sliced waxy new potatoes (instead of the flageolet beans) with the vegetables at the beginning.

Moroccan-style Lamb Shank Tagine

SERVES 4

pinch of saffron strands
1 tablespoon boiling water
1–2 tablespoons plain flour
sea salt and freshly ground black pepper
4 small lamb shanks (each around 350g)
2 glugs of vegetable oil
1 onion, chopped
4 garlic cloves, crushed
1 teaspoon ground ginger
1 teaspoon ground cinnamon
2 teaspoons ground cumin
2 teaspoons ground coriander
2 teaspoons rose harissa paste
2 small preserved lemons (or 1 large), drained, pips removed and the rest finely chopped
2 teaspoons caster sugar
600ml fresh lamb or chicken stock (or use 2 stock cubes)
a handful of semi-dried apricots or prunes, or a mixture of both
a handful of walnut halves
250g couscous
a good handful of fresh coriander, leaves and thin stems chopped
2 tablespoons fresh pomegranate seeds (optional)

The list of ingredients here looks a bit daunting, but nonetheless, most of them are straightforward store cupboard spices, and are well worth it. Very easy to make, this is a great 'get ahead' and entertaining recipe that improves with age and is better made at least a day (or up to 3) in advance. Swap 1kg diced lamb shoulder for the shanks, if you prefer.

1. Preheat the oven to 180°C/160°C fan/gas 4.

2. Put the saffron strands in a ramekin with the boiling water. Set aside to infuse. In a large bowl, season the flour with a little salt and pepper, then add the lamb shanks and toss to lightly coat them.

3. Heat a glug of vegetable oil in a deep, cast iron (lidded) casserole dish into which the shanks will fit snugly. Brown well all over on a high heat in two batches. Set aside on a plate. If some of the flour has burnt, wipe out the casserole.

4. Heat another glug of vegetable oil, add the onion and cook gently for a few minutes, until beginning to soften. Add the garlic, ground spices (I measure them all into a small ramekin while the onion is cooking) and cook gently for a few minutes until fragrant. Add the harissa paste, preserved lemons, sugar, saffron water (and strands), stock and lamb shanks. Bring to the boil, season generously, cover, transfer to the oven and cook for 1½ hours, turning the lamb shanks over halfway through cooking.

5. Add the apricots and/or prunes and walnuts and return to the oven for a further 30 minutes. The lamb will almost be falling off the bone by this stage.

6. Skim off the fat with a spoon or some kitchen paper. (Better still, cool, and chill, then take the fat off when it's set after a night in the fridge.)

7. Meanwhile, prepare the couscous (see *Hints & Tips*).

8. Serve the shanks from the casserole, or, standing bone-end up from a deep platter, sitting in the sauce and scattered with the chopped coriander and pomegranate seeds (if using). Surround with the couscous. Alternatively, serve in individual bowls with some couscous, garnished in the same way.

GET AHEAD

- Make to the end of step 5 up to 3 days in advance, then cool, cover and chill, or freeze (defrost before reheating). Reheat the tagine in the oven at 200°C/180°C fan/gas 6 for 20–30 minutes until hot throughout.

HINTS & TIPS

- To prepare the couscous, put into a serving bowl with 1 teaspoon of salt, some pepper and 1 tablespoon of vegetable oil. Pour over 375ml boiling water, stir, then cover with a clean tea towel and leave for 10 minutes. Fluff up with a fork.

Retro Beef Casserole with Horseradish & Mustard Dumplings

SERVES 6

1 head of celery, tough outer sticks discarded and stringy bits removed from the remainder
glug of vegetable oil
1 onion, sliced
1kg chuck (braising) steak, trimmed and cut into large chunks
1–2 tablespoons plain flour, for dusting (just enough to lightly coat)
sea salt and freshly ground black pepper
2 bay leaves
2 tablespoons tomato purée
1 tablespoon Worcestershire sauce
½ teaspoon dried thyme or dried mixed herbs
425ml fresh beef stock (or use 1 stock cube)
200ml red wine
300g whole Chantenay carrots, or regular carrots, peeled, halved and cut into 5cm-long wedges
1 large parsnip, halved and cut into 5cm-long wedges
roughly chopped parsley, to serve (optional)

For the dumplings
140g self-raising flour
70g shredded beef suet
¼ teaspoon sea salt
2 heaped teaspoons mustard powder
2 teaspoons creamed horseradish sauce
a large handful of parsley, chopped

Sometimes, in deepest winter, I find only a cosy, no-frills casserole will do – and this is always the recipe I turn to. Back in my catering days, we soon worked out – contrary to my cookery training and teaching days – that it wasn't vital to brown the meat first. No browning, no frills, suffice to say it makes things a whole lot quicker and it's far less messy.

1. Preheat the oven to 160°C/140°C fan/gas 2½.

2. Thinly slice two thicker celery sticks, then cut the remainder into 5cm-long chunks and set aside. Heat the vegetable oil in a large, oval, cast iron (lidded) casserole dish (around 30 x 24 x 11.5cm) and cook the onion and sliced celery on a low-medium heat for a few minutes until beginning to soften.

3. Meanwhile, put the beef into a large bowl, scatter with the flour and some salt and pepper and toss to lightly coat. Add to the casserole with the bay leaves, tomato purée, Worcestershire sauce, dried herbs, stock, wine and some seasoning. Stir everything together, bring to the boil, then cover, transfer to the oven and cook for 1½ hours.

4. Stir in the carrots, parsnip and the remaining celery, then re-cover and cook for a further 30 minutes. Check that the beef is cooked and check the seasoning. Turn the oven up to 220°C/200°C fan/gas 7.

5. Mix the dumpling ingredients in a bowl with 5 tablespoons of cold water to make a soft, slightly sticky dough. Dot (about 12) small spoonfuls of the mixture over the top of the casserole, pushing them down very slightly into the mixture. Return, uncovered, to the oven and cook for a further 30 minutes or until the dumplings are cooked through. Scatter with the parsley, if using.

GET AHEAD

- Make the recipe to the end of step 4 up to 3 days in advance, then cool, cover and chill. It also freezes beautifully (defrost before reheating). Reheat gently on the stove until hot throughout, then continue with the dumplings and finish in the oven as above.

HINTS & TIPS

- The meat might take a little more or less time to cook, depending on the quality, so check it occasionally during cooking. It should be very tender but not falling apart into shreds.

Roast Tapenade-crusted Rack of Lamb & Crispy Potatoes with Spring Onions & Asparagus

SERVES 4

olive oil, for greasing and drizzling
500g small, waxy new/salad potatoes, halved (larger ones cut into thirds)
1 head of garlic, cloves separated and left unpeeled
4 rosemary sprigs, the leaves of 2 picked and roughly chopped
sea salt and freshly ground black pepper
2 racks of lamb, chined and French-trimmed (6–7 cutlets on each), trimmed of skin and excess fat
2–3 tablespoons black olive tapenade
2 bunches of fat spring onions
about 20 thick asparagus spears, woody ends snapped off
2 mint sprigs, leaves picked, rolled and sliced into very fine ribbons (optional)

For the sauce
200g thick Greek-style yoghurt
2 tablespoons olive oil
1 tablespoon red wine vinegar
1 tablespoon freshly chopped mint
1 teaspoon ground cumin

This is one of my very favourite recipes, which I turn to time and again. A lovely 'get ahead' one-pan roast, it's ideal for Sunday lunch or entertaining, leaving little to do at the last minute. The sauce is a delicious surprise and very good with all manner of lamb recipes.

1. Preheat the oven to 220°C/200°C fan/gas 7. Lightly grease a large (lipped) baking tray around 41 x 31cm (or use a large, shallow roasting tin of a similar size) with olive oil.

2. Put the potatoes, garlic and chopped rosemary onto the baking tray, drizzle with a little olive oil, season and mix to combine everything. Spread out over half the baking tray in a single (not too crowded) layer.

3. Lay the racks of lamb on the other half of the tray, fat-side up, and smear with the tapenade. Add the remaining rosemary sprigs. Roast at the top of the oven for 18–20 minutes for pink lamb (or for a little longer if you prefer it less pink).

4. Transfer the lamb to a cold plate and leave somewhere warm to rest.

5. Turn the potatoes over, then add the spring onions and asparagus to the empty end of the baking tray. Sprinkle with a little olive oil and some seasoning and mix to lightly coat. Roast for a further 10 minutes until soft and just beginning to char.

6. Meanwhile, mix the sauce ingredients together in a serving jug and season well. The sauce can be made up to 3 days ahead and kept covered in the fridge.

7. Remove the veg from the oven and carefully mix them around on the tray. Slice the rested lamb into cutlets and arrange over the top of the veg. Scatter the mint ribbons over, if using. Spoon over a little of the sauce or serve it all separately.

GET AHEAD

- The longer the lamb has to rest, the better. Up to an hour (or more) is fine. So, this recipe can be started at least an hour ahead. Once the lamb is resting, leave the potatoes on the baking tray, then when needed, reheat them in the oven (temp as above) for 5–10 minutes until sizzling, add the spring onions and asparagus and continue as above.

HINTS & TIPS

- Replace the tapenade with a smear of Worcestershire sauce for crispy brown skin.

Roasted Chicken Orzotto Milanese-style

SERVES 5–6

½ teaspoon (a large pinch) saffron strands
good glug of olive oil
1 onion, finely chopped
1 lemon
1 whole chicken, around 1.5–1.6kg, trimmed of fat and excess skin, un-trussed (remove any giblets from cavity and use for stock or discard)
½ teaspoon sea salt, plus extra for seasoning
freshly ground black pepper
2 good knobs of butter, softened
600ml fresh chicken stock (or use 2 stock cubes)
300g dried orzo
5 tablespoons grated Parmesan cheese

HINTS & TIPS

- A dollop of crème fraîche can be stirred into the orzo with the Parmesan and butter, if you like it a bit richer and creamier.
- The ideal chicken weight is 1.5–1.6kg. Any bigger and the cooking time will need to be adjusted accordingly.
- This is best eaten when it's not piping or steaming hot.

Succulent and juicy, this is a pot-roast roast-chicken cross, with an added twist. Drawing on the classic Italian risotto Milanese flavours, namely the addition of saffron and Parmesan, renders this rustic dish seriously delicious! I hope you will agree!

1. Preheat the oven to 200°C/180°C fan/gas 6. Find a large, shallow, ovenproof or casserole dish, roughly 33 x 26 x 6cm, or large enough to hold the chicken comfortably with a little space around the edge for adding the orzo later.

2. Put the saffron into a ramekin with 1 tablespoon of warm water from the kettle and set aside to infuse.

3. Put the olive oil in the ovenproof dish, add the onion and swish around to coat. Halve the lemon, reserve one half, then cut the other in half again and stuff these two wedges into the chicken cavity. Sit the chicken on top of the onion, season it with salt and pepper and smear all over with a good knob of butter. Stir the infused saffron (including strands) and the measured salt into the stock and pour half the stock into the dish, avoiding the chicken, then roast, uncovered, for 50 minutes.

4. Remove from the oven and spoon, or tip out, as many of the juices from the chicken cavity as you can into the dish. Distribute the orzo around the chicken, followed by the remaining stock, ensuring all the orzo is submerged.

5. Return to the oven for 20 minutes, by which time the orzo will be cooked and most of the liquid absorbed. The chicken should be cooked through, too.

6. Remove from the oven and leave (uncovered) to rest and soak up the remaining liquid for 15 minutes.

7. Carefully remove the chicken to a plate, tipping any cavity juices out into the orzo. Stir the remaining good knob of butter and the Parmesan into the orzo.

8. Carve or joint the chicken as you would for roast chicken, and serve on top of the orzo (adding any juices from the chicken plate), with the remaining lemon half cut into wedges, one for each serving, for squeezing over.

Baked Sea Bass & Mediterranean Vegetables with Aïoli

SERVES 4

1 large red pepper, de-seeded and cut into chunks
1 medium aubergine, quartered lengthways and cut into 4–5cm triangular chunks
1 large red onion, quartered through the root, then each quarter cut into 3 wedges
2 courgettes, quartered lengthways and cut into 5cm chunks
450g baby waxy new/salad potatoes, halved (any larger ones cut into thirds)
8–10 baby cherry tomatoes, left whole
1 head of garlic, cloves separated and left unpeeled
4 oregano sprigs, or use 2 good pinches of dried oregano
sea salt and freshly ground black pepper
glug of olive oil, plus extra for drizzling
about 20 black olives, pitted
4 sea bass fillets, skin-on

To serve
1 x quantity Aïoli (see page 201)
extra oregano sprigs

So tasty, so easy and positively bursting with the rich colours and flavours of the Mediterranean! I like to leave the skins on the baked garlic cloves for diners to squeeze out the delicious, creamy purée within. Add a 400g tin of flageolet beans, drained and rinsed (then nestled into the veg), instead of the fish to create a lovely vegetarian main course.

1. Preheat the oven to 220°C/200°C fan/gas 7. Find a large, shallow roasting tin around 41 x 26cm and ideally no deeper than 4cm (or use a large, lipped baking tray).

2. Place all the vegetables in the roasting tin, ensuring they are roughly in a single layer, although a little overlapping is fine. (If piled up, they will stew rather than roast.) Scatter over the tomatoes, garlic and oregano, season and drizzle over a glug of olive oil. Swish everything around by shaking the tin, until the ingredients are mixed, evenly distributed and lightly coated with olive oil.

3. Roast at the top of the oven for around 45 minutes, gently turning over once halfway through, being careful not to break up the vegetables. Some will be beginning to brown and char and some won't.

4. Make the aïoli according to the recipe on page 201, then transfer to a serving bowl and set aside.

5. Nestle the black olives into the vegetables, then arrange the sea bass fillets on top, some skin-side down and some skin-side up. Drizzle the fish with a little olive oil, season, then bake for a further 8–10 minutes or until the fish is opaque and just cooked. Scatter over the oregano sprigs and serve from the tin with the aïoli served alongside (drizzling a little over, too, if you like).

GET AHEAD

- Make the recipe to the end of step 4 any time on the day, then cool and cover. Reheat the vegetables in the oven (temp as above) for 10–15 minutes or until sizzling, then continue as above with the olives and fish.

HINTS & TIPS

- Fennel bulb(s) would be a good addition instead of any of the above veg. Adjust the quantities accordingly.
- Pesto sauce drizzled over the top is a good alternative to aïoli.

Salmon, Potato, Asparagus & Cucumber Bake with Lime & Chilli Salsa

SERVES 4

1 cucumber, peeled, halved lengthways, seeds removed and cut into ½cm-thick 'boats' on a deep diagonal
sea salt and freshly ground black pepper
olive oil, for greasing and drizzling
600g waxy new/salad potatoes, cut into ½cm-thick rounds
16 asparagus spears, woody ends snapped off
4 x 110–140g skinless salmon fillets, each sliced into 5–6 pieces on a diagonal
a handful of rocket leaves or watercress (optional)

For the salsa
4 spring onions, trimmed and thinly sliced diagonally
1 green chilli, de-seeded and finely diced
juice of 1 lime
½ teaspoon sea salt
freshly ground black pepper, to taste
1 tablespoon small capers in brine, drained, plus a little of their brine
3 tablespoons olive oil
1 heaped tablespoon snipped chives or roughly chopped dill

Light, fresh, pretty and zingy, too, thanks to the lime and chilli salsa. This is an easy way to enjoy that wonderful summer combination of salmon, new potatoes, asparagus and cucumber. It's a very popular recipe, too!

1. Put the cucumber in a sieve or colander, sprinkle with a generous pinch of salt and leave to drain for 30 minutes.

2. Preheat the oven to 220°C/200°C fan/gas 7. Lightly grease a large, shallow roasting tin around 41 x 26cm and ideally no deeper than 4cm (or use a large, lipped baking tray) with olive oil.

3. Spread the potatoes out in the tin, roughly in a single layer. Swirl with a drizzle of olive oil and season with salt and pepper. Roast for 25 minutes, turning over with a fish slice after 15 minutes – some will be golden and crispy, some won't, and some might stick and break up a little, all of which is fine. At this stage (after the 15 minutes), scatter the (un-rinsed) cucumber over the top and return to the oven for the final 10 minutes.

4. Meanwhile, cut the asparagus tips off into 6.5cm lengths. Halve any thicker stems lengthways and cut all the stems in half, or into three chunks if very long. Scatter the asparagus (tips and stems) over the cucumber and potatoes, swirl over another drizzle of olive oil, sprinkle over a little salt and return to the oven for 10 minutes or until just cooked.

5. Meanwhile, mix together all the salsa ingredients in a small bowl and set aside.

6. Just before serving, arrange the salmon pieces in a single layer on top of the asparagus, then bake for a further 4 minutes or until pale pink and opaque. Remove from the oven, spoon over the salsa, scatter with rocket leaves or watercress (if using) and serve from the tin.

GET AHEAD

- Make the recipe to the end of step 3 up to 2 hours in advance, cool and cover. Reheat in the oven (temp as above) for 8–10 minutes or until sizzling, then add the asparagus and continue as above.
- The salsa can be made any time on the day, but don't add the herbs until just before serving. Cover and keep it at room temperature.

Thai-style Pot-roast Chicken & Noodles

SERVES 5

good knob of butter, softened
1 whole chicken, around 1.5–1.6kg, trimmed of fat and excess skin, untrussed (remove any giblets from cavity and use for stock or discard)
sea salt
1 red chilli, sliced into thin discs
4cm piece of fresh root ginger, peeled and finely chopped (or use 2 teaspoons ginger paste from a jar)
2 garlic cloves, thinly sliced
2 sticks of lemon grass, split lengthways (or use 2 teaspoons lemon grass paste from a jar)
8 kaffir lime leaves, fresh or dried
300ml fresh chicken stock (or use 1 stock cube)
2 tablespoons fish sauce
juice of 2 limes
bunch of spring onions, trimmed and thinly sliced diagonally
2 pak choi bulbs, cut into 2.5cm pieces
600g straight-to-wok ribbon rice noodles (or similar) or fresh egg noodles
a good handful of coriander, leaves and thin stems roughly chopped

This may appear to be quite a long list of ingredients, but please don't be put off – once everything's in the pot, this recipe pretty much looks after itself. There's also no need to brown the chicken first, which is a bonus. Fragrant, spicy, healthy and well worth cooking for its wonderful aroma alone!

1. Preheat the oven to 200°C/180°C fan/gas 6. Find a large, oval, cast iron (lidded) casserole dish (around 30 x 24 x 11.5cm) into which the chicken will fit with a little space to spare around the edges, then very lightly grease the bottom (where the chicken will sit) with a smidgen of the butter.

2. Put the chicken into the casserole, then smear it all over with the remaining butter and sprinkle with a little salt. Nestle the chilli, ginger, garlic, lemon grass and lime leaves around the chicken. Mix together the stock, fish sauce and lime juice and pour around the chicken. Bring to the boil, then cover with the lid, transfer to the oven and cook for 45 minutes.

3. Turn the oven up to 220°C/200°C fan/gas 7. Remove the lid and cook for a further 15 minutes, or until the chicken is cooked and the skin is golden brown. Larger chickens will take a little longer.

4. Carefully transfer the chicken onto a plate, having drained as much juice as possible from the cavity back into the casserole (suspending the chicken from a wooden spoon inserted into the cavity helps) and set aside somewhere warm to rest.

5. Add the spring onions and pak choi to the pot and bubble up for a few minutes until just cooked, then check the seasoning, adding a little more fish sauce or salt, if necessary. Remove from the heat, stir in the noodles and leave for a few minutes to warm through. Just before serving, scatter over the coriander.

6. Joint or slice the chicken, place on top of the noodle mixture, having added any juices from the chicken plate, and serve from the casserole.

GET AHEAD

- The chilli, ginger, spring onions and pak choi can be prepared up to 1 day in advance. Keep them separately, covered in the fridge.

HINTS & TIPS

- A good handful of finely shredded chard or whole spinach leaves can be added and wilted in the juices, instead of, or as well as, the pak choi, if you like.

Tarts & Savoury Bakes

This is savoury baking at its easiest, with the help of occasional shortcuts on the pastry front using ready-made pastry. Of course, do make your own pastry, if you prefer! You will also find some key tips on page 16 at the front of the book, which are handy to have up your sleeve for any sort of baking.

Most of these recipes are portable, making them excellent picnic or lunch box fare. Some make a striking contribution as part of a feast and others shine on their own, perhaps with just a simple mixed leaf salad to accompany.

Asparagus, Taleggio & Anchovy Tart

SERVES 4 GENEROUSLY
(or serves 6 as part of a feast)

1 x 320g ready-rolled puff pastry sheet (about 35 x 23cm)
20–24 medium thickness asparagus spears (more if the spears are thin)
200g Taleggio cheese, thinly sliced
50g anchovy fillets in oil, drained and each snipped lengthways into 3 thin slivers
olive oil, for drizzling
freshly ground black pepper

GET AHEAD

- Make to the end of step 2 up to 3 days in advance. Cool, cover with clingfilm and store on the baking sheet at room temperature.
- The anchovies can be prepared up to 3 days in advance and stored in their oil in a tub in the fridge.

HINTS & TIPS

- Replace the anchovies with soft green herbs, if you like.
- Halve any very thick asparagus spears lengthways, arranging them cut-side down.
- This tart looks very pretty garnished with snipped cress, microleaves or chive flowers, torn apart, and scattered over the top just before serving.

A very tasty and simple tart using only a few ingredients, which just happens to look pretty, too! If you leave out the anchovies and choose a creamy vegetarian cheese, it's also suitable for vegetarians.

1. Preheat the oven to 200°C/180°C fan/gas 6.

2. Unroll the pastry and place it, on its paper, on a large (lipped) baking tray. Peel it off the paper to release any bits that are stuck, and then replace it back onto the paper. Score a border about 2.5cm all around the edge to form a frame. Score a diamond pattern within the border, then prick the middle of the pastry with a fork. Bake for 10–12 minutes until puffed up and light golden brown. Remove from the oven and gently press the risen middle of the pastry frame down.

3. While the pastry is cooking, bend the asparagus spears between your hands, near their bases, until they snap naturally, then discard the woody ends (use for making soup, if you like).

4. Line the spears up inside the pastry case, tips to tails alternately. The inside should be completely filled. Tear the Taleggio slices into smaller pieces and dot them over the asparagus. Arrange the anchovies in a criss-cross pattern over the top. Drizzle with a little olive oil and season with pepper.

5. Return to the oven and bake for about 20 minutes or until the pastry is golden, the asparagus tender and the cheese is melted and bubbling. Check halfway through and turn the tart round if it's cooking unevenly.

6. Slide the tart on its paper onto a chopping board or large serving platter. Drizzle with a little more olive oil and serve.

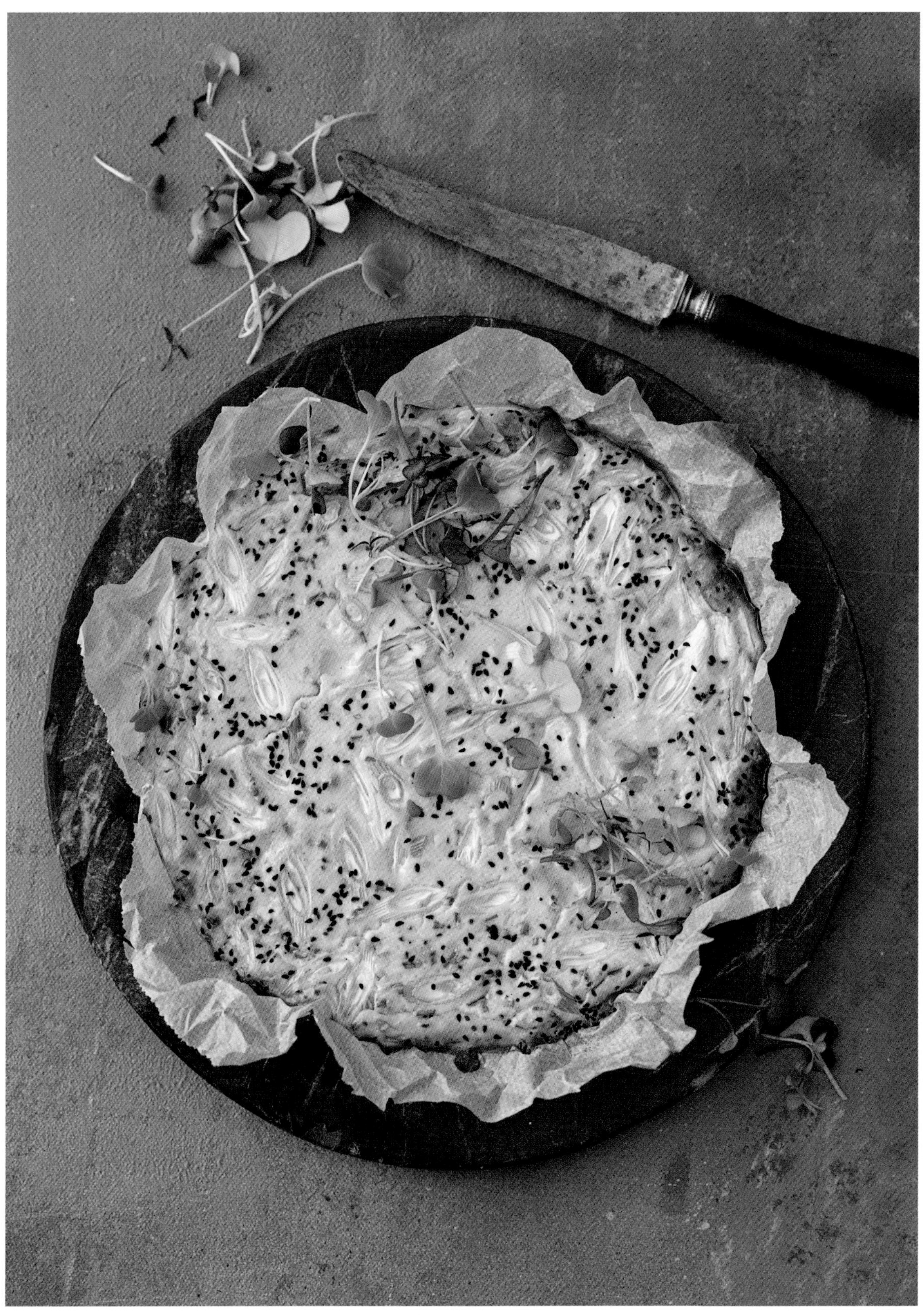

Baked Warm Roquefort Cheesecake

SERVES 4–6 as a main course (or serves 8 as part of a feast or picnic)

For the oatcake base
140g rough oatcakes, broken up
60g butter, softened at room temperature
25g walnut pieces

For the filling
250g full-fat soft cheese, at room temperature
3 eggs
100ml double cream
100g Roquefort cheese, crumbled into assorted small and larger chunks
1 heaped tablespoon snipped chives
sea salt and freshly ground black pepper
4 spring onions, trimmed and finely sliced on a diagonal
nigella or onion seeds, for sprinkling

micro leaves or salad cress, to garnish (optional)

A wobbly, crumbly, cheesey delight similar to cheese soufflé when eaten warm. Lovely eaten warm for lunch or supper, as well as cold for feasts and picnics. For a special vegetarian main course, use a vegetarian creamy blue cheese (such as Dolcelatte or Saint Agur). Being very rich, a little goes a long way.

1. Line a shallow, loose-bottomed, 24cm fluted round tart tin with baking parchment (or foil-backed baking parchment), allowing the sides to come at least 2.5cm above the top of the tin to form a collar. Put onto a baking sheet.

2. For the base, process all the ingredients in a food-processor until they come together (or bash the oatcakes into crumbs, finely chop the nuts and mix both with the butter), then press evenly over the base of the tin (the bottom of a flat glass is useful for doing this). Chill for 30 minutes, until the base has firmed up.

3. Preheat the oven to 190°C/170°C fan/gas 5.

4. For the filling, put the soft cheese into a bowl, then gradually add the eggs, one at a time, whisking with a hand whisk until smooth, before adding the next egg. Stir in the cream, followed by the crumbled Roquefort and the chives. Season, bearing in mind the filling should be well seasoned.

5. Pour the mixture into the tin over the oatcake base, then scatter over the spring onions and a few nigella or onion seeds. Bake for 30 minutes or until golden brown and just set around the edges, but barely set with a bit of a wobble in the middle. It will be risen like a soufflé but will sink down as it cools.

6. Remove from the oven and leave in the tin for 5 minutes or until it shrinks away from the sides, then, if serving it warm, carefully remove the cheesecake from the tin (see *Hints & Tips*) with the paper still in place. If serving cold, leave to cool completely in the tin. Garnish with a few micro leaves or a little salad cress (if using) and serve the cheesecake as it is or with any of the topping suggestions.

GET AHEAD

- Prepare up to the end of step 2 up to 3 days in advance, and step 4 up to 1 day in advance. Cover and keep chilled, separately.

HINTS & TIPS

- To remove the side ring from the tart, stand the tin on top of a mug, tin or small bowl; the ring will fall off onto the worktop.
- Topping suggestions: Baby cherry tomatoes on the vine snipped into bunches and roasted on the baking sheet (after the cheesecake comes out of the oven) with a little olive oil and salt for 5 minutes or so until wilted.
- Stir together a handful of walnut halves with enough honey to coat. Roast on the lined baking sheet until golden and caramelised. Cool, then pile up in the middle of the cheesecake or arrange around the edge.

Cheesey Courgette & Jalapeño Loaf

MAKES 1 LOAF
(18–20 slices)

200g courgettes
175g plain white flour
75g plain wholemeal flour
1 teaspoon sea salt
freshly ground black pepper
1 teaspoon caster sugar
1 teaspoon mustard powder
1 tablespoon baking powder
115g grated Parmesan cheese, plus an extra tablespoon for the topping
25g pickled jalapeño peppers from a jar, drained and finely chopped, including seeds
75ml olive oil, plus extra for greasing
200ml milk
2 eggs
sea salt flakes (optional)

GET AHEAD

- Steps 1 and 2 can be completed up to 2 days ahead – keep the sliced and grated courgettes separately in the fridge.
- The loaf freezes well, too. Defrost and serve cold or reheat in a medium oven for 10–15 minutes until just warmed through.

HINTS & TIPS

- Swap grated carrots for the courgettes, or use a mixture of both (reserve about a tablespoon of the grated carrots to scatter over before baking).

Over the years I have adapted this recipe, which was given to me by someone I worked with many moons ago. A cross between a cake and a loaf of bread, it's actually neither of these, but somewhere in between. A batter rather than a dough, so there's no kneading, it's damp and quite dense, with unexpected heat running throughout from the jalapeño peppers. This loaf is a great addition to summer spreads and picnics. We love it toasted, too – it becomes even more flavourful as the heat from the toaster re-ignites that irresistible taste (and smell) of cooked cheese. Lashings of butter, plain or flavoured, are essential (wild garlic is good), or a dollop of natural yoghurt is good, too.

1. Preheat the oven to 190°C/170°C fan/gas 5. Grease a 900g loaf tin (about 23 x 13 x 5.5cm) with a little olive oil, then line the base and short sides/ends with a long strip of baking parchment.

2. Cut 12 thin slices of courgette and set aside for the topping. Grate the remainder, then roll up in some kitchen paper to soak up the excess moisture.

3. Mix both flours, the measured salt, a few turns of pepper, the sugar, mustard powder and baking powder together in a bowl, then stir in the grated courgettes (gently squeezing out any excess moisture with your hands before you add them), Parmesan and jalapeño peppers. In a jug, beat the olive oil, milk and eggs together with a fork, then add to the bowl and stir everything together until well combined.

4. Transfer the mixture to the lined loaf tin and level the top, then place the reserved courgette slices on top, slightly overlapping them down the middle of the mixture. Sprinkle the remaining tablespoon of Parmesan over the entire top, plus a few sea salt flakes.

5. Bake for 50 minutes or until a skewer inserted in the middle comes out clean (if it doesn't, cook for a little longer and check again). Remove from the oven and leave to cool in the tin for 5 minutes, then turn out and transfer to a wire rack. Serve warm or cold on the day it's made (though it keeps well for several days).

Caramelised Chicory & Blue Cheese Tarte Tatin

SERVES 4 as a main course (or serves 6–8 as part of a feast)

1 teaspoon olive oil
30g butter
6–8 small thyme sprigs (or use a good pinch of dried thyme)
3 small chicory bulbs, any damaged outer leaves discarded, then bulbs halved lengthways through the root (quartered, if large)
sea salt and freshly ground black pepper
plain flour, for dusting
1 x 320g ready-rolled puff pastry sheet (about 35 x 23cm)
50g creamy soft blue cheese, such as Saint Agur

GET AHEAD

- Make the tarte tatin up to 2–3 days in advance, then turn out onto an ovenproof plate/dish (ready for reheating), cool, cover and chill. Warm through in the oven (temp as above) for 10–15 minutes or so, then dot with the cheese before serving.

HINTS & TIPS

- A good-quality tarte tatin tin is ideal for this. Or use any shallow, round, ovenproof dish or frying pan. Be very careful when turning the tarte out if using a frying pan, as the handle will be dangerously hot. Oven gloves to the ready!

Chicory is one of my favourite things, both cooked and uncooked. Here the blue cheese and buttery pastry offset the pleasing, yet slightly bitter edge to its taste. This is an easy but very tasty tarte tatin that is best eaten warm.

1. Preheat the oven to 200°C/180°C fan/gas 6. Find a 20cm tarte tatin tin or similar-sized, shallow ovenproof dish or frying pan (see *Hints & Tips*).

2. Heat the olive oil and butter in the tin/or frying pan until melted, scatter over half the thyme sprigs (or the dried thyme), then add the chicory, cut-side down and nose-to-tail. It might be a bit of a tight fit, but squeeze it in – it shrinks as it cooks. Season, then cook on a very low heat for 10–15 minutes until soft and tender, turning over when caramelised on the underside to soften the other side for the last few minutes. Don't worry if the chicory layers fall apart a bit, the end result will be fine. When cooked, carefully re-arrange the chicory, cut-side down again.

3. On a lightly floured worktop, roll out the pastry sheet slightly thinner than it is (to make it big enough to cut out the disc) and then cut out a disc around 2.5cm larger than the tin/dish or pan. Place over the top of the chicory, tucking the edges down the sides, between the chicory and the tin/dish or pan. Prick the top with a fork 3 or 4 times. Bake for 30 minutes or until golden and puffed up.

4. Remove from the oven and leave to rest for a few minutes, then loosen around the edges with a palette knife and carefully invert onto a flat, round serving plate or board. It might need a sharp shake to release it. Don't worry if a bit of chicory remains in the tin or pan, just pop it back into its empty slot! While still oven-hot, dot small pieces of the blue cheese over the top. It will begin to melt around the edges.

5. Scatter with the remaining thyme sprigs and serve warm.

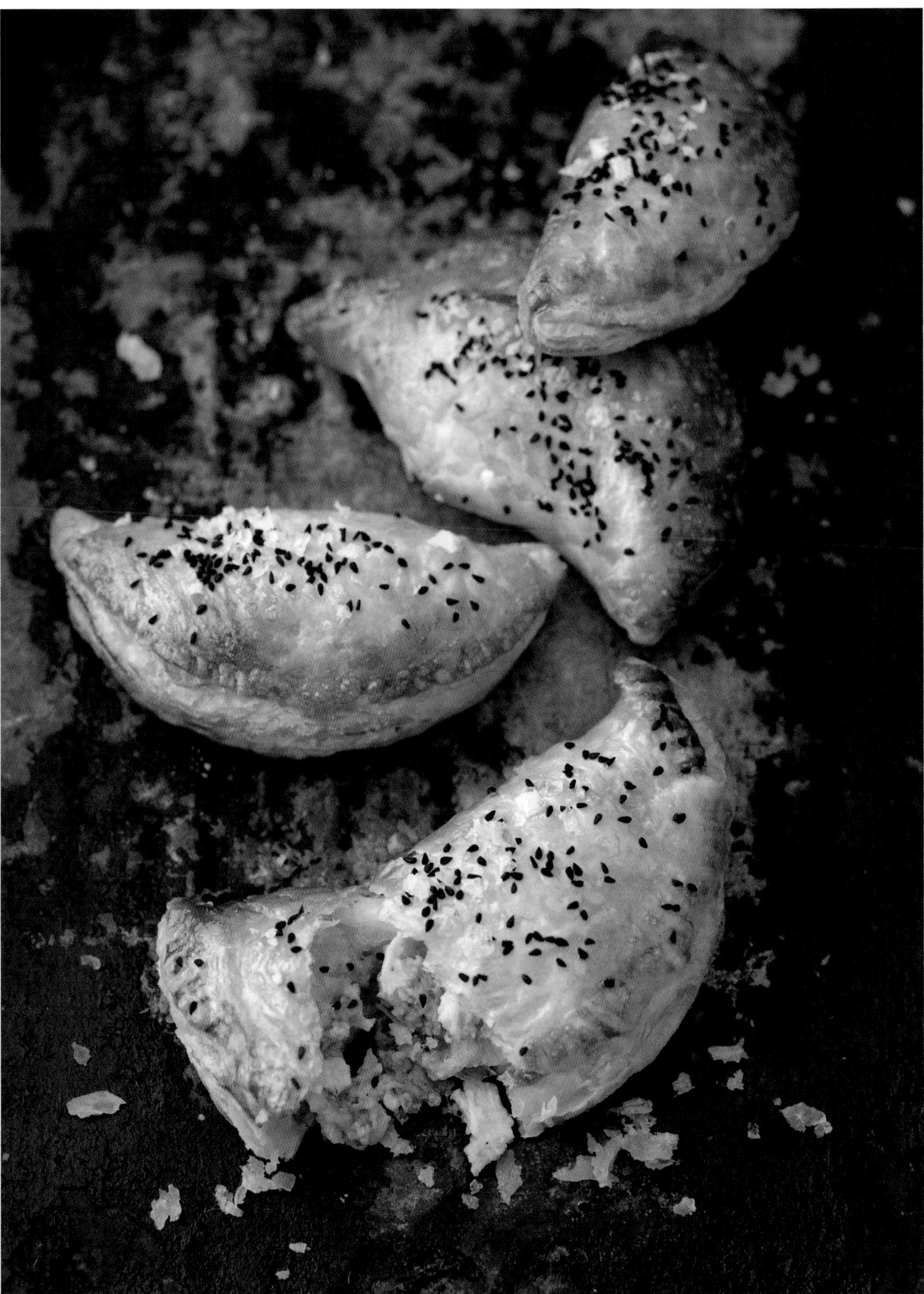

Parma Ham & Cheese Hand Pies

MAKES 4 PIES

1 x 320g ready-rolled puff pastry sheet (about 35 x 23cm)
30g full-fat soft cheese
55g soft goats' cheese log
2 slices Parma ham, each snipped into three, lengthways, then into thin strips
pinch of dried oregano or dried thyme
sea salt flakes and freshly ground black pepper
1 egg, lightly beaten with a pinch of sea salt
a few onion or nigella seeds, for sprinkling

GET AHEAD

- Make to the end of step 3 up to 2 days in advance, or complete the recipe, then cool, cover and chill.

HINTS & TIPS

- See the introductory pages (page 16) for tips on re-rolling pastry off-cuts, plus other useful pastry tricks.
- Almost any cooked meat, fish or vegetables can be used in the filling as well as any 'bin ends' of cheese.

I cannot bear waste and use up just about every single bit of food in one way or another. Sometimes we eat leftovers for days on end, until every last bit has gone. Even throwing away off-cuts of pastry goes against the grain, so I fiddle about endlessly rolling ingredients up in bits of pastry or putting things on top of it, usually to enjoy with a drink.

Hand pies fall nicely into this category and can be made with leftover pastry of any kind, if desired. Not only that, most of the contents of the fridge can be stuffed inside them, too. Sweet or savoury, they can be enjoyed for picnics or other occasions that call for portable food. They require far less filling than you would imagine, although a little seepage during cooking is fine and adds to their charm. Use these quantities as a rough guide and adjust according to how many pies you're making and what filling you have available.

1. Preheat the oven to 220°C/200°C fan/gas 7. Line a baking sheet with silicone or baking parchment (or use the pastry wrapping paper).

2. Unroll the pastry and cut out four 12.5cm circles using a pastry cutter or a small saucer as a template. Place on the lined baking sheet and chill while you make the filling.

3. Beat together both cheeses, the Parma ham and herbs in a bowl and season with salt and pepper. Divide the mixture evenly between the pastry discs, spooning it out over the lower halves and leaving the edges clear. Brush the bottom edges with egg wash and fold the top half of each disc over the filling to form a half-moon shape. Press the edges together to seal and press along the edges with the tines of a fork.

4. Brush the pies with egg wash, then scatter with onion or nigella seeds and a few flakes of sea salt. Bake for 10–15 minutes until puffed up and golden brown. Serve warm or cold (if serving for picnics, etc).

Italian-style Tomato, 'Nduja, Parma Ham & Three Cheese Galette

SERVES 4 as a main course (or serves 8 as part of a feast)

3 large, ripe tomatoes, cut across into ½cm-thick slices (discard the stem-end slices)
sea salt and freshly ground black pepper
100g full-fat soft cheese
2 teaspoons 'nduja paste from a jar
1 tablespoon fresh breadcrumbs (or use dried, such as panko)
plain flour, for dusting
½ x 500g block ready-made shortcrust pastry
1 egg, lightly beaten with a pinch of sea salt
2 heaped tablespoons grated Parmesan cheese
125g Taleggio cheese, thinly sliced
2 slices Parma ham, torn into wide strips
2 anchovy fillets in oil (from a jar), drained and snipped into pieces (optional)
a small bunch of basil, leaves picked
olive oil, for drizzling

HINTS & TIPS

- 'Nduja paste can be found in small jars in larger supermarkets or delis.

This galette could be described as pizza-esque or even a 'posh pizza'. It's certainly far easier to make than a pizza as it only requires bought ready-made pastry, rather than a bread dough base, and its components are based on Italian ingredients. It's good served warm or cold.

1. Lay the tomatoes out in one layer on a plate lined with kitchen paper, scatter with a little salt and set aside for 30 minutes to extract the excess juices.

2. Preheat the oven to 190°C/170°C fan/gas 5. Put a flat baking sheet in the oven to heat up.

3. Mix the soft cheese, 'nduja paste and breadcrumbs together in a bowl with some salt and pepper.

4. Lightly dust a large sheet of silicone or baking parchment with flour, then roll out the pastry onto it into a rough circle, about 36cm diameter (before rolling, cut the half block of pastry into two squares, put one on top of the other, offset to form a star shape, to make an easier starting point to roll out a circle). Alternatively, roll out on a worktop and then transport onto the paper.

5. Spread the 'nduja mixture over the middle of the pastry, leaving a 5cm border around the edges. Dab the top of the tomato slices dry with another piece of kitchen paper, then arrange them, slightly overlapping, over the 'nduja mixture. Bring the border of the pastry up over the outside edges of the filling, leaving most of the filling showing, pleating the edges over and over each other to form a wavy effect – it's meant to look rustic!

6. Brush the pleated pastry rim with the egg wash and scatter the rim only with the Parmesan. Tear the Taleggio into smaller pieces and dot over the filling, then drape the Parma ham over in a wavy pattern. Scatter with the anchovies (if using). Stack and roll up 8–10 of the basil leaves, then slice into thin ribbons and scatter all over the galette, followed by a drizzle of olive oil.

7. Remove the hot baking sheet from the oven, then carefully slide the galette and its paper onto it. Bake for 30 minutes or until golden brown and bubbling.

8. Remove from the oven and leave the galette for a few minutes before transferring to a serving platter or board, then leave for a few more minutes before eating. Scatter with the remaining basil leaves cut into ribbons if you like and drizzle with a little more olive oil. Serve warm or cold.

Mini Sausage, Walnut & Black Pudding Twists

MAKES AROUND 36–40

225g sausagemeat (or sausages of your choice, skins removed)
110g black pudding, crumbled
2 large sage leaves, chopped
1 pickled walnut, drained and chopped (or use a few chopped walnuts)
grating of nutmeg
good grinding of black pepper
1 x 320g ready-rolled puff pastry sheet (about 35 x 23cm)
plain flour, for dusting
Dijon mustard, for spreading
1 egg, lightly beaten with a pinch of sea salt

Topping suggestions
sea salt flakes; nigella or onion seeds; dried chilli flakes; black and/or white sesame seeds

GET AHEAD

- Make to the end of step 3 up to 3 days ahead and store, covered, in the fridge (halve the rolls diagonally to make them easier to store).

HINTS & TIPS

- 'Nduja & Parmesan Sausage Twists: make as above using 340g sausagemeat, but replace the black pudding with 25g 'nduja paste from a jar. Omit the walnut and mustard. Before cooking, sprinkle with grated Parmesan cheese, salt and fennel seeds.

There's a huge amount of flavour packed into these tasty little morsels, as well as very good meat to pastry ratio and their own convenient 'picking-up' handles. These twists or 'straws' always go down a storm, so I would advise making more than you think you need. A cross between a sausage roll and a canapé, they're good to eat at almost any time of the day, and cut into longer lengths, they're just the job for lunch. I have included an alternative, very tasty Italian-style version as well (see *Hints & Tips*).

1. Line a large baking sheet (or 2 smaller ones) with silicone or baking parchment.

2. In a bowl, mix together the sausagemeat, black pudding, sage, pickled walnut, nutmeg and pepper. Unroll the pastry, peel off its paper, dust the paper with flour and then place the pastry back in position on top. Cut the pastry in half lengthways and spread each half thinly with Dijon mustard, leaving a 2.5cm border along both long edges.

3. Halve the sausagemeat mixture and roll it into two long, thin sausages to the same length as the long side of the pastry (this is easiest done in sections, if you prefer). Place (and join up) the sausage(s) down the middle of each pastry strip. Brush the border of one side of each pastry strip with egg wash, then fold the other side over the filling to cover the egg-washed border. Press a finger down along the sausage to form a seam. Press the seams together to seal using the tines of a fork.

4. Brush the rolls with egg wash, avoiding the cut end edges. Sprinkle with any, or some, of the topping suggestions. Chill in the fridge for 30 minutes to firm up before slicing.

5. Preheat the oven to 220°C/200°C fan/gas 7.

6. Cut each roll at a very deep diagonal angle into approximately 18–20 x 1cm-thick slices (they then twist slightly during cooking, hence the name). Transfer to the prepared baking sheet(s), leaving a little space between each one for expansion during cooking. Cook at the top of the oven for 8–12 minutes or until puffed up, golden brown and crisp.

7. Remove from the oven and transfer to a serving platter. Best served warm as is, or with some sriracha sauce, mustard mayonnaise or puréed piccalilli for dipping into. (If serving cold, transfer to a wire rack to cool.)

Petit Pois & Mint Tart with Parmesan & Thyme Pastry

SERVES 4–6 (or serves 8–10 as part of a feast)

For the pastry
55g cold butter, diced
85g plain flour, plus extra for dusting
pinch of sea salt
good pinch of dried thyme
40g Parmesan cheese, grated
1 egg yolk

For the filling
200g frozen petit pois
250g mascarpone cheese
3 tablespoons grated Parmesan cheese
150ml double cream
3 egg yolks
sea salt and freshly ground black pepper
1 tablespoon snipped chives
about 20 mint leaves, rolled up and finely shredded, plus a few extra (optional) to garnish
nutmeg, for grating
pea shoots, cress or borage flowers, to garnish (optional)

GET AHEAD

- The tart can be made fully up to 3 days in advance, cooled, covered and chilled, or frozen (defrost before serving). Serve at room temperature or reheat in a medium oven for 10–15 minutes or until warm.

This pretty and very tasty tart incorporates that great summer combo of petit pois and mint – here, encased in crisp, biscuit-like cheesey pastry. The pastry is very malleable, therefore forgiving of any blips, which are simply repaired with a little finger-moulding. For vegetarians, swap the Parmesan for a vegetarian Italian-style hard cheese.

1. Find a loose-bottomed tart tin, either rectangular (about 36 x 13 x 2 .5cm) or round (about 24 x 2.5cm) and a baking sheet. Cut a piece of baking parchment large enough to line the tin with a collar slightly higher than its sides. Scrunch the paper up to soften it, then open it out again and set aside.

2. To make the pastry, place the butter, flour and salt in a food-processor and whizz together briefly until the mixture resembles fine breadcrumbs. Add the remaining ingredients along with 1½ tablespoons of cold water and whizz until beginning to come together. Turn out onto a floured worktop, knead lightly into a ball, then flatten into a rectangular or round shape. Wrap and rest in the fridge for 30 minutes.

3. Roll out the pastry on a lightly floured worktop into a rectangle or circle large enough to line the tin, allowing for it to come up a little higher above the sides. Line the tin, trim the edges to neaten and prick the base all over with a fork. Place on the baking sheet and chill for a further 30 minutes.

4. Preheat the oven to 190°C/170°C fan/gas 5.

5. To bake it blind, line the pastry case with the baking parchment and fill with enough baking beans (or dried rice or pulses) to cover the bottom and halfway up the sides of the tin. Bake for 15 minutes until the pastry is firm, then remove the beans and paper. Return to the oven for a further 5–10 minutes until the case is a pale biscuit colour and cooked through. Reduce the oven to 180°C/160°C fan/gas 4.

6. Meanwhile, boil a kettleful of water. Put the petit pois in a heatproof bowl, cover with boiling water, then immediately drain and gently roll in kitchen paper to dry. Mix the mascarpone, Parmesan, cream and egg yolks together in a jug or bowl and season well with salt and pepper.

7. Stir in the chives, shredded mint and petit pois, then pour into the pastry case and grate a little nutmeg over the top. Bake for 25–30 minutes until golden brown and just set. Remove from the oven and cool in the tin until you are ready to serve, then remove and serve warm or at room temperature, garnished with any of the suggestions.

Ridiculously Easy Flatbreads

MAKES 6
(or 8 smaller ones)

225g self-raising flour, plus extra for dusting
200g thick Greek-style yoghurt
½ teaspoon sea salt
a few nigella or onion seeds (optional)

GET AHEAD

- Make any time on the day and serve as they are, or warmed through. Cooled and tightly wrapped, they last very well until the next day.

HINTS & TIPS

- A generous knob of butter or ghee, melted, then brushed over the warm flatbreads when they come out of the pan is delicious, made even better with a sliced or crushed garlic clove added at the melting stage. A handful of freshly chopped parsley or coriander leaves, or a tablespoon of snipped chives, stirred into the melted butter/ghee is a lovely addition, too.

- A few jarred anchovies, drained of their oil, arranged over the top and scattered with any of the above herbs turn the flatbreads into a very tasty snack. Brush the warm flatbreads with a little melted butter or ghee as above, or with a drizzle of olive oil, first.

The clue is in the title! These are so easy and quick to make and no kneading is required, which in my book is a huge plus. This recipe isn't strictly a 'bake' because it's cooked/'baked' in a frying pan, not in the oven. Made from store cupboard staples, flatbreads are endlessly versatile, either served as an accompaniment for 'mopping up', or piled with all sorts of goodies on top, making them a great base on which to build a delicious mélange of leftovers from the fridge, too.

1. Put the flour, yoghurt and salt into a bowl, then mix, bringing them together with your hands to make a soft dough. If it's too sticky, add a little more flour and if too dry, a little more yoghurt.

2. Tip the dough onto a lightly floured worktop, then briefly and gently work the dough into a pliable, smooth-ish ball. Cut it in half, then cut each half into three (or four) triangular shapes.

3. Heat a small dry frying pan.

4. Thinly roll out each piece of dough into a 'slipper', pitta or triangular shape. If using nigella or onion seeds, scatter a few over the flatbreads before cooking and lightly roll them into the dough.

5. Cook one flatbread at a time in the pan for a few minutes on each side. Flip it over when it's puffed up and flecked with brown on the underside, then repeat on the other side. Transfer to a plate and keep warm in a low oven if using immediately (stack the cooked flatbreads wrapped in a clean tea towel in a pile on a plate), or transfer to a wire rack to cool.

Ham & Cheese Savoury Bread & Butter Pudding

SERVES 5–6

softened butter for spreading, plus extra for greasing and for dotting over the top
8 slices bread, preferably stale, or a few days old at least
Dijon mustard, for spreading (or use other mustard of your choice)
4 generous slices ham
110g Gruyère or mature Cheddar cheese, grated
4 eggs
600ml milk
2 tablespoons grated Parmesan cheese
2 tablespoons snipped chives
sea salt and freshly ground black pepper

GET AHEAD

- Complete the recipe up to 3 days in advance, cool, cover and chill. Reheat in the oven (temp as above) for about 15 minutes or until hot throughout.

HINTS & TIPS

- All sorts of things can be added to the 'sandwiches'. Swap the mustard for your favourite chutney or some Marmite®, replace the ham with thinly sliced tomatoes, or try a different hard cheese, such as Emmental in place of the Gruyère or Cheddar.

Nothing fancy here, just a tasty way of using up stale bread, plus any odds and ends of cheese, as well as ham, for that matter. This is a great weekend brunch, Saturday lunch or supper. It's delicious served with a green salad, made even better with a few walnut pieces and perhaps a little walnut oil in the dressing.

1. Butter a shallow, ovenproof dish about 31 x 20 x 5cm (about 1.7 litre volume).

2. Generously butter one side of each slice of bread, then spread four of the slices with mustard, to taste.

3. Using the ham and half the Gruyère or Cheddar cheese, make four sandwiches in the usual way. Cut each sandwich into four triangles (leaving the crusts on). Arrange the sandwiches overlapping in the greased dish, pointed sides uppermost. Gather up any stray bits of cheese and scatter over.

4. Put the eggs, milk, Parmesan, chives and some salt and pepper into a jug and beat together well with a fork – it should be well seasoned. Pour this mixture over the sandwiches, ensuring that the tops of the sandwiches are protruding out above the liquid. These will crisp up during cooking. Scatter over the remaining cheese, then leave to stand for 15 minutes, to allow the bread to soak up some of the liquid.

5. Meanwhile, preheat the oven to 200°C/180°C fan/gas 6.

6. Dot the top of the pudding with butter, then bake for 25–30 minutes or until just set, puffed up, golden and a little bit crispy in places. Remove from the oven and leave to cool for 10–15 minutes before serving. This is best served warm.

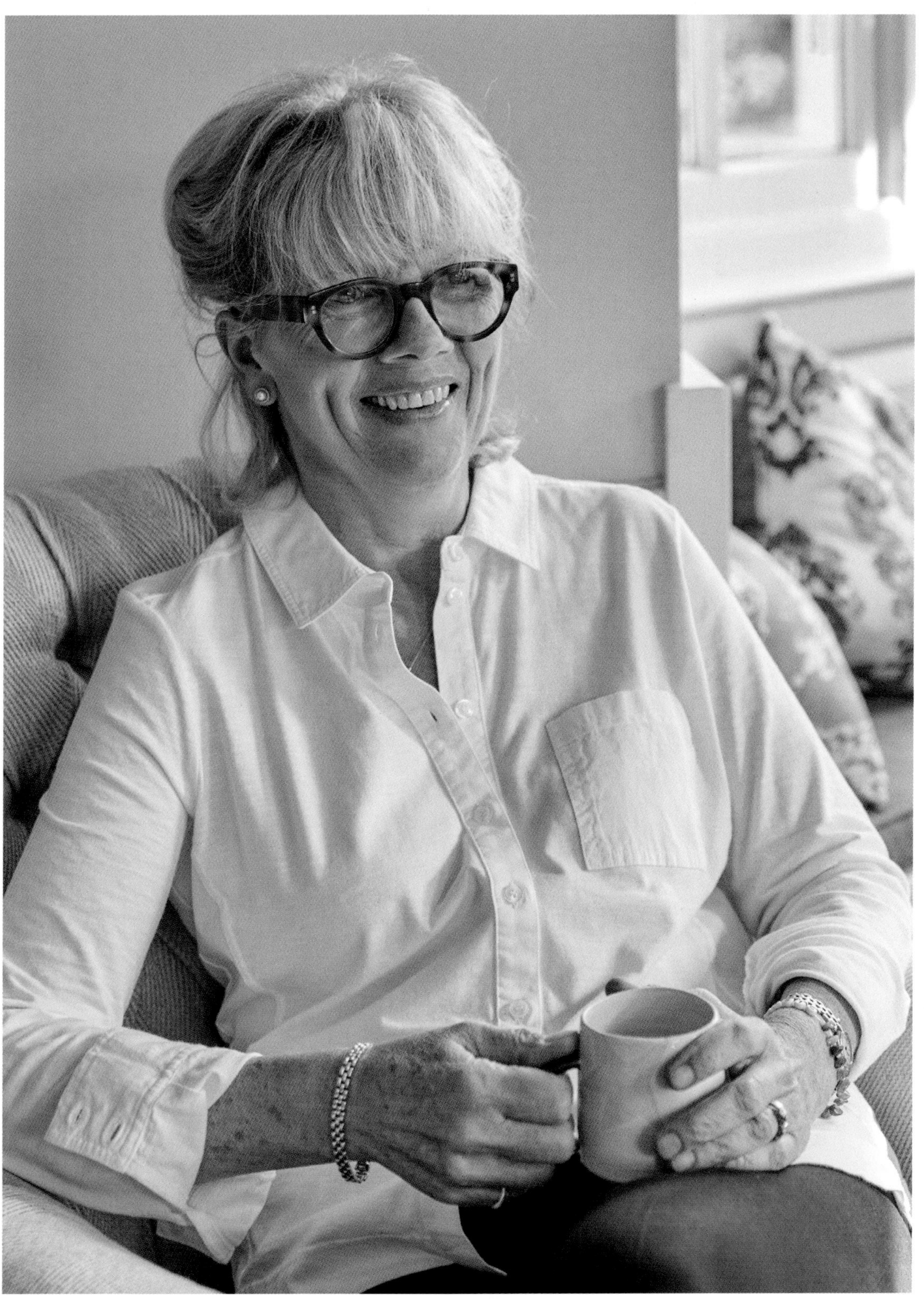

Seedy Soda Bread

MAKES 1 LOAF (8–10 slices)

35g pumpkin seeds
35g sunflower seeds
225g plain white flour
225g plain wholemeal flour, plus extra for dusting
1 teaspoon bicarbonate of soda
2 teaspoons cream of tartar
1 tablespoon caster sugar
1 teaspoon sea salt
1 tablespoon olive oil
225g natural yoghurt
200ml milk
good pinch each of black and white sesame seeds

GET AHEAD

- The seeds can be toasted in advance (they keep well in an airtight tub for up to a week).
- The bread can be baked in advance on the day, then cooled. If serving warm, reheat in the oven at 180°C/160°C fan/gas 4 for about 10 minutes or until warmed through.

HINTS & TIPS

- The weight of the pumpkin and sunflower seeds used can be varied, but just stick to 70g in total of the combined seeds.
- This is best eaten on the day it's made, but it's also great toasted and spread with butter a day or so later. It is especially good served with smoked salmon.

This classic Irish bread is one of the simplest breads to make as it contains no yeast, which means no kneading or proving. Better still, overworking makes it tough, ensuring it's a very quick and easy way to produce a tasty loaf of bread. It's also the ideal accompaniment for one-pan dishes, such as casseroles, stews and soups, and for mopping up anything with tasty juices that are too good to waste.

1. Preheat the oven to 190°C/170°C fan/gas 5.

2. Spread the pumpkin and sunflower seeds out on a baking sheet and cook in the oven for around 5 minutes, until fragrant and toasted. Watch them as they can burn quite quickly! Tip onto a plate and leave to cool.

3. In a large bowl, sift together the flours, bicarbonate of soda, cream of tartar, sugar and salt. Reserve 1 tablespoon of the toasted seeds and add the remainder to the bowl. Mix together the olive oil and yoghurt, then stir into the dry ingredients with a wooden spoon, adding enough milk and mixing to make a soft dough (you may not need all the milk). Knead together gently with your hands in the bowl, just to bring it together and no more, as overworking makes it tough.

4. Put onto the same baking sheet and shape into a round about 20cm in diameter. Scatter the reserved pumpkin and sunflower seeds and the mixed sesame seeds over the loaf, gently pressing them down into the dough a little. Push the handle of a wooden spoon down into the dough to form a cross in the top, then dust the top with a little extra wholemeal flour.

5. Bake for 30–45 minutes. When cooked, the loaf will have a slightly coloured crust and will sound hollow when tapped on the bottom. Remove from the oven, transfer to a wire rack and leave to cool. Serve warm or cold.

Smoked Haddock & Saffron Tart

SERVES 8

large pinch of saffron strands
2 teaspoons boiling water
½ x 500g block ready-made shortcrust pastry (see *Hints & Tips* in the Crostata recipe on page 219)
plain flour, for dusting
300ml double cream (or use crème fraîche)
5 egg yolks
1 tablespoon snipped chives or freshly chopped parsley
sea salt and freshly ground black pepper
340g skinless smoked haddock fillets (un-dyed), roughly snipped into 1cm dice
bunch of spring onions, trimmed and finely sliced
55g Gruyère or mature Cheddar cheese, grated

To garnish (optional)
a few extra cut chives; torn chive flowers; fresh borage flowers; a scattering of micro leaves or salad cress

GET AHEAD

- The tart can be made up to 3 days in advance, cooled, covered and chilled, or frozen (defrost before serving). Serve at room temperature or reheat for 10–15 minutes or until warm.

Very savoury and moreish, this tart is also, rather conveniently, just an assembly job. None of the ingredients for the filling need cooking before adding to the pastry case. I've suggested using ready-made shortcrust pastry here as a timesaver, but also with such a rich, savoury filling, a straightforward pastry case is all that's needed. By all means make your own, if you prefer.

1. Find a loose-bottomed, 28 x 2.5cm round tart tin and a baking sheet. Cut a piece of baking parchment large enough to line the tin with a collar slightly higher than its sides. Scrunch the paper up to soften it, then open it out again and set aside.

2. Put the saffron and the boiling water into a ramekin and set aside.

3. Roll out the pastry on a lightly floured worktop into a circle large enough to line the tin, allowing for it to come up a little higher above the sides. Line the tin, trim the edges to neaten and prick the base all over with a fork. Place on the baking sheet and chill for 30 minutes.

4. Preheat the oven to 200°C/180°C fan/gas 6.

5. To bake it blind, line the pastry case with the baking parchment and fill with enough baking beans (or dried rice or pulses) to cover the bottom and halfway up the sides of the tin. Bake for 15–20 minutes until the pastry is firm, then remove the beans and paper. Return to the oven for a further 5–10 minutes until the case is a pale biscuit colour and cooked through. Reduce the oven to 170°C/150°C fan/gas 3.

6. Meanwhile, mix the cream (or crème fraîche), egg yolks, saffron (with its liquid), chives or parsley and some seasoning together in a jug or bowl.

7. Place the haddock pieces evenly over the bottom of the pastry case, followed by the spring onions. Pour over the cream mixture, then scatter the cheese evenly over the top. Bake for 35 minutes or until just set. Don't worry if it's not quite set in the very middle, it will continue to cook in the residual heat.

8. Remove from the oven and cool in the tin until you are ready to serve, then remove and serve warm or at room temperature. Garnish with any of the suggestions, if you like.

Salads & Platters

My preferred way of serving food, where appropriate, is on large platters, with all the different tasty components on show. This style looks bountiful and generous as well as appealing, plus it's a lot less fiddly for a main course than several small bowls of this and that. A few of these recipes hardly even require a pan at all, just one platter. Others involve the use of more than one mixing bowl, but are well worthy of inclusion all the same.

Some are little more than an assembly job and once you've got into the hang of it, it's easy to put together an inviting and delicious platter that requires no cooking at all. A trip to a delicatessen for cured and cold meats, some cheeses, ripe tomatoes, olives, olive oil and fresh herbs can create a fabulous summer lunch or supper, perhaps with a fresh loaf of bread and the best butter to accompany.

Baked Beetroot, Walnut & Cumin Seed Salad with Whipped Feta

SERVES 6–8
as an accompaniment

50g pumpkin seeds
1½ teaspoons cumin seeds
100g walnut pieces (or use walnut halves, roughly chopped)
600g raw beetroot (approx. 8 medium beets)
1 teaspoon olive oil, plus extra for drizzling
sea salt and freshly ground black pepper
200g good-quality feta cheese (see *Hints & Tips* in One-pan Whole Feta recipe on page 52)
100g full-fat soft cheese
4 spring onions, trimmed and thinly sliced diagonally
rocket leaves or freshly chopped mint, dill or parsley leaves, to serve (optional)

GET AHEAD

- Make to the end of step 5 up to 3 days in advance. Cool, cover and chill separately.

HINTS & TIPS

- This salad is very good made with raw beetroot, too, in which case, peel and finely grate the beetroot, then continue as above.

Fresh, tangy, crunchy and healthy! Serve as part of a feast, or as an accompaniment or a starter. If you're vegan, just omit the whipped feta.

1. Preheat the oven to 190°C/170°C fan/gas 5. Find a shallow roasting tin or (lipped) baking tray into which the beetroot parcel (see below) will fit comfortably.

2. Spread the pumpkin and cumin seeds and the walnuts in the tin/tray and cook in the oven for 4–5 minutes until fragrant and beginning to brown. Tip onto a plate and leave to cool.

3. Cut any leaves from the beetroot, leaving 2.5cm of stalks attached and the roots intact. Wash well, then place (unpeeled) onto a large sheet of foil, drizzle over a little olive oil, season with salt and pepper and wrap up loosely, forming a large, airy 'tent'. Transfer to the same roasting tin/tray and roast for 1 hour or until tender (the skins will slip off easily when cooked).

4. Meanwhile, put the feta and soft cheese in a food-processor with 1 teaspoon of olive oil and process until smooth. Set aside.

5. Remove the beetroot from the oven, then when cool enough to handle, slide off the skins (wearing gloves to prevent stained hands, if you like). Cut the beetroot into matchsticks either by hand or using the 'julienne' blade of a food-processor, or coarsely grate or finely dice and put into a large bowl.

6. Reserving a few of each for the garnish, add the pumpkin seeds, cumin seeds, walnuts and spring onions to the beetroot. Season well, add a glug of olive oil and gently mix together.

7. Pile the beetroot mixture up high on a platter or in a pretty, shallow bowl and then scatter with the reserved ingredients. Spoon small blobs of the whipped feta over the top, serving the remainder separately. Alternatively, spread the feta over the base of a platter or individual plates as a starter and pile the beetroot salad on top. Drizzle with olive oil and scatter with rocket (if using) and serve.

Burrata, Charred Broccoli & Parma Ham Crumble with Basil Vinaigrette

SERVES 4 as a main course (or serves 6 as a starter or part of a feast)

olive oil, for greasing and drizzling
300g purple sprouting broccoli or tenderstem broccoli
sea salt flakes and freshly ground black pepper
pinch of dried chilli flakes
4 slices Parma ham (2 left whole and 2 snipped lengthways into 4 strips each)
1 tablespoon pine nuts
1 x quantity of Basil Vinaigrette (see page 192)
2–3 good handfuls (around 100g) of rocket leaves or other soft salad leaves
2 burrata cheeses, drained
4 anchovy fillets in oil (from a jar), drained and snipped into small strips
micro leaves, pea shoots, cress and/or edible flowers, such as borage, to garnish (optional)

GET AHEAD

- The Parma ham and pine nuts can be cooked up to 2 days in advance. Store individually, covered, at room temperature.

HINTS & TIPS

- The Parma ham strips can be added to the salad, uncooked, if you prefer.

A pretty and very tasty salad inspired by Italian ingredients. Delicious, creamy burrata is now more readily available and is well worth seeking out. This makes a very good starter as well as a main course salad, either served on one platter or individual plates.

1. Preheat the oven to 220°C/200°C fan/gas 7. Lightly grease a large (lipped) baking tray with olive oil.

2. Cut off and discard the tough bottom sections of the broccoli stems, then roughly shave off the remaining outer layer with a knife. Split any thick stems in half, forming two 'trees', and spread out on the greased baking tray. Drizzle over a little olive oil, and sprinkle with salt and the chilli flakes. Mix around with your hands, then spread out in a single layer.

3. Roast at the top of the oven for about 5 minutes or until beginning to char on the bottom. Turn over and push to one end/half of the tray, still in a single layer. Lay the Parma ham strips and whole slices flat over the empty half, find a little space to add and spread out the pine nuts, then roast for a further 4–5 minutes.

4. Remove from the oven and transfer the Parma ham to a plate lined with kitchen paper – it will crisp up further as it cools. Transfer the broccoli and pine nuts to another plate and leave to cool. When cold, crumble the whole slices of Parma ham in your fingers. Set aside.

5. Make the vinaigrette according to the recipe on page 192. You may like to thin it with a little extra olive oil for a looser consistency.

6. Spread the rocket or salad leaves out on a platter. Tear the burrata into small (bite-sized) chunks and arrange over the leaves. Criss-cross the broccoli over the top, then drape over the anchovies. Scatter over the pine nuts and Parma ham crumble. Drizzle over a little of the vinaigrette (you may not need it all), a grinding of pepper and a drizzle of olive oil. Finish with the Parma ham strips propped up artistically on the platter, and any of the garnishes (if using).

Butterflied Lamb with Preserved Lemon, Chilli & Mint Drizzle

SERVES 8–12 as a main course (depending on the size of lamb leg)

1 large leg of lamb (about 1.6–2.7kg boned weight), butterflied/de-boned and trimmed of excess fat (your butcher can do this for you)
olive oil, for greasing
sea salt
pea shoots or rocket leaves, cress or micro leaves, and/or caperberries (from a jar), to serve (optional)

For the marinade
2 bay leaves
4 garlic cloves, sliced
a few thyme or rosemary sprigs
2 tablespoons dark soy sauce
4 tablespoons olive oil

For the drizzle
30g pitted green olives, thinly sliced
30g pitted black olives, thinly sliced
8 anchovy fillets in oil (from a jar), drained and chopped
2 red chillies, halved, de-seeded and thinly sliced across
1 large or 2 small preserved lemons (approx. 85g) quartered, pips removed and chopped
2 tablespoons liquid from preserved lemon jar
90ml olive oil
a good handful of freshly chopped parsley
a good handful of freshly chopped mint

This summer recipe was inspired after eating wonderful lamb, olives and lemons during a lovely holiday in Greece. Perfect for the barbecue, ideally it needs to be started a day in advance. It's a very popular recipe, so I hope you'll give it a try, too!

1. The day before open out the leg of lamb, slashing and spreading out any thicker areas to make it roughly of an even thickness. Place it, skin-side down, in the smallest mixing bowl into which it will fit. Sprinkle over all the marinade ingredients, then fold the wings back over into the middle to encase the marinade. Cover and leave to marinate at room temperature for an hour or so, then refrigerate overnight, turning over occasionally.

2. The next day, to make the drizzle, stir all the ingredients, except the parsley and mint, together in a bowl. Set aside.

3. Preheat the oven to 240°C/220°C fan/gas 9. Lightly grease a shallow roasting tin with olive oil (choose one into which the lamb fits comfortably but not too snugly, allowing a little space around it).

4. Drain and discard the marinade and bits from the lamb, then place flat, skin-side up, in the greased roasting tin. Rub plenty of salt into the skin. Roast at the very top of the oven for 30 minutes for the largest leg (or see other cooking weights and times in *Hints & Tips*). When it's ready, the lamb should be deep golden brown and crispy on the outside but still pink inside. Immediately transfer to a cold plate or board and leave somewhere warm to rest for at least 30 minutes (up to an hour or a little more is fine). Skim the fat from the juices in the tin and keep them warm (or reheat).

5. Slice the lamb into very thin slices and arrange, slightly overlapping, over a large platter. Spoon over any juices from the rested meat, along with the reserved roasting juices (reheated, if necessary). Stir the chopped herbs into the drizzle, then spoon it over the lamb. Eat warm, decorated with your chosen leaves, and/or caperberries (if using), just before serving.

HINTS & TIPS

- Lamb cooking times (these are for boned weights and assume the oven or barbecue is very hot): 2.7kg x 30 minutes (feeds 12); 2.3kg x 20–25 minutes (easily feeds 10); 1.8kg x 20 minutes (easily feeds 8); 1.6kg or less x 20 minutes (feeds 8).

Red Camargue & Wild Rice Salad with Chicken & Avocado

SERVES 6 as a main course (or serves 8–10 as part of a feast)

250g pre-mixed red Camargue and wild rice, or plain red Camargue rice
sea salt and freshly ground black pepper
2 tablespoons pumpkin seeds
6 boneless, skinless chicken thigh fillets, trimmed of any fat
olive oil, for drizzling
4 celery sticks, stringy bits removed, very thinly sliced on a deep diagonal
1 large or 2 small ripe avocados, halved, stoned and diced (in their skins)
4 spring onions, thinly sliced diagonally
½ small red onion (optional), very thinly sliced
a handful of coriander, parsley or mint leaves, roughly chopped
2–3 tablespoons fresh pomegranate seeds
nigella seeds, for sprinkling
sea salt flakes
thick Greek-style yoghurt, seasoned, to serve (optional)

For the dressing
75ml olive oil
2 tablespoons vegetable oil
1 tablespoon red or white wine vinegar
2 teaspoons Dijon mustard
1 small garlic clove, crushed
½ teaspoon sea salt

So many different textures in this salad – chewy, crunchy and creamy – and it's very tasty! Treat the quantities below as a loose guide, and add or substitute according to whatever you have to hand, and how many people you are feeding. A leafy green salad is a lovely accompaniment.

1. Put the rice into a 24cm sauté pan (that's ideally about 6cm deep), cover with plenty of well-salted water, then bring to the boil, cover and cook according to the packet instructions (about 30 minutes) until just tender but still a little chewy with some bite. Drain, rinse and cool under cold running water, then drain again and tip into a bowl lined with kitchen paper to remove the excess water. Remove the kitchen paper, scraping off any grains that have stuck. Set the rice aside in a cool place. Rinse and dry the pan.

2. Toast the pumpkin seeds in the same dry pan on a medium heat for a few minutes until fragrant and beginning to brown. Tip onto a plate and leave to cool.

3. Snip both sides of the chicken thighs to stop them curling, then rub all over with a little olive oil and some salt. Heat the same pan on a high heat until very hot, then fry the chicken thighs for 4–5 minutes on each side or until cooked through and golden. Transfer to a plate and leave to cool, then slice into diagonal strips.

4. Whisk (or shake) the dressing ingredients together to form an emulsion. Set aside.

5. An hour or so before serving, stir a little olive oil and some salt and pepper into the rice, then spread it over a large platter. Scatter over the celery, then arrange the chicken on top, followed by the avocado (removing the diced flesh from the skin as you go), the spring onions, red onion (if using) and toasted pumpkin seeds. Ensure all the components are visible. Set aside somewhere cool. Just before serving, spoon over the dressing and any juices from the chicken, and scatter with the herbs, pomegranate and nigella seeds and some sea salt flakes. Serve with the seasoned yoghurt (if using).

Edamame, Maftoul & Feta Salad

SERVES 6 as an accompaniment (or serves 8 as part of a feast)

110g maftoul (giant couscous or Mograbiah)
sea salt and freshly ground black pepper
350g frozen edamame beans
4 spring onions, trimmed and roughly chopped
1 garlic clove, chopped
a small handful of parsley leaves, chopped
a small handful of mint leaves, chopped, plus an extra sprig to garnish
juice of ½ lemon
115g good-quality feta cheese (see *Hints & Tips* in One-pan Whole Feta recipe on page 52), broken up into rough chunks
1–2 tablespoons olive oil

Delightfully fresh, this is a lovely salad for any time of the year, but is especially good on a hot day. Maftoul, also known as giant couscous or Mograbiah, bears no resemblance to its miniscule cousin. It is larger, with the appearance of small pearls, and has a nice chewy bite to it. For a more substantial salad, I sometimes add a 400g tin of drained and rinsed chickpeas.

1. Cook the maftoul in a large pan of well-salted, boiling water, according to the packet instructions (usually around 6–8 minutes). 2–3 minutes before the end of the cooking time, add the edamame beans, bring back to a simmer and cook for the final few minutes. Drain, cool under cold running water, drain well again and transfer to a serving bowl.

2. Add all the remaining ingredients, setting aside a little feta for garnishing, and adding enough olive oil just to moisten the salad, mixing everything together. Season well with salt and pepper. Top the salad with the reserved feta cheese and the leaves from the sprig of mint, and serve.

GET AHEAD

- The salad can be completed up to 1 day in advance and kept covered in the fridge.

HINTS & TIPS

- Swap frozen baby broad beans for the edamame beans or use a mixture of both.
- A handful or two of baby spinach leaves could be added to the salad with the herbs just before serving, if you like.
- If you have vegetarian guests, ensure you choose feta that is suitable for vegetarians.

Fillet of Beef Carpaccio with Herby Mustard Rémoulade Sauce

SERVES 8 as a main course (or serves 16 as a starter or as part of a feast)

- 900g well-hung beef fillet tails, trimmed of the thin outside membrane and any fat
- 75ml thick Mayonnaise (see page 198)
- a few drops of Tabasco® sauce
- 1 heaped teaspoon English mustard
- a little warm water, for thinning
- 1 small shallot, finely chopped
- 2 teaspoons small capers in brine, drained
- 1 tablespoon finely chopped parsley
- 1 tablespoon freshly chopped tarragon or 1 teaspoon dried tarragon, or more to taste
- 1 tablespoon finely snipped chives, plus a few extra to garnish (optional)
- sea salt flakes
- a few caperberries (from a jar), to garnish (optional)

Oh, how I love this! An excellent way of stretching an expensive cut of meat to feed a lot of people and it can be prepared several days in advance. It doesn't actually use a pan at all (just a platter), but it is so simple and quick to prepare and saves on washing-up, too! Arranged on a large platter, the beef looks as gorgeous as it is delicious for entertaining. I use fillet tails, which are cheaper than a piece of middle-cut fillet (ask your butcher as they are not always on display). The tarragon is non-negotiable in the sauce, so use (a little less) dried if you can't find fresh.

1. Slice the beef as thinly as you possibly can, using a large, heavy, very sharp knife. Lay the slices on a chopping board, then with the knife, press and spread the blade down over the beef with the heel of your hand. This will make the slices even thinner. Run the back of the knife over any lingering thicker bits, as if spreading butter with it. The slices don't need to be wafer-thin, just as thin as you can manage.

2. Arrange the beef, slightly overlapping, on a large serving platter (or two if you prefer), or individual plates, then cover and chill (for up to 3 days) until required.

3. To make the sauce, whisk the mayonnaise, Tabasco® and mustard together. Thin with a little warm water until the consistency is slightly thicker than double cream, then stir in the shallot, capers, parsley, tarragon and chives.

4. When you are ready to serve, sprinkle the beef with a few sea salt flakes, then drizzle over some of the sauce (serve the remainder separately). Scatter over the extra snipped chives and the caperberries (if using) to garnish.

GET AHEAD

- Prepare step 3 up to 1 day in advance, then cover and chill.

HINTS & TIPS

- When buying, the beef may not look enough, but I assure you it will be!
- It's easier to slice the beef straight from the fridge.
- The recipe is easily halved, particularly to serve as a starter for eight.
- Spread small, individual slices of the beef with a little of the rémoulade sauce, then roll them up to create delicious, bite-sized canapés.

French Beans with Toasted Hazelnuts & Baby Mâche

SERVES 8–10 as an accompaniment (or serves 12 as part of a feast)

55g whole blanched hazelnuts
sea salt
600g very fine French/green beans, topped but not tailed
drizzle of hazelnut or olive oil, plus extra for serving
knob of butter (if serving warm)
60g baby mâche (corn salad, lamb's lettuce)
60g pea shoots

A very simple, yet delightful vegetarian platter (and vegan, too, if you omit the butter), this can be served warm as an accompaniment or as part of a feast, or served cold as a salad. If you buy ready-toasted hazelnuts, you can skip browning them yourself. If serving cold, I use hazelnut or olive oil and omit the butter. It's very important to ensure the beans retain their bright green colour, which is achieved by refreshing or cooling them under cold water as soon as they are cooked.

1. Choose a saucepan that is large enough for cooking the beans in. Toast the hazelnuts in the dry saucepan on a medium heat until golden and fragrant, about 5 minutes. Tip onto a plate and leave to cool, then roughly chop. Set aside.

2. Add enough salted water to the same pan for cooking the beans in and bring to the boil, then add the beans and cook for a few minutes until just tender. Drain and refresh quickly under cold running water, then drain again.

3. If serving warm, heat the hazelnut or olive oil and butter in the same pan until melted, return the beans to the pan and briefly toss to coat and heat through. Tip onto a serving platter or into a shallow dish and scatter over the baby mâche, nestling it into the beans. Scatter over the pea shoots and finally the hazelnuts, plus an extra drizzle of oil at the last minute.

4. If serving cold, simply toss the beans in a generous drizzle of hazelnut or olive oil, tip onto a serving platter, then finish and serve as above.

GET AHEAD

- Cook the beans up to 1 day in advance, refresh and cool immediately, then drain and wrap in kitchen paper or cover with clingfilm and chill. If serving warm or cold, follow the instructions above.

HINTS & TIPS

- Griddled tuna steaks, seared for just a minute or two on each side, then sliced on a slant, turn this into a tasty, light main course. Fan out the tuna slices on top of the salad and finish with a grinding of pepper and a swirl of olive oil.

- Swap pine nuts for hazelnuts, if you like (but I prefer the hazelnuts!).

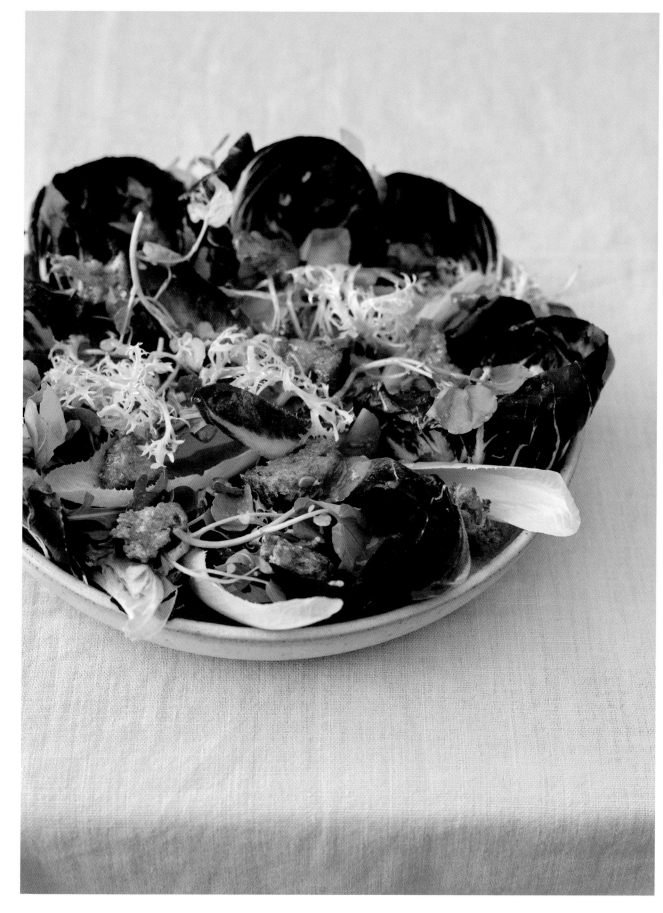

Italian Bitter Leaf Salad with Sourdough Croûtons & Mustard Vinaigrette

SERVES 8–10 as an accompaniment (or serves 10–12 as part of a feast)

2 slices sourdough bread
olive oil, for drizzling
sea salt
300g mixed bitter radicchio and chicory leaves (see *Hints & Tips*)
½ bunch of watercress or 1 x 80g bag of watercress
2 handfuls of rocket leaves

For the mustard vinaigrette
150ml olive oil
2 tablespoons white balsamic vinegar
1 tablespoon Dijon mustard
1 teaspoon sea salt
freshly ground black pepper, to taste

This mixed chicory and bitter leaf salad can be used as a useful part of your menu for counteracting rich dishes, cutting through them and offering a lovely contrast. Happily, when used in place of a vegetable, and unlike vegetables, it requires very little last-minute effort. It's quite substantial and makes a lovely salad as part of a feast, too, plus it's suitable for vegetarians.

1. Preheat the oven to 220°C/200°C fan/gas 7.

2. Roughly tear the bread into pieces (leave the crusts on). Spread out on a baking sheet, then drizzle with a little olive oil and scatter with some salt. Bake for 6–8 minutes or until golden and crispy, turning once. Remove from the oven, drain on kitchen paper and set aside to cool.

3. Place all the vinaigrette ingredients in a small bowl (or clean jam jar) with 1 tablespoon of water and whisk (or shake) together to form an emulsion. Set aside.

4. Separate the salad leaves, tearing larger ones into smaller pieces. Arrange the leaves on a platter and nestle in the watercress and rocket. Just before serving, spoon over the dressing to taste (you may not need it all) and scatter with the croûtons.

GET AHEAD

- The croûtons can be made up to a week ahead and stored in an airtight container. You may like to warm them through to crisp and freshen them up a bit before using.
- The vinaigrette can be made up to 3 days in advance and stored, covered, in the fridge (although it will keep for a few days longer).

HINTS & TIPS

- There are many varieties of radicchio and chicory leaves, including tight round red and white heads of radicchio, heads of long, thin, oval-leaved radicchio, white chicory, red chicory, escarole, endive, frisée (curly chicory), Castelfranco radicchio, to name but a few.

Middle-Eastern Chicken & Chickpea Salad with Cumin Yoghurt Sauce & Quick Pickles

SERVES 6–8 (6 big appetites!) as a main course salad (or serves 10 as part of a feast)

1 whole cooked chicken (900–950g cooked weight), or poach your own (see *Hints & Tips*)
160g baby spinach leaves
1 x 400g tin chickpeas, drained, rinsed and dried on kitchen paper
ground sumac, for sprinkling
1 teaspoon onion or nigella seeds
warm, chargrilled or griddled pitta breads or flatbreads, to serve (optional)

For the quick pickles
70g raisins
1 red onion, halved and very finely sliced (I use a mandolin)
90ml white wine vinegar
3½ tablespoons granulated sugar
1 teaspoon sea salt

For the sauce
1 tablespoon olive oil
2 teaspoons cumin seeds
¼ teaspoon ground cinnamon
300g thick Greek-style yoghurt
sea salt, to taste

This is unbelievably quick and easy to put together and enormously popular. It is also an inexpensive way of feeding a lot of people, and if you use ready-cooked chicken, it is really just an assembly job.

1. The quick pickles need to be made at least 2 hours in advance. Put the raisins and red onion separately into two small bowls. Put the vinegar, sugar and salt in a small pan and bring to the boil, stirring occasionally to dissolve the sugar, then simmer for 1 minute. Remove from the heat and pour just enough of the pickling liquid over the raisins to barely cover, then pour the remainder over the onion. Set aside, stirring from time to time. Wash the pan.

2. When you are ready to eat, make the sauce. Heat the olive oil in the same pan on a medium heat, add the cumin seeds and stir for a minute or so, until fragrant. Tip into a heatproof bowl, then add the remaining sauce ingredients, plus some (drained) raisin pickle syrup to taste (you may not need it all). Taste, adjust the salt or syrup as necessary and let down with a little cold water to the desired consistency, if necessary. Set aside.

3. Remove the skin and bones from the chicken and tear the meat into pieces.

4. Spread the spinach leaves over a large platter, followed by the chicken and a sprinkling of salt, then the chickpeas, a drizzle of the sauce, the drained raisins, and pickled red onion (discard the pickling syrup), some more sauce, then, lastly, a sprinkling of sumac and the onion or nigella seeds. Serve the remaining sauce separately, with warm, chargrilled or griddled pitta breads or flatbreads, if you like.

HINTS & TIPS

- A whole 1.3–1.5kg (raw weight) chicken (900–950g whole cooked weight) yields around 500g of meat.
- To poach a whole chicken, place the untrussed oven-ready chicken (about 1.3–1.5kg) in a saucepan into which it fits fairly snugly. Barely cover it with water, add a quartered onion, and a bouquet garni. Cover, bring to the boil, then reduce the heat and simmer gently for 1 hour or until cooked through. Remove the pan from the heat and leave the chicken to cool completely in its liquid. When cooled, remove the chicken, retain the stock for another use, then skin, de-bone and shred the meat.

Moroccan Aubergine Salad with Mint & Olive Oil

SERVES 4 as a side dish

- a small handful of pine nuts (optional)
- 2 large aubergines, each cut lengthways into 4 wedges, then across into 2.5cm dice
- 1 teaspoon ground cumin
- sea salt and freshly ground black pepper
- olive oil, for drizzling
- 1 garlic clove, crushed
- 1 tablespoon white wine vinegar
- good pinch of dried oregano
- 3 large mint sprigs, leaves picked
- thick Greek-style yoghurt, to serve (optional)

GET AHEAD

- Make to the end of step 4 up to 2 days in advance. Store, covered, in the fridge, but bring back to room temperature before serving.

HINTS & TIPS

- A mixture of courgettes and aubergines is very good, as are a few dried chilli flakes, scattered over with the mint, just before serving.
- Dukkah also makes a tasty alternative to the cumin.
- Garnish with a few fresh thyme sprigs if you have them to hand.

This vegetarian salad is so much tastier than the sum of its parts, and the mint brings it alive. Eat it warm, if you prefer, but it's delicious either way. This also makes a tasty addition to a meze and it's vegan if you leave out the yoghurt to serve (or use vegan yoghurt).

1. Preheat the oven to 220°C/200°C fan/gas 7. Find a large (lipped) baking tray around 41 x 26 x 2.5cm, or use a large, shallow roasting tin of a similar size.

2. If using, add the pine nuts to the baking tray, then toast in the oven for 4–5 minutes or until pale brown. Watch them as they burn easily! Tip onto a plate and set aside.

3. Put the diced aubergines on the same baking tray, scatter with the cumin and some salt and pepper, and drizzle with a swirl or two of olive oil. Mix together so that everything is evenly coated, then give the tray a good shake, ensuring the aubergine is in a single layer. Roast at the top of the oven for 20–25 minutes or until golden brown, caramelised and beginning to go crispy, turning over with a fish slice once or twice.

4. Remove from the oven and transfer to a shallow serving dish or platter and, while still hot, sprinkle over the garlic, vinegar and oregano. Chop two-thirds of the mint leaves and add to the aubergine mixture with a drizzle of olive oil, gently mixing them into the salad. Leave to marinate at room temperature for 2–3 hours.

5. Just before serving, top the salad with a few blobs of yoghurt, if you like, and scatter with the toasted pine nuts (if using). Stack up the remaining mint leaves, roll them into a tight cigarette shape, cut into fine strips and then scatter over the salad. Finish with a drizzle more olive oil.

Puy Lentil & Feta Salad

SERVES 6 as a side dish
(or serves 4 as a main course)

175g dried Puy lentils
½ small red onion, halved and very thinly sliced
2 tablespoons olive oil, plus extra for drizzling
2 teaspoons Dijon mustard
1 whole roasted red pepper from a jar, drained and thinly sliced
1 garlic clove, chopped
a squeeze of fresh lemon juice
sea salt and freshly ground black pepper
a good handful of parsley, roughly chopped
110g good-quality feta cheese (see *Hints & Tips* in One-pan Whole Feta recipe on page 52), broken into chunks

---

GET AHEAD

- Make up to the end of step 3 up to 2 days in advance, then cool, cover and chill. Bring back to room temperature before serving.

HINTS & TIPS

- Soft goats' cheese is a good alternative to the feta – use either rind-on cheese, sliced, or blobs of soft, creamy cheese.

- If you have vegetarian guests, ensure the feta you use is suitable for vegetarians. Oozing slices of fried or grilled halloumi cheese on top (instead of feta) creates a delicious vegetarian supper, too.

This simple recipe is so versatile, plus if you're whizzing around with little time to spare, a ready-cooked pouch of Puy lentils can be used instead of cooking them yourself. Parma ham, salami or other dried or cured meats, rolled up or arranged in 'waves' around the edge of the platter, would make a delicious main course for lunch, served with some warm, crusty bread and a green salad.

Or this healthy salad can easily be transformed into a delicious supper (with or without the feta cheese), served warm with some grilled, fried or baked white fish fillets sitting on top. Cut a lemon into four wedges and cook with the fish until charred, then squeeze over.

1. Put the lentils into a medium saucepan and cover with roughly double their volume of water. Bring to the boil, then reduce the heat and simmer gently (uncovered) for 15–20 minutes or until just soft but still with some bite and not bursting open.

2. Drain and rinse briefly under cold running water until the water runs clear (you want to keep them warm). Line a mixing bowl with one or two pieces of kitchen paper, tip in the drained lentils and toss around until the excess moisture has been absorbed. Remove and discard the kitchen paper.

3. While the lentils are still warm, add all the remaining ingredients, except the parsley and feta, and mix well, seasoning to taste with salt and pepper.

4. Reserve a little chopped parsley to garnish, then stir in the remainder. Pile the lentil salad onto a serving platter. Scatter the feta cheese over the top, followed by the reserved parsley, then add a last-minute drizzle of olive oil. Serve either warm or at room temperature.

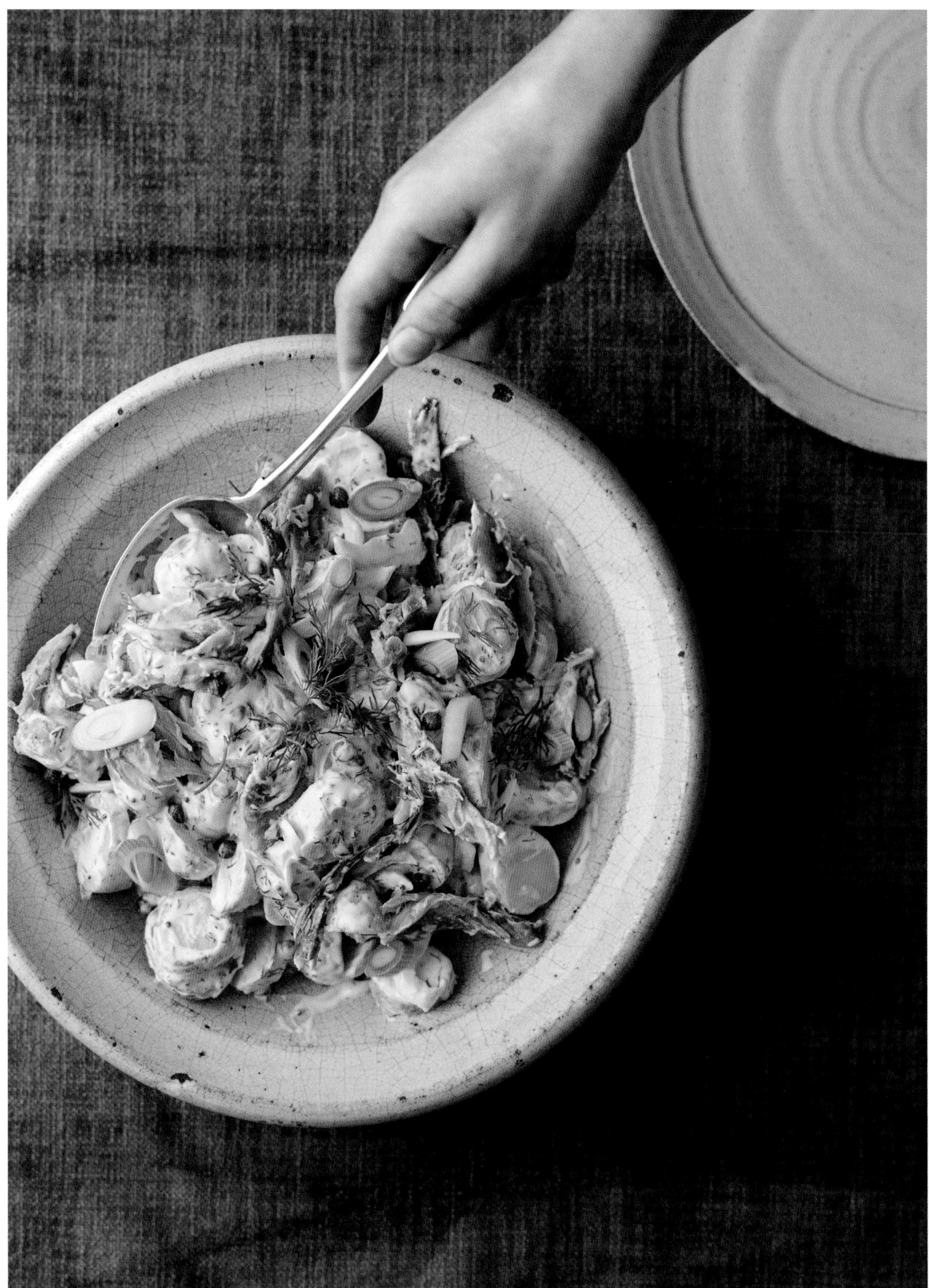

Smoked Mackerel & New Potato Salad with Horseradish, Celery & Dill

SERVES 6–8 as a main course (or serves 10–12 as part of a feast)

500g small new potatoes, skin-on and washed (larger ones halved)
sea salt and freshly ground black pepper
½ bunch spring onions, trimmed and thinly sliced diagonally
2 celery sticks, stringy bits removed and thinly sliced diagonally
1 tablespoon small capers in brine, drained, plus a few extra to garnish
3–4 tablespoons thick Mayonnaise (see page 198)
3–4 tablespoons thick Greek-style yoghurt
1 heaped teaspoon whole grain (seedy) mustard
1 heaped teaspoon creamed horseradish sauce
30g dill sprigs, 2–3 sprigs reserved to garnish, the remainder roughly chopped
2 smoked mackerel fillets

The addition of smoked mackerel turns this into a main course potato salad, plus the celery adds a welcome bit of crunch. Yoghurt combined with mayonnaise makes a much lighter dressing, too.

1. Put the potatoes into a medium saucepan, cover with plenty of well-salted water and bring to the boil, then reduce the heat and simmer until just tender. Drain and leave to cool. Cut into ½cm-thick slices and put into a large mixing bowl with the spring onions, celery and capers.

2. In a separate small bowl, mix together the mayonnaise, yoghurt, mustard, horseradish sauce and chopped dill and, if necessary, thin with a little warm water to a consistency that coats the back of a spoon. Add salt and pepper to taste, bearing in mind it should be very well seasoned – almost over-seasoned at this point. Pour the dressing over the vegetables and gently fold together.

3. Remove the skin from the mackerel fillets, carefully picking over and removing any stray bones. Break the flesh into largish chunks and carefully fold into the potato salad. Pile up on a platter, garnish with the reserved dill sprigs and a few extra capers, and serve.

GET AHEAD

- Complete the recipe up to 2 days in advance, then cover and chill, but garnish just before serving.

HINTS & TIPS

- Use this as a base recipe. Almost anything can be added in place of, or as well as, the smoked mackerel – cooked, peeled prawns, roughly chopped hard-boiled eggs, cooked bacon or chicken, smoked, cured sausages, raw or cooked vegetables, jarred/tinned anchovies . . .

Sauces & Dressings

Sauces and dressings can be the crowning glory, particularly with one-pan cooking. Rich or plain, they're often an important addition to seamlessly bind flavours together, or a secret weapon to elevate a recipe, providing the final flourish, enhancement or embellishment!

The recipes in this chapter don't include a 'pan' as such and I encourage you to be playful, explorative and experimental. Use these recipes simply as a guide, an ideas board, a foundation upon which to build. Please do pick, choose and add your own ingredients and quantities as you see fit and, as always, to your taste.

I find, quantity-wise, that sauces and dressings aren't an exact science as some people only like a modest amount (my husband) and others devour them with gusto (me). It's probably safest to err on the side of generosity, especially since they go with all sorts of things (not just recipes in this book), and generally keep well in the fridge, too, so can often be made a few days in advance.

Most of these sauces and dressings are interchangeable and go with myriad recipes throughout the book. As a rough guide, yoghurt-based sauces sit well with Middle Eastern-style recipes and spicy flavours, and mayonnaise-based ones go with Mediterranean food and salads. Creamy savoury sauces are good with meat, fish and barbecued food, and sweet versions provide the perfect accompaniment to many puddings and desserts.

Basil Vinaigrette

SERVES 8

90ml olive oil
1 tablespoon red wine vinegar
1 small shallot, chopped
1 small garlic clove, chopped
about 20 basil leaves
generous pinch of sea salt
a little freshly ground black pepper

I hope you will agree when you taste this that it's a delicious dressing to enhance many things – not just with its taste, but with its colour, too.

Blitz all the ingredients together using a mini herb chopper, a very small food-processor or a stick blender and its beaker, until vibrant green and smooth. Check and adjust the seasoning, if necessary. If it tastes too oily, add more salt, and vice versa. Serve.

GET AHEAD

- Make the vinaigrette up to 2 hours in advance, then transfer to a bowl, cover and keep at room temperature until you are ready to serve.
- Keep any leftover vinaigrette in a covered container in the fridge for up to 3 days (but it will keep for a few days longer, although it will lose a little of its vibrant colour as time goes by).

HINTS & TIPS

- Swap the basil leaves for parsley or coriander leaves or snipped chives.

Crème Fraîche Sauces

The lovely, slightly sour tang of crème fraîche makes it very versatile and both savoury and sweet sauces can be made using crème fraîche.

These sauces are for when you want to enrich a recipe with something creamy. There is no end to the additions and variations. For savoury sauces, think horseradish and mustards for meats, lemon and lime for fish, freshly chopped herbs and/or jarred/tinned anchovy fillets (or anchovy essence) for meat, fish and vegetables, spice for Middle-Eastern-style recipes, or just olive and garlic for Mediterranean ones. All will need seasoning, too.

For sweet sauces, liqueurs of all sorts can be stirred in. Try matching them to the ingredients in the pudding (e.g. Cointreau for orange or chocolate puddings, and fruity cordials or syrups for fruity puddings). Lemon curd crème fraîche is a perfect accompaniment to fresh raspberries, and vanilla crème fraîche goes with most desserts and looks particularly good with vanilla paste stirred in (as the vanilla seeds are visible). Other sweet suggestions include grated orange or lime zest, clear honey, chopped stem ginger, ground nutmeg or cinnamon.

QUANTITIES

For all of the above, and indeed any other additions, allow 200g crème fraîche for serving 4–6 people. I recommend stirring in your chosen flavouring gingerly to begin with – say a teaspoonful at a time (depending on what it is) and taste as you go along, adding more, if necessary, and seasoning along the way with sea salt and freshly ground black pepper (for savoury sauces) or icing or caster sugar (for sweet sauces).

GET AHEAD

- The sauces will keep for up to 3 days in a covered container in the fridge.

HINTS & TIPS

- Different brands of crème fraîche vary hugely in texture, so I recommend finding one you like and sticking with that.

Lucy's Green Sauce

SERVES 8

150ml olive oil
2 tablespoons red wine vinegar
1 shallot, roughly chopped
2 garlic cloves, roughly chopped
1 green chilli, halved and de-seeded
50g coriander leaves (including tender stems)
50g parsley, stems removed
2 teaspoons sea salt flakes
½ teaspoon dried oregano
juice of ½ lemon

This vivid, hot green sauce is my daughter, Lucy's, loosely based version of Argentinian chimichurri, which is traditionally served alongside barbecued meat and chicken. Fresh, zingy, fragrant and moreish, its piquancy cuts through the richness of meat. However, it's delicious with all manner of other things, too, including boiled new potatoes, grilled/baked fish or roast/barbecued vegetables, so a bowlful in the fridge never goes amiss!

Whizz all the ingredients together into a smooth sauce – I find a stick blender and its beaker is best for this. Alternatively, use a very small food-processor or a spice or herb grinder. Taste and adjust the seasoning accordingly. Serve.

GET AHEAD

- Although this is at its brightest and best when freshly made, the sauce keeps for up to 3 days, covered, in the fridge (but it will keep for a few days longer – although the colour won't be as vibrant, it will still be delicious and it might need thinning with a little olive oil before serving).

HINTS & TIPS

- Leave the seeds in the chilli if you like more heat, or use two chillies.
- Add a little more olive oil at the end for a looser sauce.
- Adjust the flavour to your taste, adding more or less of any of the ingredients.

1
2

1. MAYONNAISE
2. WATERCRESS MAYONNAISE
3. SMOKED PAPRIKA MAYONNAISE
4. TARTARE SAUCE
5. MUSTARD MAYONNAISE
6. SAFFRON MAYONNAISE
4
3
5
6

Mayonnaise

MAKES ABOUT 600ML

1 whole egg
1 egg yolk
1 heaped teaspoon English mustard
1 teaspoon sea salt
425ml vegetable oil (possibly more)
150ml olive oil
1 tablespoon white wine vinegar or fresh lemon juice

GET AHEAD

- Store the mayonnaise in a covered container in the fridge – it will keep for up to 3 days (or a bit longer).

HINTS & TIPS

- If the mayonnaise curdles at any stage, pour the curdled mixture into a jug. Wash out the processor/blender bowl or other bowl, and put two new egg yolks into the bowl. With the processor running (or whisking continuously by hand), very, very slowly drip, drip, drip the curdled mixture onto the yolks. As the mixture becomes emulsified, you can pour the curdled mixture in a little faster.
- If it is only on the verge of curdling, a splash of boiling water added while the processor is running (or if whisking by hand) usually does the trick and brings it back to a stable emulsion.
- To thin mayonnaise, whisk in small amounts of warm water from the kettle until it's the desired consistency.

This recipe produces a good batch of mayonnaise (around 600ml), which keeps happily covered in a container in the fridge for up to 3 days (or a bit longer), as long as no 'foreign bodies' enter via a dirty spoon, to contaminate it.

I like to make mayonnaise thick, the texture of 'ointment' rather than 'lotion', and let it down to the required consistency with warm water from the kettle, as I need it. Adding ingredients to mayonnaise thins it, such as with sauces like tartare, cocktail or watercress; therefore, a thin mayonnaise base becomes too runny. Likewise, vegetables (think coleslaw, and celeriac for rémoulade) release lots of moisture when mixed with mayonnaise, which, if thin to start with, becomes far too runny for coating the vegetables. Equally, runny egg or tuna mayonnaise sandwiches are a messy business. Shop-bought mayonnaise in jars is generally on the thinner side.

It's worth noting that the runnier the mayonnaise is, the more people it feeds, so if you're a bit short, whisk in a little warm water from the kettle to thin it and stretch it a little further. Quantifying mayonnaise is tricky but I would allow around 200ml for four people (or 2 good tablespoons per person).

The trick to mayonnaise is to start with all the ingredients at room temperature and add the oil very slowly, and remember that well-seasoned mayonnaise is the beginning of a good sauce.

1. Put the whole egg, the egg yolk, mustard and salt into the bowl of a small food-processor and whizz together until well amalgamated. Alternatively, use a stick blender, or whisk together in a bowl by hand.

2. Mix the oils together, then, with the processor/blender running, or whisking continuously by hand, very, very slowly trickle the mixed oils into the egg mixture in a thin stream. As the emulsion thickens, you can add it a tad faster.

3. When all the oil is incorporated, the mayonnaise will be very thick. Add the vinegar or lemon juice and whizz/whisk to mix it in. This will thin it down a little. Check the seasoning – it should be very flavourful, but if it's too salty, add a little more oil, or if it's too oily and bland, add a little more salt. Serve.

Mayonnaise-based Sauces

All of these variations can be made lighter and healthier by substituting half the quantity of mayo with natural yoghurt. All these sauces keep for up to 3 days in a covered container in the fridge.

Watercress Mayonnaise

SERVES 4–6

80g watercress, including stalks (discard any very thick ones)
200ml thick Mayonnaise (see page 198)
sea salt and freshly ground black pepper
fresh lime juice, to taste (optional)

Peppery watercress mayo makes a delicious sauce to serve with many things – hot or cold cooked fish or chicken and boiled new potatoes, to name but a few. If made ahead, it retains its bright green colour, too. It's very good with a squeeze of fresh lime juice added to taste before serving, especially if serving with fish. If you're in a hurry, there's no need to blanch the watercress, but it does give the most gorgeous bright green colour, which lasts for longer, too.

1. Put the watercress into a sieve over the sink and pour a kettleful of boiling water over to blanch and wilt it. Cool under cold running water, then squeeze out all the liquid using your hands.

2. Roughly snip the watercress with scissors, then either whizz it with the mayonnaise in the beaker or bowl of a stick blender or very small food-processor until smooth and bright green (or finely snip/chop the watercress by hand and then stir into the mayonnaise).

3. Add salt and pepper, then squeeze in a little lime juice to taste, if you like. Thin with a little warm water from the kettle, if necessary.

Tartare Sauce

SERVES 4–6

200ml thick Mayonnaise (see page 198)
1 small round shallot, finely chopped
1 tablespoon gherkins (5 cocktail gherkins), drained and finely chopped
1 tablespoon capers in brine, drained and finely chopped
1 tablespoon finely chopped parsley
1 teaspoon finely chopped tarragon (or use a good pinch of dried tarragon)

There's never enough tartare sauce, whatever it comes with, and for me, it's the whole point of fish and chips, goujons and pretty much anything fried. A classic and delicious sauce.

Mix all the ingredients together in a bowl, then thin to your preferred consistency with a little warm water from the kettle, if necessary.

HINTS & TIPS

- Optional additions include: 1 anchovy fillet from a jar (or tin), drained and finely chopped; a squeeze of fresh lemon juice; 1 tablespoon snipped chives or finely chopped dill.

THE FOLLOWING RECIPES EACH SERVE 4

Aïoli

Crush 2 garlic cloves and stir into 200ml thick Mayonnaise (see page 198). Add more or less crushed garlic, if you like. (The garlic is best crushed to a paste on a chopping board under a round-bladed knife with some sea salt.)

Curried Mayonnaise

Add 1 teaspoon of your favourite curry paste (not powder) to 200ml thick Mayonnaise (see page 198). A little lime pickle or mango chutney, added to taste, is a good addition, too.

Mustard Mayonnaise

I like to add 1 teaspoon each of Dijon, English and whole grain (seedy) mustard to 200ml thick Mayonnaise (see page 198) (or use 3 teaspoons of one mustard).

Smoked Paprika Mayonnaise

Stir 1 teaspoon of smoked paprika into 200ml thick Mayonnaise (see page 198). I like to use hot smoked paprika for heat as well as the lovely smoky flavour. It's very good with hot or cold cooked meat, fish and vegetables (particularly boiled new potatoes) and barbecued food.

Saffron Mayonnaise

In a ramekin, infuse a small pinch of saffron strands in 1 tablespoon of boiling water for 10 minutes, then stir the saffron water (including the strands) into 200ml thick Mayonnaise (see page 198).

HINTS & TIPS

- Other ingredients to add, to taste, to thick Mayonnaise (see page 198) include: grated lime zest; preserved lemons, chopped; jarred/tinned anchovy fillets, drained and chopped; freshly chopped basil, dill or mixed herbs; crumbled or creamy blue cheese.

Pistachio, Parsley & Green Chilli Pesto

MAKES ABOUT 125ML

25g unsalted shelled pistachio nuts
2 good handfuls of parsley leaves (roughly 25g)
1 mild green chilli, de-seeded and roughly chopped (or leave seeds in for more heat)
1 garlic clove, roughly chopped
generous ¼ teaspoon sea salt
90ml olive oil, plus a little extra

A lovely, verdant and herby pesto, with a gentle heat from the chilli. Parsley, being an easily accessible herb, makes this a versatile and everyday sauce. The chilli and pistachios also add an intensity to the flavour.

1. Put the pistachio nuts into a small, dry frying pan and toast on a medium heat for a few minutes until they are fragrant and just beginning to brown. Tip onto a plate and leave to cool.

2. To make the pesto, put all the ingredients, except the olive oil, into a small food-processor and whizz together until amalgamated but still a little chunky. Add half the olive oil, whizz again, then add the remainder and whizz to combine. Check and adjust the seasoning, if necessary, and stir in a little more oil if you prefer a slightly sloppier consistency. Serve.

GET AHEAD

- All pesto-style sauces keep well in small bowls or jars in the fridge for up to 3 days (or a little longer if covered with a slick of oil) or they freeze well (cover with the oil before freezing, and defrost before use). The one caveat is to ensure the mixture is covered with the olive oil at all times, to keep it fresh and its colour vibrant. After using some sauce from the container, level the top and cover with oil again.
- If freezing in jars, leave a little room for expansion at the top and freeze with the lid off, then screw the lid back on when frozen. Defrost before use.

HINTS & TIPS

- If you don't have a small food-processor, a pestle and mortar will do the job, too.
- Swap the pistachios for other nuts, such as hazelnuts or cashew nuts for a sweeter, more creamy pesto. Any other soft, green herbs you have to hand, in any combination, can be used in place of the parsley.

Quick Pickles & Relishes

These are so handy to have in the fridge to enhance all sorts of things. By nature, they keep for a long time as they're pickled and therefore preserved, although as time goes by, their colour, but not their flavour, will begin to fade. Offering a sweet and sharp tangy crunch, I think they're a must to have up your sleeve! A jar of pickles makes a lovely present, too.

Quick Pickles

SERVES 4–6 as an accompaniment or topping

4 tablespoons white wine vinegar
2½ tablespoons granulated sugar
1 teaspoon sea salt
1 red onion, halved and very finely sliced, or 1 cucumber, finely sliced (I use a mandolin)

Quick pickles can be used almost as soon as they're made, but I think they are better made at least 2 hours in advance.

1. Put the vinegar, sugar and salt in a small saucepan and heat together on a low heat, stirring to dissolve the sugar, then simmer for 1–2 minutes until syrupy.

2. Put the red onion or cucumber in the smallest heatproof bowl into which it will fit, then pour over the hot pickling liquid. Set aside for at least 2 hours, stirring from time to time until they've softened. Drain before serving.

GET AHEAD

- Make these quick pickles a few days in advance (although they will keep for longer), then cool, cover and chill.

HINTS & TIPS

- Other vegetables, sliced or cut into batons, such as radishes, fennel and carrots, can be quickly pickled, too.
- ½ teaspoon each of yellow and black mustard seeds and 1 star anise (or other whole spices) are a lovely addition to the pickling liquid.

Cucumber, Spring Onion, Chilli & Dill Relish

SERVES 4–6 as an accompaniment or topping

1 large cucumber
large pinch of sea salt
2 heaped teaspoons granulated sugar
4 tablespoons white wine vinegar
½ bunch of spring onions, thinly sliced diagonally
1 green chilli, halved, de-seeded and thinly sliced
½ bunch of dill, chopped

This relish is delicious spooned over or alongside warm or cold cooked salmon fillets or bashed-out cooked chicken fillets, complete with the tasty sweet and sour pickling juices. When peeling the cucumber, I like to leave every other strip of the skin intact, giving the fleshy half-moons a lovely, appealing stripy pattern.

1. Peel the cucumber, leaving behind the odd strip of skin (see recipe introduction, above). Halve lengthways, scoop out the seeds with a teaspoon and slice the flesh into 1cm-thick half-moons. Put into a sieve, sprinkle with the salt and leave to drain for 30 minutes.

2. Put the unrinsed drained cucumber slices into a small bowl, stir in the sugar and vinegar, then leave for 1 hour, giving it the odd stir. Just before serving, stir in the spring onions, chilli and dill.

3. Serve as is (with the pickling juices) if serving as an accompaniment, but drain first if using as a topping.

GET AHEAD

- Make this relish a few days in advance (although it will keep for longer), then cover and chill.

HINTS & TIPS

- Use rice vinegar instead of white wine vinegar, and swap the green chilli for a red chilli if this is what you have to hand.

Romesco Sauce

SERVES 6–8

40g blanched hazelnuts, toasted
3 small, or 2 large, whole roasted red peppers from a jar, drained and roughly chopped
1 garlic clove, roughly chopped
½ red chilli, de-seeded and roughly chopped
1 ripe tomato, roughly chopped
4 tablespoons olive oil
1 tablespoon sherry vinegar or red wine vinegar
sea salt and freshly ground black pepper

This is my version of this classic Spanish sauce, which, as it goes with just about everything, is very handy to have in the fridge!

1. If you can't find ready-toasted hazelnuts, toast them yourself in a small, dry frying pan on a medium heat for a few minutes until light golden brown. Tip onto a plate and leave to cool.

2. Put the hazelnuts and the remaining sauce ingredients into a small food-processor, adding salt and pepper to taste, and blitz together to make a textured sauce. Check and adjust the seasoning accordingly and add a little more oil, if you prefer it runnier.

GET AHEAD

- Make this sauce up to 3 days in advance (although it will keep for a few days longer), cover and chill.

Yoghurt-based Sauces

Yoghurt-based sauces make delicious accompaniments to many things. Healthier than mayonnaise, they are no less delicious as long as they are seasoned generously. They offer a lovely counterbalance and freshness to rich and spicy foods and can also be served as dips for dunking vegetable crudités, etc.

All of these recipes require unsweetened natural yoghurt. My preferred choice is thick Greek-style yoghurt, which is tangier and thicker than standard natural yoghurt, and with a bit of seasoning it makes a perfectly tasty sauce or accompaniment on its own.

Each of these recipes serves 4–6. They can all be made in advance and will keep for up to 3 days in a covered bowl in the fridge. Give each sauce a quick stir before serving.

Cucumber Raita

½ cucumber, coarsely grated (skin, seeds and all)
good pinch of sea salt
200g thick Greek-style yoghurt
a large handful of mint leaves, chopped

Put the cucumber into a sieve set over a bowl, sprinkle with the salt and leave to drain for 30 minutes. Squeeze the excess liquid from the cucumber, put into a clean bowl and then mix with the yoghurt and mint. Taste and add a little more salt, if necessary. Thin with a little cold water, if you prefer a runnier sauce. Serve.

HINTS & TIPS

- 2 spring onions, finely sliced or chopped, or a handful of chopped coriander leaves, are lovely additions or substitutes to ring the changes.

Saffron Yoghurt

small pinch of saffron strands
1 tablespoon boiling water
200g thick Greek-style yoghurt
sea salt and freshly ground black pepper

Put the saffron strands in a ramekin with the boiling water and leave to infuse for 10 minutes. Mix the saffron water (including the strands) into the yoghurt and season well with salt and pepper. Serve.

Harissa Yoghurt

200g thick Greek-style yoghurt
1 teaspoon rose harissa paste, plus a little extra to serve
sea salt
a few fresh mint leaves, roughly chopped

Mix the yoghurt and harissa paste together in a small serving bowl and season well with salt. Swirl a little extra harissa paste over the top. Scatter with the chopped mint leaves and serve.

Lime, Coriander & Chilli Sauce

200g thick Greek-style yoghurt
1 green chilli, de-seeded and roughly chopped
juice of 1 lime
30g fresh coriander
sea salt and freshly ground black pepper

Put the yoghurt and chilli into a small food-processor and whizz together, then add the lime juice. Twist off the fat lower stems from the coriander and discard. Snip the remainder into chunks and whizz with the yoghurt and some salt and pepper until bright green – this will take a few minutes. Thin with a little cold water, if you prefer the sauce a little runnier. Serve.

Garlic & Mint Yoghurt Sauce

200g thick Greek-style yoghurt
1 garlic clove, crushed
2 tablespoons olive oil
juice of ½ lemon
2 mint sprigs, leaves picked and chopped
sea salt and freshly ground black pepper

Stir all the ingredients together in a serving bowl, adding salt and pepper to taste. Serve.

OPINEL
SAVOIE FRANCE

Sweet Things

The variety of these very tempting pudding, dessert and baking recipes is wide-ranging – from fruit to chocolate, creamy to more healthy, baked and comforting to more indulgent – so there's something for everyone, including recipes for every season. Some are large for sharing as part of a feast and some are served individually. All of them can be made in advance, too, thus considerably lightening the load when entertaining.

Consider what you have served before when choosing which pudding to make, and remember that, even if you're a chocoholic, it doesn't necessarily mean everyone else is (however odd that may seem!). Some might prefer creamy treats and others fruity ones.

Pots Au Chocolat with a Twist

MAKES 8–10 POTS

8–10 small amaretti biscuits
4–5 teaspoons Amaretto liqueur or brandy, plus 3 tablespoons
300ml double cream
3 tablespoons icing sugar, sifted
200g dark chocolate (minimum of 70 per cent cocoa solids)
2 egg yolks
30g butter, diced
seasonal berries, to serve (optional)

This is a very rich pudding so only small helpings are necessary – even for chocoholics! In France, chocolate puddings of this intensity are traditionally served in tiny, individual ceramic pots, sometimes with lids, specially designed for the purpose. Small coffee or espresso cups work just as well, or small ramekins. I've added a little twist, putting Amaretto-soaked amaretti biscuits at the bottom of each pot, providing a nice surprise when you dig into this delectable, silky-smooth, glossy lusciousness.

1. Place one amaretti biscuit at the bottom of 8 or 10 of your chosen small serving pots, then pour ½ teaspoon of Amaretto or brandy over each biscuit. Leave to soak for 30 minutes.

2. Put the cream into a saucepan with the icing sugar and heat gently until it's just under boiling point, then remove from the heat.

3. Break the chocolate into pieces (within its packet is easiest), add to the hot cream and stir until melted. Stir in the remaining 3 tablespoons of Amaretto or brandy, the egg yolks and then the butter until combined. Pour the chocolate mixture into the pots over the soaked biscuits, dividing it evenly and leaving quite a generous rim free at the top of each pot.

4. Leave to cool, then cover and chill in the fridge for at least 4 hours (but preferably overnight) before serving.

5. Serve the chilled pots as they are, or with some seasonal berries either on top or alongside, if you like.

GET AHEAD

- This is an ideal 'get ahead' pudding for entertaining as it can be made up to 3 days in advance (but will keep for a few days longer). Whisper it, but it actually lasts a lot longer than that, although I'm not suggesting you actually set out to make it 2 weeks before it's required!

HINTS & TIPS

- For Christmas and other special occasions, a little edible gold leaf (sheets – broken up, flakes or dust) on top looks wonderful and festive against the rich, dark, glossy chocolate. You can find it in larger supermarkets or online.

Baked Toffee Peaches

SERVES 4

4–6 ripe peaches or nectarines, halved and stoned
4–6 generous knobs of butter, plus extra for greasing
4–6 generous teaspoons dark muscovado sugar
4–8 amaretti biscuits

To serve (optional)
a few fresh raspberries for scattering; double cream or crème fraîche; a scoop of vanilla ice cream atop each cavity

A lovely and simple way to transform a humble ingredient into an irresistible, buttery, toffee-like delight. Magic!

1. Preheat the oven to 200°C/180°C fan/gas 6. Butter a shallow, ovenproof dish large enough to take the halved fruit in one layer, snugly but not tightly packed.

2. Place the peach or nectarine halves, cut-side up, in the prepared dish. Place a generous knob of butter in each cavity and then sprinkle ½ teaspoon of sugar over the top of each half.

3. Bake for 20 minutes or until the fruit is just soft when pierced with a knife and the juices have turned into a toffee, butterscotch-like sauce. The timing will depend on the size and ripeness of the peaches/nectarines.

4. Remove from the oven. Roughly crush the amaretti biscuits (fingers will do), then scatter them over the peaches/nectarines and serve warm, with any of the serving suggestions, if you like.

GET AHEAD

- Complete the recipe up to 1 day in advance (but don't scatter with the crushed amaretti until just before serving), then cool, cover and chill. Reheat in the oven (temp as above) for 5–10 minutes until just warm, before serving.

HINTS & TIPS

- For the best results, use perfectly ripe fruit. Extracting the stone from unripe fruit is not easy and it will also take longer to cook.

Black Cherry Trifle

SERVES 10–12 (or more!)

1 x 285g ready-made Madeira cake
black cherry jam or confit, for spreading
4 tablespoons sherry
2 tablespoons brandy
2 x 390g jars black cherries in kirsch (from larger supermarkets or delis), or use tinned black cherries in syrup (around 450g drained weight)
1 x 500g carton of chilled fresh ready-made vanilla custard
300ml double cream
2 tablespoons pomegranate seeds
a handful of shelled pistachio nuts, roughly chopped

GET AHEAD

- Make up to the end of step 3 up to 2–3 days in advance, cover and chill the trifle and syrup separately.

HINTS & TIPS

- Bowls: trifles look best in (round) glass bowls to show off their beautiful layers. Around 23 x 12cm is a good size, but it depends on what you have in the way of glass bowls. A traditional glass trifle bowl on a short stand looks wonderful.

- Substitute other jarred/tinned fruit for the black cherries, such as peaches or apricots.

This is a bit of a cheat to say the least, as it's made using ready-made cake and ready-made custard! It couldn't be much easier though and is just an assembly job really, with the most arduous part possibly being the shopping. Ready-made fresh custard is runnier than the home-made custard traditionally used, but apart from the convenience, I like it for giving the trifle a slightly looser texture. This is best made the day before (or even 2–3 days before), as it improves with age and is festive for Christmas with its red and green toppings. Just as trifle should be, this is quite alcoholic, so bear this in mind if serving to children. See *Hints & Tips* for trifle bowl sizes.

1. Slice the Madeira cake in half horizontally and spread quite generously with cherry jam or confit. Sandwich back together, slice down vertically into about 1cm-thick slices and then arrange in the bottom of the trifle bowl. You will need to cut/break some of the slices to roughly fill in the gaps – it's a bit of a jigsaw but doesn't need to be perfect! Pour the sherry and brandy evenly over the cake.

2. Tip the cherries into a sieve set over a small saucepan and drain them well, then scatter the cherries over the Madeira cake, followed by 4 tablespoons of the cherry syrup. Spoon over the custard, covering the fruit completely, then cover and chill for several hours or ideally overnight.

3. Meanwhile, heat the remaining cherry syrup on a high heat and boil it fast for a few minutes until it becomes fairly thick and syrupy, bearing in mind it will thicken up more as it cools. Pour into a heatproof jug to cool, then cover and chill until you are ready to serve.

4. Any time on the day of eating, lightly whip the cream until it forms very soft peaks. Be careful – it's important to under-whip, as it will thicken more as you spread it. Spoon the cream in a mass of little blobs all over the custard, and then carefully join the blobs with a spoon or spatula. As the custard is runny, this is the only way you will be able to 'spread' the cream layer. Return to the fridge until ready to serve.

5. Just before serving, scatter the trifle with the pomegranate seeds and pistachios and a swirl of the cherry syrup too, if you like. The remaining syrup can be handed separately (with perhaps some pouring cream, too, if you like!). Trifle is best served very cold and straight from the fridge.

Blackberry & Almond Crostata

SERVES 6–8

½ x 500g block ready-made shortcrust pastry (see *Hints & Tips*)
plain flour, for dusting
170g good-quality 'ready-to-roll' natural marzipan, chilled
400g fresh blackberries
50g demerara sugar
1 egg, lightly beaten with a pinch of sea salt
a small handful of flaked almonds
icing sugar and mint leaves (optional), to decorate
250g crème fraîche or vanilla ice cream, to serve

GET AHEAD

- Make to the end of step 3 any time on the day. Or, make to the end of step 5 up to 2 days ahead, then cool, cover and chill. Reheat in the oven (temp as above) for 5–10 minutes until warm throughout, or serve at room temperature.

HINTS & TIPS

- If using chilled fresh pastry, the spare half can be frozen for later use. If using frozen pastry, halve it while still partially frozen, wrap the spare half and immediately return to the freezer.
- Before rolling out, cut the half block of pastry into two squares, put one on top of the other, offset to form a star shape, to make an easier starting point to roll out a circle.

This rustic tart couldn't be easier and, furthermore, the filling can be changed along with the seasons, making it a year-round winner. Just bear in mind when choosing that some fruit can be watery. A sprinkling of cornflour over the bottom of the pastry helps to absorb juices. Also known as 'free-form' tarts, these are very handy to have in your pudding armoury.

I like to sprinkle lots of sugar round the rim, which then sweetens the pastry and caramelises during cooking, making it delicious enough to pass off as home-made! This crostata is best served warm or at room temperature, not piping hot.

1. Roll out the pastry directly onto a large lightly floured sheet of silicone or baking parchment roughly into a circle, about 38cm in diameter (wobbly edges are fine!), then transfer to a medium (lipped) baking tray (the pastry may overhang the edges of the paper a bit, but that's fine as they will be folded over shortly). Alternatively, roll out on a floured worktop and then transport onto the paper.

2. Coarsely grate the marzipan over the pastry, leaving a 5cm border around the edges. Arrange the blackberries on top of the marzipan in the middle of the pastry. Reserve 1 tablespoon of the demerara sugar and scatter the remainder over the fruit.

3. Bring the border of the pastry up over the outside edges of the filling, leaving most of the blackberries showing, pleating the edges over and over each other to form a wavy effect. Chill for 20–30 minutes or until required.

4. Preheat the oven to 200°C/180°C fan/gas 6. Brush the pleated pastry rim with the egg wash and then sprinkle it with the reserved demerara sugar. Scatter the flaked almonds over the whole crostata. Bake for 20–25 minutes or until golden and bubbling. It doesn't matter if some of the filling spills out – it's meant to be rustic and this will depend on the ripeness and water content of the fruit.

5. Leave to cool for 15 minutes or so on the baking tray, before sliding onto a flat serving platter or board. If using baking parchment, I like to serve it on this.

6. Just before serving, dust with icing sugar and scatter with a few mint leaves (if using). Serve warm or at room temperature with crème fraîche or ice cream.

Cherry Clafoutis

SERVES 6

a little butter for greasing, plus extra for dotting over the top
450g fresh red or black cherries (or 2 x 400g tins black cherries), stoned or left un-stoned
3 tablespoons plain flour
pinch of sea salt
6 tablespoons caster sugar, plus a little extra for dusting (for tinned cherries, use only 2–3 tablespoons sugar, as they're very sweet)
3 eggs
425ml milk
1 teaspoon vanilla extract
icing sugar, for dusting (optional)
crème fraîche or double cream, to serve (optional)

A French classic for a reason! Juicy cherries gently baked in the most delicate of trembling custards. I don't stone the cherries – just issue lots of warnings and leave guests to do all the work!

1. Preheat the oven to 190°C/170°C fan/gas 5. Lightly butter a shallow, ovenproof dish (mine is round and 24 x 5cm), then scatter the cherries over the base. They should cover the base in a single layer, but not be crammed in, hugger-mugger. If using tinned cherries, drain them very well before use.

2. Put the flour, salt, caster sugar, eggs, milk and vanilla extract into a blender (this will not work in a food-processor) and whizz together until smooth and combined. Alternatively, put the flour into a bowl with the salt and sugar. Make a well in the centre, add the lightly beaten eggs, then, using a wooden spoon, stir the eggs into the flour mixture, gradually drawing the flour into the middle. Whisk or stir in the milk and vanilla extract to make a smooth batter. Pour the batter over the cherries, then dot the surface with a little butter.

3. Bake for 25–30 minutes or until the batter is just set, yet still wobbly in the centre, and rich, golden brown on top (the cooking time will depend on the size of the dish and how deep the batter is).

4. Remove from the oven, then sprinkle with a little extra caster sugar. Leave to cool and serve lukewarm, not hot. This is also good served cold, in which case dust with a little icing sugar before serving. Serve with crème fraîche or double cream (if using).

GET AHEAD

- The batter can be made up to 1 day in advance and kept covered in the fridge until required. Give it a quick whisk/stir before use.
- Make the whole recipe up to 2 days in advance, then cool, cover and chill. Serve chilled or at room temperature, or reheat in the oven (temp as above) for 5–10 minutes until just warm throughout.

HINTS & TIPS

- Swapping 450g fresh blackberries, raspberries or blueberries for the cherries, stretches this delicious pudding out over another season.

Chocolate, Raspberry & Sea Salt Brownies

MAKES 24 LARGE SQUARES OR 48 SMALL SQUARES

325g butter, diced
125g cocoa powder
4 eggs
500g caster sugar
1 teaspoon vanilla extract
250g plain flour
250g fresh raspberries
a few sea salt flakes

To decorate (optional)
icing sugar
freeze-dried raspberry powder (and/or freeze-dried raspberry pieces)
fresh or dried edible flowers, such as fresh borage or viola flowers or dried rose petals

---

GET AHEAD

- The brownies will keep for up to 3 days in an airtight container in the fridge. Minus the raspberries, they will last up to a week (no need to chill), or they can be frozen.

HINTS & TIPS

- If you don't have a microwave, put the butter and cocoa powder into a large, heatproof bowl. Set the bowl over a slightly smaller heatproof bowl containing boiling water (ensuring the bottom of the top bowl doesn't touch the water underneath) and leave until melted and combined, stirring occasionally.

These are irresistibly fudgy and combine one of my favourite pairings – chocolate and raspberries – not to mention a touch of sea salt. I like to cut a tray this size into 48 small squares, pile them up high in a pyramid and decorate.

1. Preheat the oven to 180°C/160°C fan/gas 4. Line a 30 x 23 x 4.5cm baking tin with baking parchment, foil, or better still, foil-lined baking parchment, which is easier to handle. It is simpler to line a tin upside down – mould the parchment/foil over the outside of the tin, remove (keeping its shape), then turn the tin over and slot in the moulded 'case'.

2. Place the butter and cocoa powder in a microwave-safe bowl, then microwave (uncovered) on low, for a few seconds at a time, stirring occasionally, until melted and combined. Remove from the microwave and set aside. If you don't have a microwave, see *Hints & Tips*.

3. Whisk the eggs and caster sugar together, using a stand mixer or an electric hand-held whisk, until thick, pale and fluffy. Stir the egg mixture and vanilla extract into the cocoa mixture, then stir in the flour until combined.

4. Pour the mixture into the prepared baking tin and level it out. Dot the raspberries over the top, pushing them down slightly into the mixture, then sprinkle with a little sea salt.

5. Bake for about 30 minutes or until crusty around the edges but still squidgy in the middle (it will firm up a little as it cools).

6. Leave to cool completely in the tin, then remove from the tin using the baking parchment or foil, cut into squares and peel off the parchment/foil. Cutting the brownies is even easier after a spell in the fridge (about 2 hours) – they are quite soft with the addition of raspberries, so I recommend eating them cold from the fridge.

7. Decorate with any, or a selection, of the suggestions (a very light sprinkling of sea salt flakes looks pretty too), then serve.

Gooseberry & Amaretti Crumble Cake

SERVES 8

110g butter, softened, plus extra for greasing
110g self-raising flour
110g caster sugar
½ teaspoon baking powder
2 large eggs
225–250g fresh gooseberries, topped and tailed
55g amaretti biscuits, roughly crushed into varying sizes of 'gravel'
1 tablespoon demerara sugar

To serve
icing sugar, for dusting
crème fraîche mixed with a little elderflower cordial to taste, or double cream (optional)

Always astonishingly popular, this cake or pudding can be made in advance and warmed through before serving, but it is equally delicious served cold. It's both sweet and sharp and I love it with lashings of crème fraîche mixed with a little elderflower cordial, to taste.

1. Preheat the oven to 160°C/140°C fan/gas 2½. Lightly butter a loose-bottomed, 20cm round cake tin and line the base with a disc of baking parchment.

2. Put the butter, flour, caster sugar, baking powder and eggs in a food-processor and whizz together for 20–25 seconds until well mixed (or, put them into a bowl and beat together by hand or with an electric hand-held mixer to make a soft cake mixture). Spoon the cake mixture into the prepared tin and spread evenly. Arrange the gooseberries on top, pushing them slightly into the cake mixture. Scatter all but 1 tablespoon of the crushed amaretti evenly over the top, then sprinkle over the demerara sugar.

3. Bake for 50–60 minutes or until a skewer inserted in the middle comes out clean. If it's not ready, bake it for a little longer. Remove from the oven and leave to cool in the tin for 5 minutes, then remove from the tin (keeping it gooseberry-side up) and transfer to a wire rack. Serve warm or cold.

4. Just before serving, scatter the cake with the reserved amaretti crumble, then dredge the top with icing sugar. Serve with elderflower crème fraîche or double cream, if you like.

GET AHEAD

- The cake keeps very well in an airtight container for 2–3 days. It also freezes beautifully, as does the compote (if using) – defrost both before serving. Serve the cake at room temperature or reheat in the oven (temp as above) for 10–15 minutes until warm throughout.

HINTS & TIPS

- Gooseberry compote is a lovely accompaniment – put a spoonful on top of the cake just before serving and serve the remainder separately. To make, put 450g topped and tailed fresh gooseberries into a small saucepan with 1 tablespoon of undiluted elderflower cordial or water and 6 tablespoons of caster sugar, and cook on a very low heat for about 5 minutes or so until just softened. Add a little more sugar, if necessary. Set aside to cool. Keep in a covered bowl in the fridge for up to 3 days.

- Swap the gooseberries for Victoria plums. You will need about 6 plums (halved and stoned) and the cake will take about 1 hour, 20 minutes to cook.

Strawberry & Pistachio Mini Pavlovas

MAKES 8 MINI PAVLOVAS
(or 10 slightly smaller ones)

3 egg whites
pinch of sea salt
170g caster sugar
1 teaspoon cornflour
1 teaspoon white wine vinegar
½ teaspoon vanilla extract
60g shelled pistachio nuts, roughly chopped
pink food colouring
300g crème fraîche, clotted cream or lightly whipped double cream
450g fresh strawberries, 8 (or 10) hulled and sliced, the remainder left whole (un-hulled)

To serve (optional)
freeze-dried strawberry powder and/or freeze-dried strawberry pieces; icing sugar; dried or fresh rose or cornflower petals; crystallised rose petals; mint leaves; pouring cream

GET AHEAD

- The pavlovas can be topped with the crème fraîche or cream (but don't decorate) up to 4 hours in advance and kept chilled, although last minute is better.
- The baked (un-decorated) pavlova bases keep for several days in an airtight container and they last for months in the freezer (defrost before use), so are excellent for getting ahead when entertaining, and for (impressive!) emergencies!

Ever-popular pavlovas, here in individual helpings, look stylish, elegant and very appealing arranged on a platter, and the fact that they can be made months in advance (the pavlova bases freeze well) makes them a great choice for entertaining. The nuts and the fruit topping can be varied according to the season, transforming them into a lovely year-round dessert.

1. Preheat the oven to 120°C/100°C fan/gas ½. Line a large baking sheet with silicone or baking parchment.

2. Whisk the egg whites and salt together in a bowl until stiff. Gradually add the caster sugar, a tablespoon at a time, whisking very well between each addition and ensuring it is fully incorporated before adding more. The mixture should be thick and shiny once all the sugar has been added. Whisk in the cornflour, vinegar and vanilla extract. Set aside 2 tablespoons of the pistachios, then gently fold the remainder into the meringue with a large metal spoon.

3. Secure the silicone/baking parchment to the baking sheet with a tiny blob of meringue underneath at each corner. Spoon the meringue into 8 (or 10) well-spaced blobs on the baking sheet, then form into round shapes with a slight dip in the middle using the back of a spoon. They don't need to be perfect – higgledy-piggledy equals character!

4. Using a skewer, flick 2–3 tiny droplets of food colouring onto each pavlova and swirl to form a marbled effect. Scatter half the reserved pistachios over the top edges and sides of each one.

5. Bake for 1 hour for a slightly gooey, chewy middle, or for 1¼–1½ hours for dry, crunchy middles. The pavlovas should lift off the paper easily and cleanly. If not, cook for a little longer. Leave to cool completely on the baking sheet.

6. Arrange the pavlovas on a large, pretty platter or individual plates and top each with a spoonful of crème fraîche or clotted or whipped cream. Arrange a sliced strawberry on top of each one, then scatter the remaining whole strawberries on the platter/plates, along with the last of the pistachios. If using, sprinkle with the freeze-dried strawberry powder and/or pieces, dust with icing sugar and/or add any of the other serving suggestions.

No-bake White Chocolate, Ginger & Blueberry Cheesecake

SERVES 12–16

vegetable oil, for greasing
200g ginger biscuits
100g butter, melted
300g good-quality white chocolate broken into pieces
700g full-fat soft cheese
300ml double cream
1 large piece of stem ginger in syrup, drained and finely chopped
300g fresh blueberries

GET AHEAD

- The cheesecake can be made up to 3 days ahead and kept chilled.

HINTS & TIPS

- If you don't have a microwave, put the chocolate into a large, heatproof bowl. Set the bowl over a slightly smaller heatproof bowl containing boiling water (ensuring the bottom of the top bowl doesn't touch the water underneath) and leave until melted, stirring occasionally.

Rich, luscious and indulgent sums up this lovely, ridiculously easy (and very deep) cheesecake. A great way to feed and impress a crowd, it's ideal for making ahead as it needs making at least a day in advance. For a change I sometimes can't resist adding a little twist and topping it with blueberry compote, even though it does use another pan.

1. Line the base of a 20 x 7cm round springform cake tin with a square piece of baking parchment, leaving the excess sticking out from the sides. To do this, unclip and remove the side of the tin, lay the paper over the base, then replace the side and clip it up. Lightly grease the sides of the tin with vegetable oil.

2. Put the ginger biscuits into a food-processor and whizz to make fine crumbs, then pour in the melted butter and whizz again until the mixture comes together (or, bash the biscuits in a polythene bag, then combine with the melted butter). Tip into the prepared tin and press over the base, using the base of a flat glass for even distribution and getting into the edges. Chill for at least 30 minutes or until firm.

3. Meanwhile, place the chocolate pieces in a microwave-safe bowl, then microwave (uncovered) on low, for a few seconds at a time, until melted. Remove and set aside. If you don't have a microwave, see *Hints & Tips*.

4. Using a stand mixer or hand-held electric whisk, whisk the soft cheese in a bowl until smooth, then add the cream and whisk briefly until thickened. Whisk in the melted chocolate, then fold in the ginger. Spoon the mixture into the tin and shake it to level the top, then cover and chill overnight. As the cheesecake is on the soft side, it should be eaten straight from the fridge.

5. If cooking the blueberries put into a small, non-reactive pan, with 2 tablespoons of granulated sugar and 1 tablespoon of water, on a low heat for 3–5 minutes, shaking occasionally. The juices will begin to run but the blueberries should remain whole. Transfer to a bowl, cool, cover and chill (for up to 3 days).

6. To serve, unclip the tin, then use the overhanging baking parchment to transfer the cheesecake to a flat serving plate (leaving the tin base behind). Tumble, or arrange (lightly pressing them in) the uncooked blueberries over the top, or spoon over the compote if using. Serve immediately.

Pears Poached in Spiced Dessert Wine

SERVES 8

4 firm pears (preferably Williams or Conference), peeled but left whole, stalks left on and as long as possible
1 bottle (75cl) dessert wine
1 tablespoon caster sugar, or more to taste, depending on the wine
1 cinnamon stick, split in half lengthways
2 star anise
10 green cardamom pods, cracked under a heavy knife
a handful of flaked almonds, toasted (see *Hints & Tips*)
crème fraîche, to serve

This lovely classic French pudding is delicious in its simplicity. Use a dessert wine of your choice, but I would recommend choosing a good-quality one. Sometimes I use Gewürztraminer. Omit the nuts, if you like, but they do add a nice bit of crunch. I think this is best eaten cold and straight from the fridge.

1. Put the pears into a saucepan into which they fit neatly (about 20cm diameter), then add all the remaining ingredients, except the almonds and crème fraîche. Cover, slowly bring to the boil, then taste for sweetness, adding a little more sugar, if necessary. Simmer very gently for 5–20 minutes or until soft and tender when pierced into the middle with a sharp knife. The cooking time will depend on the ripeness of the pears (the firmer the pear, the longer the cooking time).

2. Remove from the heat and leave the pears and liquid to cool completely in the saucepan.

3. Transfer the pears, spices and cooking liquor to a pretty serving bowl (they look pretty in a glass bowl) and chill for at least 4 hours (overnight is even better) before serving. Serve with the almonds scattered over the top and a bowl of crème fraîche to accompany.

GET AHEAD

- The recipe can be completed up to 3 days in advance and kept chilled in the fridge (but will keep for a day or two longer, if required), but don't scatter the almonds over until just before serving.

HINTS & TIPS

- Most large supermarkets sell ready-toasted flaked almonds. However, if toasting your own, toast them in the (same) dry saucepan on a medium heat for 3–5 minutes, before or after cooking the pears. Cool and store any leftover toasted nuts in the freezer to prevent them from going rancid.

Pistachio Biscotti

MAKES ABOUT 15–18

110g plain flour
110g caster sugar
½ teaspoon baking powder
pinch of sea salt
100g shelled whole pistachio nuts
½ teaspoon vanilla extract
1 egg, lightly beaten

These are deliciously moreish and that's speaking as someone who doesn't have much of a sweet tooth! Biscotti are good for any time of the day, dunked into coffee or tea, or served alongside jellies and creamy puddings. They make a lovely present, too, and happily they are far easier to make than you might imagine.

1. Preheat the oven to 180°C/160°C fan/gas 4. Line a medium baking sheet with silicone or baking parchment.

2. Mix the flour, sugar, baking powder, salt and whole pistachios together in a bowl. In a cup, mix the vanilla extract into the egg, add this to the dry ingredients and mix in with a spoon as best you can, then form into a dough with your hands. Transfer to the lined baking sheet and mould into a log shape about 25 x 5cm.

3. Bake for 20–25 minutes until pale golden and firm on the top. Remove from the oven, turning it down to 150°C/130°C fan/gas 2.

4. Transfer the log to a wire rack and leave to cool for 10 minutes, then while it's still warm, transfer to a board and carefully slice diagonally into 1cm-thick slices using a bread knife and a gentle sawing motion.

5. Return the slices to the same lined baking sheet and bake for a further 20 minutes until pale golden, then turn over and bake the other side for another 5–10 minutes until the biscuits are almost dried out, bearing in mind they will harden more when cold.

6. Transfer to a wire rack and leave to cool completely. Store in an airtight Kilner-style jar or tin.

GET AHEAD

- Biscotti keep well in an airtight container for up to a week. They also freeze well (defrost before eating).

HINTS & TIPS

- In Italy, biscotti are traditionally dunked into sweet Vin Santo wine at the end of a meal, instead of a pudding, or into black coffee.
- Any other nuts and/or dried fruit can be added instead of, or as well as, the pistachios. Just try to stick to around 100g total weight.

Oven-poached Rhubarb with Elderflower

SERVES 8 (as an accompaniment – see *Hints & Tips*)

450g rhubarb stems (either pink rhubarb or main crop stems)
4 tablespoons elderflower cordial
3 tablespoons caster sugar

GET AHEAD

- The rhubarb, once cooled, will keep in the fridge for up to 3 days (but will keep for a day or two longer). Cover and store in the dish it's cooked in, in a single layer.

HINTS & TIPS

- Oven-poached rhubarb has so many uses: served on its own as a compote with cream, crème fraîche or custard; as an accompaniment to individual puddings, such as panna cotta; as a topping for pavlovas and meringues, both large or individual ones; served for breakfast with natural yoghurt; whizzed up with cream to make a fool; spooned over the top of a cheesecake; use for making ice cream.

The beauty of this recipe is in its simplicity and because the rhubarb remains perfectly in shape, rather than stewed into a shredded mush, which tends to happen if cooked in a saucepan. I like to poach most soft fruit using this oven method. It makes all the difference.

1. Preheat the oven to 190°C/170°C fan/gas 5.

2. Wipe the rhubarb stems, then cut them on a slant into 4cm lengths and place in a shallow, ovenproof dish big enough to take them mainly in one layer (a little bit of overlapping is fine). Drizzle over the elderflower cordial and sprinkle over the sugar.

3. Bake for 10–15 minutes until the rhubarb is just cooked but still holding its shape and is soft when pierced with the tip of a sharp knife. The exact cooking time will depend on the thickness of the stems. New season's tender, thin stems will take far less time than the thicker late season ones.

4. Leave to cool in the dish before serving warm or chilled.

Prune & Armagnac Ice Cream

SERVES 4–6

170g semi-dried prunes
125ml sweet dessert wine
2 tablespoons Armagnac or brandy
375ml milk
50g caster sugar
¼ teaspoon vanilla extract
125ml tinned sweetened condensed milk
250ml double cream
pinch of sea salt

GET AHEAD

- Make up to 3 months in advance.
- To make life easier when entertaining, I pre-scoop balls of ice cream, pile them up in a pretty bowl and re-freeze, ready to serve when required. Alternatively, spoon the churned ice cream mixture into a loaf tin lined with clingfilm (wet the tin first), cover the top with clingfilm and freeze until firm. Turn out, peel off the clingfilm, cut the ice cream into slices, then arrange them overlapping on a plate and return to the freezer until required.

HINTS & TIPS

- Redcurrants on the stem look pretty draped over the ice cream.

Although delicious at any time of the year, I make this every Christmas to enjoy on its own or with the Prune & Armagnac Frangipane Tart (see page 239). Both recipes have the bonus of being immensely easy to make in advance – a huge plus any time, but it's particularly useful at Christmas to have two puddings stashed away in the freezer that were made a month or two beforehand.

1. Put the prunes into a bowl, pour over the wine and Armagnac or brandy and leave to soak for at least 4 hours or preferably overnight.

2. Put the milk and sugar in a saucepan and heat together gently to just below boiling point, stirring occasionally. Remove from the heat, stir in the vanilla extract and leave to cool. Once cool, stir in the condensed milk, double cream and salt. Take the prunes out of their liquid using a slotted spoon and roughly chop, either using a food-processor or by hand. They should still be fairly chunky. Stir the prunes into the cream mixture along with their syrup.

3. Pour the mixture into a chilled ice-cream machine (see below, if making by hand) and churn for about 20 minutes or until the ice cream is the consistency of very softly whipped cream. Scrape the mixture into a suitable freezerproof container, leaving ½cm rim to spare at the top, to allow for expansion. Cover with baking parchment (or freezer dividing tissue), placing it directly onto the ice cream to exclude any air and stop ice crystals forming. Cover with a lid and freeze until firm.

4. If you are making the ice cream by hand, pour the creamy prune mixture into a shallow, freezerproof container, then cover and freeze for 1½ hours or until a frozen ring has formed around the edge of the container. Remove from the freezer and beat the ice cream for a few seconds with an electric hand-held mixer (or by hand using a balloon whisk) until the mixture forms a uniform slush. Quickly cover and return to the freezer for another 1½ hours, then repeat this beating and freezing process twice more. For the final freezing, leave a ½cm rim spare at the top of the container. Cover with baking parchment as above, then cover with a lid and freeze until firm (about 1 hour).

5. Serve the ice cream in scoops.

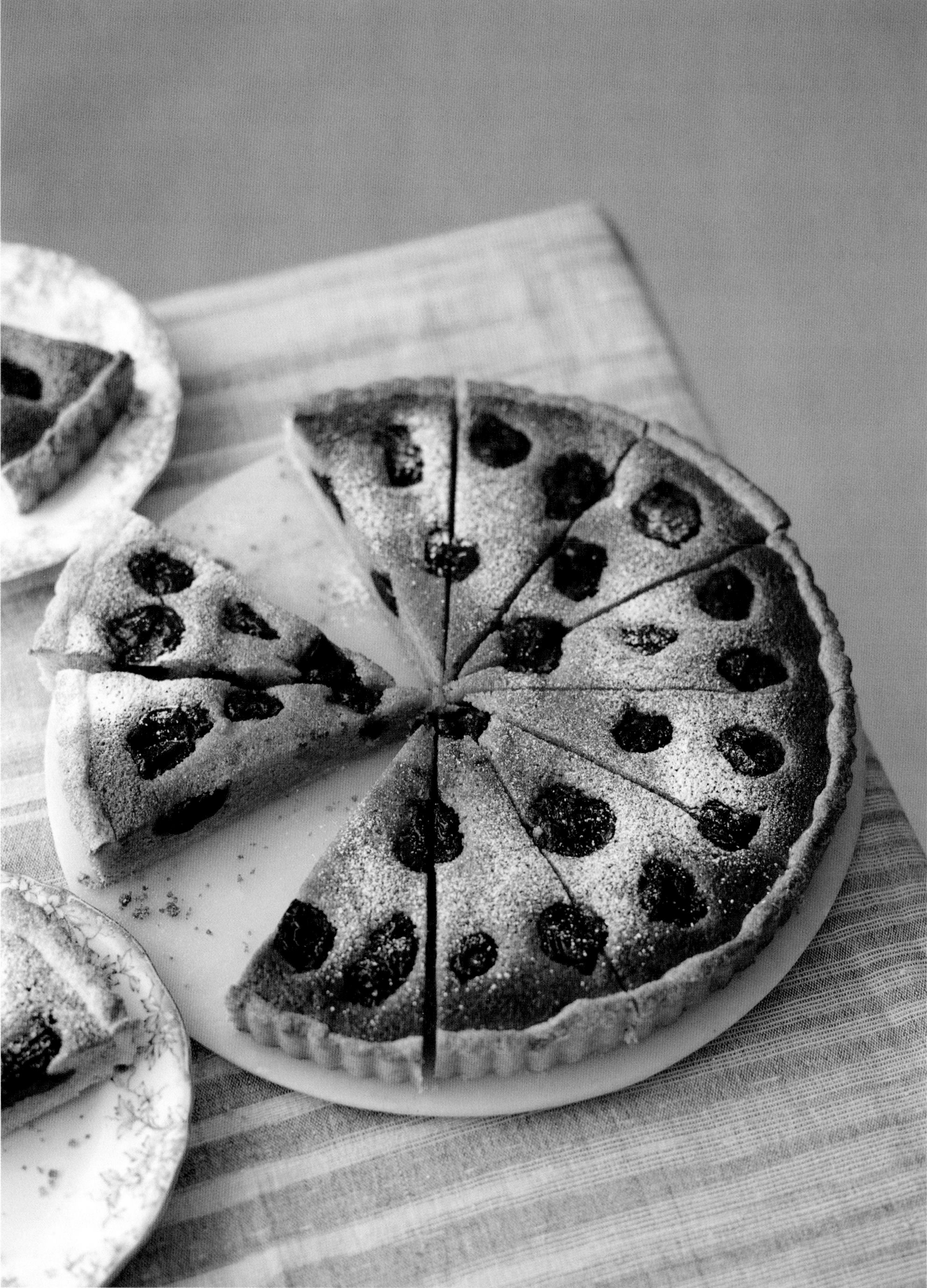

Prune & Armagnac Frangipane Tart

SERVES 12

200g (about 30) semi-dried prunes
90ml Armagnac or brandy
icing sugar, for dusting
crème fraîche or double cream, to serve

For the pastry
225g plain flour, plus extra for dusting
110g cold butter, diced
110g caster sugar, plus extra for sprinkling
3 egg yolks

For the frangipane
170g butter, softened
170g light muscovado sugar
170g ground almonds
3 eggs
2 tablespoons plain flour
2 tablespoons Armagnac or brandy

GET AHEAD

- The tart can be made fully up to 3 days in advance, then cooled, covered and chilled, or frozen (defrost before serving).

HINTS & TIPS

- If you don't have a food-processor, make the pastry by hand. Mix the flour and sugar in a bowl, lightly rub in the butter until the mixture resembles breadcrumbs, then add the egg yolks and water, mixing until just coming together. For the frangipane, beat all the ingredients together in a bowl to make a smooth paste.

This very easy tart can be made entirely in a food-processor and freezes like a dream. An impressive 'get ahead' pudding to have up your sleeve, it's also very good served with the Prune & Armagnac Ice Cream (see page 236) – together they make a lovely pairing for festive Christmas eating, as well as entertaining. The light muscovado sugar gives a lovely caramel flavour and slightly softer texture to the frangipane.

1. Put the prunes and Armagnac or brandy into a bowl and set aside to soak for 4 hours (or overnight), giving them the odd stir when you remember.

2. Preheat the oven to 190°C/170°C fan/gas 5. Find a loose-bottomed, 28cm round tart tin and a baking sheet.

3. Put all the pastry ingredients into a food-processor (see *Hints & Tips*), along with 1 tablespoon of cold water, and whizz together gently until everything just begins to come together into a crumbly ball. Tip onto a lightly floured worktop and knead lightly until it has formed a smooth-ish ball. Flatten it into a disc, wrap in clingfilm and chill for 30 minutes (but if you work quickly, you won't need to chill the pastry – see step 5).

4. Meanwhile, make the frangipane. Using the un-washed processor bowl (see *Hints & Tips*), briefly whizz all the frangipane ingredients together to make a smooth paste (but don't worry if it curdles). Set aside.

5. Roll out the pastry on a lightly floured worktop as best you can, as it will be very short and crumbly, and use it to line the base and sides of the tart tin. It may fall apart, but it is very malleable, so you can just mould it into the tin using your fingers (treat it gently and don't overwork it though).

6. Spoon the frangipane into the pastry case and smooth the surface. Drain the soaked prunes, then arrange them on top, not touching each other. Slide the tin onto the baking sheet. Bake for 25–30 minutes or until golden and just set in the middle and darker around the edges.

7. Remove from the oven and cool in the tin until you are ready to serve, then remove and serve warm or at room temperature (it can also be served chilled), dusted with icing sugar. Serve with crème fraîche or double cream (or with ice cream – see recipe introduction, above).

Rhubarb & Pistachio Tarts with Stem Ginger Crème Fraîche

SERVES 8

1 x 320g ready-rolled puff pastry sheet (about 35 x 23cm)
plain flour, for dusting
300g young rhubarb stems (see intro)
caster sugar, for sprinkling
clear honey, for brushing
1 piece of stem ginger in syrup, drained and finely chopped, plus a little of the syrup (to taste)
250g crème fraîche

To serve
icing sugar, for dusting
a handful of shelled pistachio nuts, roughly chopped
Rhubarb Ribbons (see *Hints & Tips*) (optional)

These little tarts are a doddle to make and are at their prettiest when made with tender, new season forced 'champagne' rhubarb. If using later season (main crop) rhubarb, try to pick out the pink and thinner stems.

1. Preheat the oven to 200°C/180°C fan/gas 6.

2. Unroll the pastry and peel it from its paper. Put the paper onto a large baking sheet and lightly dust with flour. Replace the pastry on its paper and cut into 8 even-sized rectangles. Re-position each one very slightly so that they're marginally separated from their neighbours. With the point of a sharp knife, score a border about 1cm in around the edge of each tart, being careful not to cut right through the pastry. Score a criss-cross pattern within the borders, then prick the centre of the tarts with a fork.

3. Cut the rhubarb stems into even-sized pieces that fit exactly into the middle of the tarts, then arrange, side-by-side, in the middle of each tart (roughly 6 pieces per tart, depending on the thickness of the stems). Cut fatter stems in half and arrange them cut-side down. Scatter the tarts all over quite generously with caster sugar (about 1 teaspoon per tart).

4. Bake for 30 minutes or until puffed up and golden brown. Remove from the oven and immediately brush the tarts all over with honey. Set aside (still on the baking sheet).

5. Mix the stem ginger, plus a little of its syrup to taste, into the crème fraîche.

6. Serve the tarts warm, dusted with icing sugar and scattered with the pistachios and the rhubarb ribbons (if using). Serve the stem ginger crème fraîche separately or spoon a neat 'quenelle' shape into the middle of each tart.

GET AHEAD

- The tarts can be made fully up to 3 days in advance. Cool, cover and chill on the baking sheet. Reheat in the oven at 180°C/160°C fan/gas 4 for 5–10 minutes until warm. The crème fraîche can be made up to three days ahead (cover and chill).

HINTS & TIPS

- To make Rhubarb Ribbons: using a potato peeler, peel long, thin strips off the length of a young (pink) rhubarb stem(s). Put onto a baking sheet lined with silicone or baking parchment, in a single layer, then cook in a low oven (120°C/100°C fan/gas ½), for an hour or so until completely dried out (cooking time will depend on the thickness). Leave to cool, then store in an airtight container – they will keep crisp for several weeks.

Index

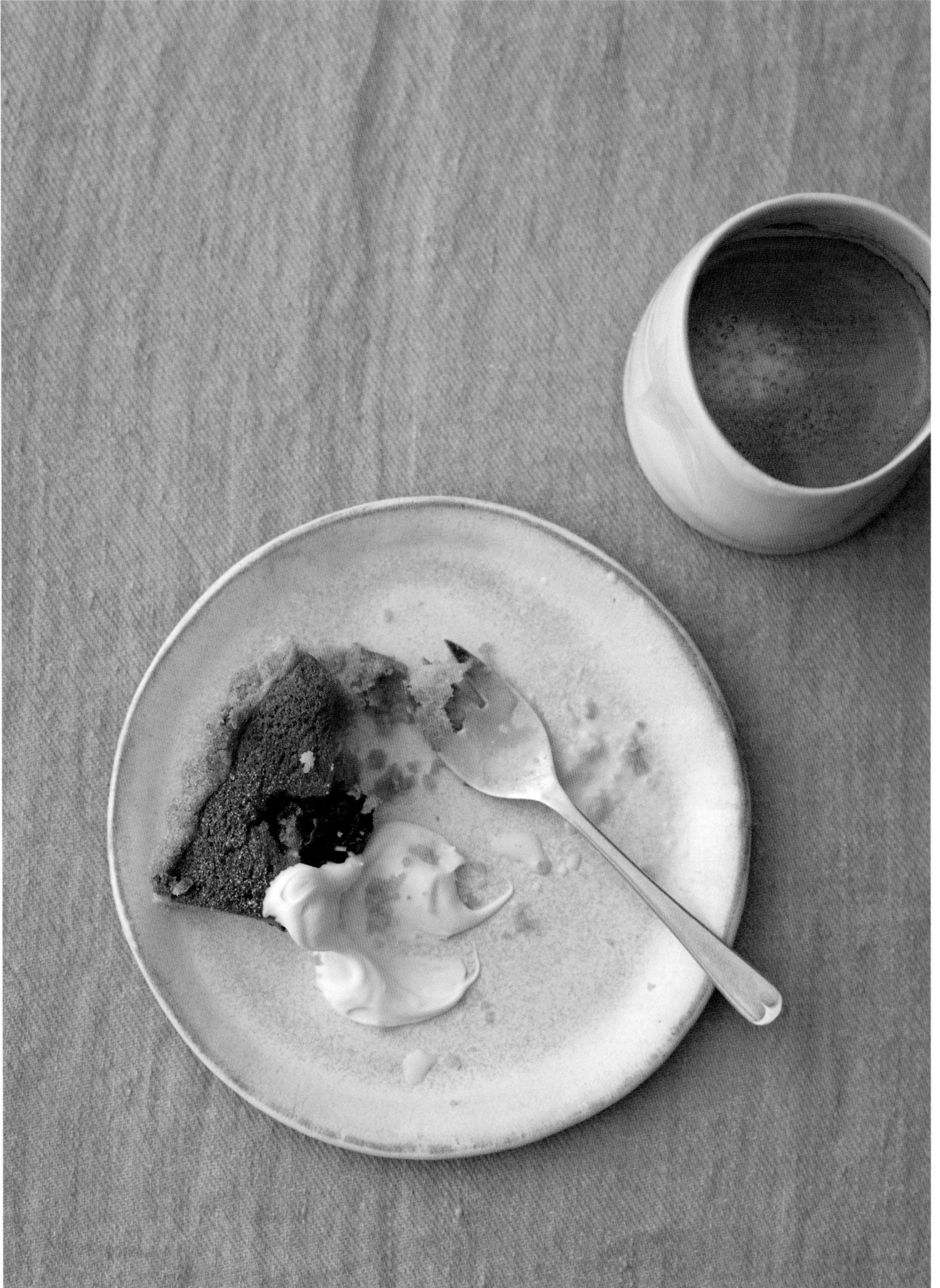

Acknowledgements

I am indebted and grateful to so many people . . .

Enormous thanks to the dream Headline Home team, Lindsey Evans, Anna Steadman and Kate Miles, for commissioning *Just One Pan*, and for their wonderful enthusiasm and vision for this book. With particular thanks to my brilliant editor, Kate Miles, for her expertise, patience, and never-ending kindness and support.

Anne Sheasby, copy editor extraordinaire who offers new meaning to the word 'thorough', navigating my shortcomings with great tolerance, resulting in a much-improved book.

Nathan Burton for his delightful design and the time and trouble he so patiently and painstakingly took with the layout and the graphics.

Tony Briscoe for his brilliant photographs as well as his excellent styling eye – and for leaving his family and studio for the wilds of north Northumberland for weeks at a time. This is the third book we've worked on together and what a happy team we are.

Hannah Wilkinson for her prop-styling vision and excellent choice of props, as always.

Alice Joicey for keeping us neat and tidy in the kitchen during the shoots, overseeing the props and thus enabling the rest of us to concentrate on the job in hand.

Tina Paul for production, Rosie Margesson for publicity, Shadé Owomoyela for marketing, and Margaret Gilbey for proofreading.

My family, John, Flora, Freddie and Lucy, for being willing (most of the time!) guinea pigs, testers and tasters and never complaining when (quite often) eating a particular recipe for the umpteenth time. They were a captive audience during lockdown when I was developing most of these recipes, but I'm forever grateful to them for being unfailingly supportive of everything I do.

Particular thanks go to my younger daughter, Lucy. Apart from her kindness and support while at home during lockdown, her quite extraordinary input made such a difference to many of the recipes and other aspects of the book – not to mention her contribution to, and project management of, the photo shoots, keeping us all on target and much more, which was no mean feat.

Sally Poltimore, my oldest friend, who is always by my side as we travel around the country giving demonstrations, and whose contribution, without doubt, enhances them. She's always supportive, unbelievably hardworking and makes it fun, even when we're exhausted, and she never lets her high standards slip.

Amanda Finley, my dear friend, who tested many of these recipes with her usual commitment, diligence and attention to detail. Her feedback consistently makes all the difference. As has that of the Poltimore family who also kindly tested some recipes during lockdown.

Heather Holden-Brown, whom I'm fortunate enough to be able to call my agent, whose advice is always spot-on, who believes in me, always has my best interests at heart and is endlessly encouraging, as well as wise, kind and always fun.

Karen Miller, without whose fantastic help, support and thoughtfulness in the office and beyond I would be totally lost.

Lastly, to all those who kindly come to my demonstrations, I would like to say your valuable feedback keeps me in touch with the sort of food and recipes you like cooking and your families like eating – I love devising these recipes. You also keep me on my toes, which is why I'm able to guarantee my recipes are tested, re-tested and fail-safe.

Thank you to you all.

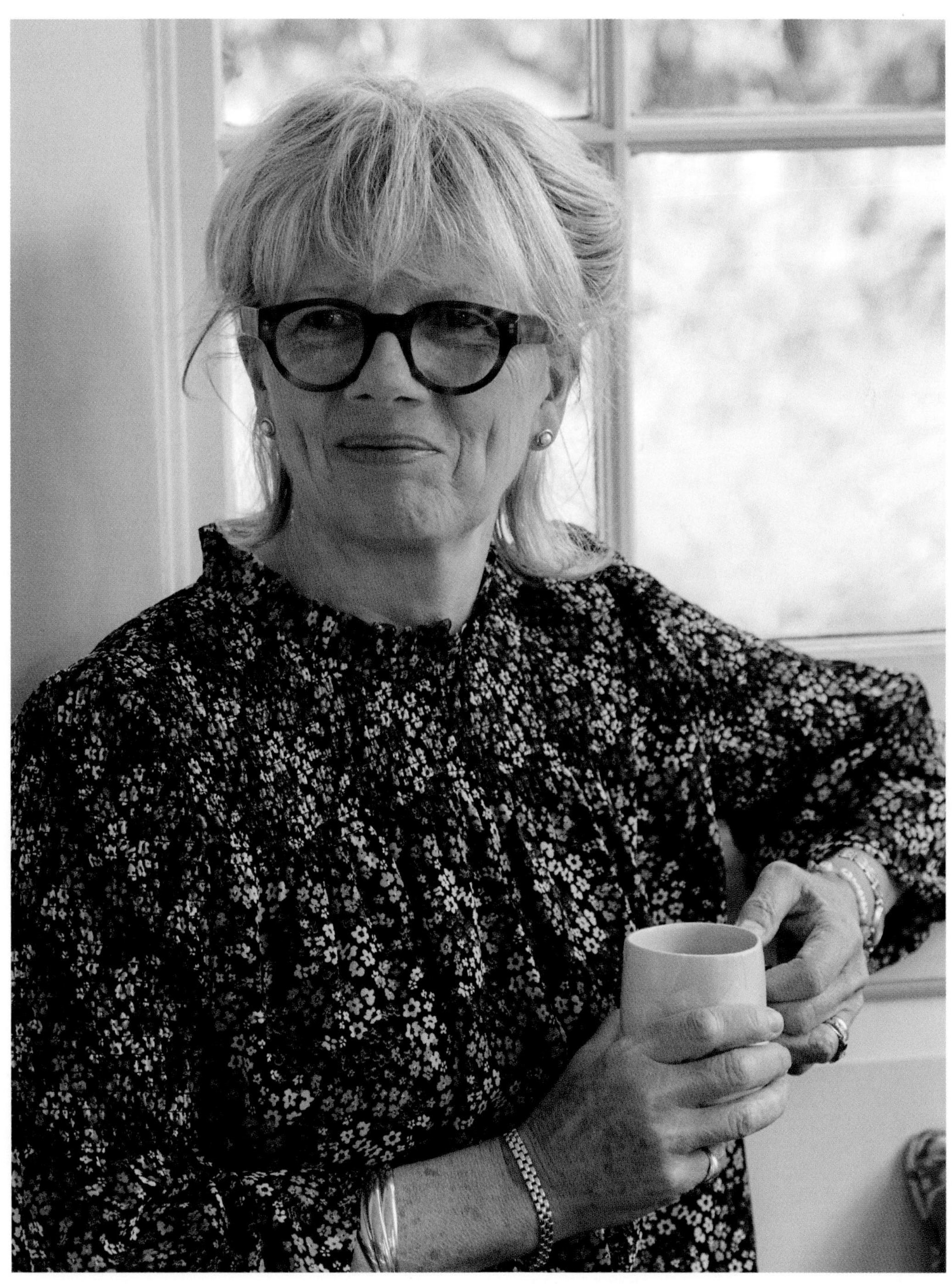

Conversion Charts

Conversions are approximate and have been rounded up or down. Follow one set of measurements only – do not mix metric and imperial.

WEIGHT CONVERSIONS

METRIC	IMPERIAL
10g	¼oz
15g	½oz
20g	¾oz
25g/30g	1oz
35g	1¼oz
40g	1½oz
50g	1¾oz
55g	2oz
60g	2¼oz
70g	2½oz
75g/80g	2¾oz
85g	3oz
100g	3½oz
110g	3¾oz
115g	4oz
120g	4¼oz
125g	4½oz
140g	5oz
150g	5½oz
160g	5¾oz
170g/175g	6oz
180g	6¼oz
200g	7oz
225g	8oz
250g	9oz
280g/285g	10oz
300g	10½oz
320g	11¼oz
325g	11½oz
340g	11¾oz
350g	12oz
375g	13oz
390g	13½oz
400g	14oz
425g	15oz
450g	1lb
500g	1lb 2oz
600g	1lb 5oz
750g	1lb 10oz
900g	2lb
1kg	2lb 4oz
1.3kg	3lb
1.5kg	3lb 5oz
1.6kg	3lb 8oz
2kg	4lb 8oz
2.7kg	6lb

VOLUME CONVERSIONS (LIQUIDS)

METRIC	IMPERIAL	IMPERIAL/CUPS
5ml	1 teaspoon	
15ml	1 tablespoon	
30ml	1fl oz	2 tablespoons
45ml	3 tablespoons	
50ml	2fl oz	
60ml	4 tablespoons	¼ cup
75ml	2½fl oz	⅓ cup
90ml	6 tablespoons	
100ml	3½fl oz	
120ml/125ml	4fl oz	½ cup
150ml	5fl oz (¼ pint)	⅔ cup
175ml	6fl oz	¾ cup
200ml	7fl oz	
225ml	8fl oz	1 cup
250ml	9fl oz	
300ml	10fl oz (½ pint)	
350ml	12fl oz	1½ cups
400ml	14fl oz	
425ml	15fl oz (¾ pint)	
500ml	18fl oz	2 cups
600ml	20fl oz (1 pint)	
700ml	1¼ pints	
900ml	1½ pints	
1 litre	1¾ pints	4 cups
1.2 litres	2 pints	
1.7 litres	3 pints	

VOLUME CONVERSIONS (DRY INGREDIENTS – AN APPROXIMATE GUIDE)

Flour	125g	1 cup
Sugar	200g	1 cup
Butter	225g	1 cup (2 sticks)
Breadcrumbs (dried)	125g	1 cup
Nuts	125g	1 cup
Seeds	160g	1 cup
Dried fruit	150g	1 cup
Dried pulses (large)	175g	1 cup
Grains & small pulses	200g	1 cup

LENGTH

METRIC	IMPERIAL
5mm/½cm	¼inch
1cm	½ inch
2cm	¾ inch
2.5cm	1 inch
3cm	1¼ inches
4cm	1½ inches
5cm	2 inches
5.5cm	2¼ inches
6cm	2½ inches
7cm	2¾ inches
7.5cm	3 inches
8cm	3¼ inches
9cm	3½ inches
10cm	4 inches
11cm	4¼ inches
12cm	4½ inches
13cm	5 inches
15cm	6 inches
18cm	7 inches
20cm	8 inches
23cm	9 inches
24cm	9½ inches
25cm	10 inches
26cm	10½ inches
27cm	10¾ inches
28cm	11 inches
30cm	12 inches
31cm	12½ inches
33cm	13 inches
34cm	13½ inches
35cm	14 inches
36cm	14¼ inches
38cm	15 inches
40cm	16 inches
41cm	16¼ inches
43cm	17 inches
44cm	17½ inches
46cm	18 inches

OVEN TEMPERATURES

°C	°C WITH FAN	°F	GAS MARK
110°C	90°C	225°F	¼
120°C	100°C	250°F	½
140°C	120°C	275°F	1
150°C	130°C	300°F	2
160°C	140°C	325°F	3
170°C	150°C	340°F	3½
180°C	160°C	350°F	4
190°C	170°C	375°F	5
200°C	180°C	400°F	6
220°C	200°C	425°F	7
230°C	210°C	450°F	8
240°C	220°C	475°F	9

First published in 2021 by Headline Home
an imprint of Headline Publishing Group

4

Cataloguing in Publication Data is available from the British Library

ISBN 978 1 4722 7787 9
eBook ISBN 978 1 4722 7788 6

Commissioning Editor: Anna Steadman
Senior Editor: Kate Miles
Design: Nathan Burton
Photography: Tony Briscoe
Home Economist: Jane Lovett
Home Economist Assistant: Lucy Lovett
Prop Stylist: Hannah Wilkinson
Copy Editor: Anne Sheasby
Proofreader: Margaret Gilbey
Indexer: Caroline Wilding

Printed and bound in China by C&C Offset Printing Co., Ltd.
Colour reproduction by Alta Image

Headline's policy is to use papers that are natural, renewable and recyclable products and made from wood grown in sustainable forests. The logging and manufacturing processes are expected to conform to the environmental regulations of the country of origin.

HEADLINE PUBLISHING GROUP
An Hachette UK Company
Carmelite House
50 Victoria Embankment
London EC4Y 0DZ

www.headline.co.uk
www.hachette.co.uk